Crisis Narratives in International Law

Nijhoff Law Specials

VOLUME 104

The titles published in this series are listed at *brill.com/nlsp*

Crisis Narratives in International Law

Edited by

Makane Moïse Mbengue and Jean d'Aspremont

BRILL

NIJHOFF

LEIDEN | BOSTON

Library of Congress Cataloging-in-Publication Data

Names: Mbengue, Makane Moïse, editor. | D'Aspremont, Jean, editor.
Title: Crisis narratives in international law / edited by Makane Moïse
    Mbengue and Jean d'Aspremont.
Description: Leiden ; Boston : Brill Nijhoff, [2022] | Series: Nijhoff law
    specials, 0924-4549 ; volume 104 | Includes bibliographical references
    and index.
Identifiers: LCCN 2021038934 (print) | LCCN 2021038935 (ebook) |
    ISBN 9789004472358 (paperback) | ISBN 9789004472365 (ebook)
Subjects: LCSH: International law. | COVID-19 (Disease)–Law and
    legislation. | Crisis management–Political aspects. | International
    relations.
Classification: LCC KZ3410 .C749 2022 (print) | LCC KZ3410 (ebook) |
    DDC 341–dc23
LC record available at https://lccn.loc.gov/2021038934
LC ebook record available at https://lccn.loc.gov/2021038935

Typeface for the Latin, Greek, and Cyrillic scripts: "Brill". See and download: brill.com/brill-typeface.

ISSN 0924-4549
ISBN 978-90-04-47235-8 (paperback)
ISBN 978-90-04-47236-5 (e-book)

Printed by Printforce, United Kingdom

Contents

Crisis and Its Curators: A Preface

Philippe Sands

Few would quibble with the idea that the SARS-CoV-2 virus strain has caused a crisis that affects just about everybody on the planet. As lawyers active in the field of international law, our reading and teaching, writing and thinking, law-making and adjudication have been profoundly affected. These nineteen essays, individually and as a group offer a range of reactions and insights, touching on the impact on international law in its present incarnation and in a broader historic context, a snapshot on the state of thinking about international law. They offer a reminder too, as Benedict Kingsbury tells us, of the wisdom of others, of the Maori insight about our propensity to walk backwards into the future with our eyes on the past.

The essays are likely to cause many readers to pause and reflect on the project in which we are collectively engaged, and their own roles. Why we do what we do, how we do it, whether it matters. If these essays tell us anything it is that the current moment is inscribed into a longer historical continuum, a consequence which tends to reinforce impressions of the utilities and futilities of the enterprise in which we are engaged. International law follows and reacts, rather than lead or catalyse.

I thought about this on the morning walk I recently took around Hampstead Heath with a friend, a retired member of the English judiciary with a deep knowledge of international legal matters. I mentioned the challenge of writing this short preface, not sure what I could say that might be of interest or offer insight. 'It's not a new problem', my friend observed, explaining how one of his first writings was indeed a contribution to a book about crisis and international law, five decades earlier. Back home, he sent through a few pages from his essay in the collection, published in 1968 with an introduction by Stanley Hoffmann. The book evoked the Berlin blockade, Suez, Kashmir and the missiles in Cuba, as well as the confusion of the World Court in dealing with matters that led to the Advisory Opinion on Certain Expenses.[1] A crisis may take many forms, in the eyes of its beholders.

The conversation on the Heath caused me to dig deeper. My Colombian research assistant excavated a few nuggets that lay close to the surface,

---

1   Wolfgang Friedmann and Lawrence Collins, 'The Suez Canal crisis of 1956' in Lawrence Scheinman and David Wilkinson (eds), *International law and political crisis; An analytic casebook* (Little Brown 1968) 91.

including various courses given at the Hague Academy over a century. Take your pick! You might start with Professor Zimmermann's excursus into the crisis of international organisation during the Middle Ages (1933);[2] move onto Professor Kunz's exploration of the crisis in the post-war law of nations (1955);[3] and finish with Ms Reed's more recent journey into the contribution of private and public international law to the resolution of international crises (2003).[4]

I could offer more examples, but you get the point. Crisis is ever present and all around. It is, in a way, the lifeblood of international law, offering moments for reflection and decision, a journey into the past that offers possible lessons for the future. Crisis is our *raison d'être*, a thing that gives meaning to our existence, reinforcing our senses of marginality and purpose. Crisis nourishes us, as we muddle on, incrementally re-constructing and re-imagining, until some true disaster befalls – 1815, 1919, 1945 – causing the shaky edifice that stands above the not-so-firm foundations to collapse, requiring another exercise in rebuilding.

Digging deeper into my own memory, I recalled the first 'crisis' I encountered as a novice international lawyer, back in the summer of 1983. I had moved to America, in pursuit of love, and managed to park myself as a visiting scholar at a law school at the moment the Soviet Union shot down a Korean passenger airliner that had strayed off course and accidentally entered prohibited airspace. The incident caused me to write my first article – *The Legal Fallout from KAL 007* – which I found and read again for the first time in decades. 'Even in situations where a common perception of the law does broadly exist', I noted as a twenty-two-year-old, 'our procedural system is unable to avert crisis'.[5]

Plus ça change, plus c'est la même chose. Looking back over four decades, I am surely not alone in recognising the place of crisis in intellectual and professional developments, from Chernobyl in 1986, to the war in Iraq in 2003, to the mistreatment of the Rohingya and the need for a new crime of ecocide to help in the struggle against climate change.

This collection reflects a common experience: 'crisis' is in our blood and guts, and our engagement with international law is deeply informed by the moments of 'crisis' that intrude into our lives as lights illuminating a runway. In this way, the international lawyer is not unlike a pathologist, for whom, as

---

2 Michel Zimmermann, 'La crise de l'organisation internationale à la fin du Moyen Age' (1933) 44 Recueil des Cours 315.

3 Josef L Kunz, 'La crise et les transformations du droit des gens' (1955) 88 Recueil des Cours 1.

4 Lucy Reed, 'Mixed Private and Public International Law Solutions to International Crises' (2003) 306 Recueil des Cours 177.

5 Philippe Sands, 'The Legal Fallout from KAL 007' (1983) 6 Harvard International Review 44.

the Oxford English Dictionary tells us, 'crisis' has operated since the sixteenth century to identify 'the point in the progress of the disease when an important development takes place which is decisive of recovery or death'.

The pandemic of 2020, like the financial downturn of 2008, like the 'war on terror' launched in 2001, will no doubt come to be seen as a crisis rather than a disaster that requires a total rebuild. A few tweaks here and there, until the real disaster lands. In the meantime, as I observed in my immediate post-teenage years, each crisis makes us cognisant of the fragility of the enterprise and its dependence on matters of political will. Perhaps we are, as James Crawford noted in his own reflections on such moments, merely like the curator at the assembly hall who, after the assembly is over, turns up to clear the mess and get the place ready for the next performance.[6]

---

6 James Crawford, 'Reflections on Crises and International Law' in George Ulrich and Ineta Ziemele (eds), *How International Law Works in Times of Crisis* (Oxford University Press 2019) 10, 14.

Notes on Contributors

Laurence Boisson de Chazournes
is Professor of international law at the University of Geneva, Director of the Geneva LLM in International Dispute settlement (MIDS) and co-Director of the Geneva Center for International Dispute Settlement (CIDS). She is a Member of the Institute of International Law. She acts as adviser to international organizations, governments and law firms and as arbitrator and counsel in various dispute settlement fora.

Edith Brown Weiss
is University Professor at Georgetown University and past President of the American Society of International Law She was awarded the Manley Hudson Medal (ASIL), Elizabeth Haub Medal (IUCN/Free University of Brussels) and Doctorate Honoris Causa Heidelberg University. Her book *In Fairness to Future Generations* received the ASIL Certificate of Merit. From 2003 to 2007 she chaired the World Bank Inspection Panel, a Vice President level appointment. She is former President of the IADB Administrative Tribunal and a Judge on the IMF Administrative Tribunal.

B.S. Chimni
is Distinguished Professor of International Law, O.P. Jindal Global University, Sonipat, India. He has been elected Associate Member, Institut de Droit International.

Eliana Cusato
is a Marie Skłodowska Curie post-doctoral fellow at the Amsterdam Center for International Law (University of Amsterdam). She holds a Ph.D. in international law from the National University of Singapore and serves as a member of the editorial board of the Asian Journal of International Law. Prior to joining UvA, Eliana was a lecturer in the School of Law, Essex University (UK).

Jean d'Aspremont
is Professor of International Law at Sciences Po Law School. He also holds a chair of Public International Law at the University of Manchester. He is General Editor of the *Cambridge Studies in International and Comparative Law* and Director of *Oxford International Organizations* (OXIO). He is a member of the Scientific Advisory Board of the *European Journal of International Law* and

series editor of the *Melland Schill Studies in International Law*. He writes on questions of international law and international legal theory.

Malgosia Fitzmaurice

holds a chair of public international law at the Department of Law, Queen Mary University of London. Since 2019 she has been elected an Associate Member of the Institue de Droit International and in 2021 she was awarded the Doctorate Honoris Causa of the University of Neuchâtel. She specialises in international environmental law; the law of treaties; and indigenous peoples. She publishes widely on these subjects.

In 2020, Professor Fitzmaurice has published (with Professor Panos Merkouris) a book Treaties in Motion: The Evolution of Treaties from Formation to Termination (Cambridge University Press, 2020). She is Editor in Chief of International Community Law Review journal and of the book series published by Brill/Nijhoff *Queen Mary Studies in International Law*.

Iga Joanna Józefiak

holds an M.Sc in Environmental Sciences with a specialization in Climate Impacts from the University of Geneva. Currently starting her PhD, focusing on the relationship between climate science and international law, using the case study of the Arctic. She is the author of scientific publications, specializing in sustainable development and environmental protection of polar regions.

Catherine Kessedjian

is Professor Emerita of the University Panthéon-Assas Paris II. She acts as arbitrator or mediator in a selected number of International Commercial and Investment Disputes, including in Business and Human Rights disputes. She is a member of numerous professional organisations, notably the American Law Institute (ALI) and the Institut de droit international. She is the Honorary President of the French Branch of the International Law Association and Vice Chair of the global ILA. She is the President of the Organizing Committee for ASI/ILA 2023.

Benedict Kingsbury

is Director of the Institute for International Law and Justice and the Program in the History and Theory of International Law at NYU Law School.

Jan Klabbers

teaches international law at the University of Helsinki, having earlier taught at the University of Amsterdam. He is currently mostly involved in a research project on international organizations and their relations to the private sector. His forthcoming monograph is Virtue in Global Governance: Discretion and Judgment (Cambridge University Press).

Frédéric Mégret

is a Full Professor and Dawson Scholar and co-Director of the Centre for Human Rights and Legal Pluralism, Faculty of Law, McGill University.

Makane Moïse Mbengue

is Professor of International Law at the Faculty of Law of the University of Geneva and Director of the Department of International Law and International Organization. He is also an Affiliate Professor at Sciences Po Paris (School of Law). He is a Member of the Curatorium of The Hague Academy of International Law. Since 2017, he is the President of the African Society of International Law (AfSIL). He is the author of several publications in the field of international law.

Anne Peters

is a director at the Max Planck Institute for Comparative Public Law and International Law, Heidelberg (Germany), a professor at the universities of Heidelberg, Freie Universität Berlin, and Basel (Switzerland), as well as a L. Bates Lea Global Law professor at the University of Michigan Law School.

Mónica Pinto

is Professor Emerita, Universidad de Buenos Aires. Member of the Institut de droit international. Counsel in international law cases; arbitrator, member of ad hoc Committees in foreign investment cases. Member of the Committee on Experts on the Application of ILO Conventions and Recommendations.

Hélène Ruiz Fabri

is Director of the Max Planck Institute Luxembourg for Procedural Law, where she heads the Department of International Law and Dispute Resolution, and Professor at the Sorbonne Law School (University Paris 1 Panthéon-Sorbonne)

Iain Scobbie

is Professor of Public International Law and Director of the Manchester International Law Centre, University of Manchester. He was formerly the Sir Joseph Hotung Research Professor in Law, Human Rights and Peace Building in the Middle East at SOAS, University of London. He studied at the Universities of Edinburgh and Cambridge, and at the Australian National University.

Yuval Shany

is the Hersch Lauterpacht Chair in International Law and former Dean of the Law Faculty of the Hebrew University of Jerusalem. Prof. Shany directs the CyberLaw program at the Hebrew University Federmann Cyber Security Research Center and is also Vice President for Research at the Israel Democracy Institute and Co-director of the International Law Forum at the Hebrew University Law Faculty. He served until recently as a member of the UN Human Rights Committee (Member 2013–2020; Vice Chair 2017–2018, 2019–2020. Chair 2018–2019).

Christian J. Tams

is Professor of International Law at the University of Glasgow where he directs GCILS, the Glasgow Centre for International Law & Security. (weblink: https://gcils.org//) He is an academic member of Matrix Chambers, London, and sits on the Board of ESIL, the European Society of International Law.

Fuad Zarbiyev

is an associate professor of international law at the Graduate Institute of International and Development Studies in Geneva. His research interests include the politics and sociology of international law and institutions, treaty interpretation, international judicial behavior, as well as philosophy, critical theory and post-structuralist discourse analysis as applied to international law.

Introduction

Makane Moïse Mbengue and Jean d'Aspremont

International lawyers have always shown a great confidence in their ability and that of their craft to change and manage the world according to preferences and necessities they define. And they have generally found in the experience of crises a formidable confirmation of their power to intervene and manage the world. It is no surprise that crises have been a convenient narrative for international lawyers to reaffirm their managerial power and that crisis narratives have continuously populated the literature and the case-law for more than a century.

As the world emerges from a very severe pandemic and prepare to a severe climate catastrophe, crises narratives are back in international law circles. Yet, as crisis narratives again dominate the international legal discourse, there is a strong sense that we have been here before and that the current pandemic and upcoming climate catastrophe may be just crises like all those which international lawyers capitalize on to reaffirm their managerial ambitions. Crisis narratives seem to be a very mundane referent of the international legal discourse. At the same time, the pandemic as well as the upcoming environment catastrophe cannot be dismissed as part of a certain ordinarity of the international legal discourse. There seems more to them than just the crisis narratives that the pandemic as well as the upcoming environment catastrophe generate. Such crises seem to seriously bear on the functioning of international law and international legal institutions, the meaning they convey, and the vocabularies around which international law is articulated. International law, the international lawyers and the international legal discipline seem to be simultaneously craving for crises and battered by crises.

It is the purpose of this collection of short essays to reflect on this fundamental ambivalence permeating the way in which international lawyers, international law, and the international legal discipline engage with the recent Covid 19 pandemic and the upcoming climate catastrophe.

This volume includes nineteen short and highly self-reflective essays by a diverse range of junior and leading international lawyers. They offer new and original reflections on international law and its relation to crises. Together these essays provide a unique stocktaking about the role, limits, and potential of international law as well as the worlds that are imagined through international lawyers' vocabularies.

In his chapter, Jan Klabbers takes issue with the very idea of crisis narratives, and suggests that such narratives are inevitable parts of our political culture. International law can always be said to be in crisis – which says something about international lawyers as well. If there currently is a crisis, he argues, it is a crisis of liberal democracy, not of international law. For him, international law is perfectly capable of propping up all sorts of projects, whether benign or malign.

Iain Scobbie starts his chapter by recalling that Governments often try to harness a 'crisis', whether real or imagined, in order to ride on its wings to achieve a transformation of substantive international law to something which they think might be more amenable to their concerns, interests, or freedom of action. For Iain Scobbie, this can amount to a blatant attempt at norm manipulation or norm entrepreneurship. But governments can control the narrative to decide when a 'crisis' exists, setting the terms of a debate which is often weaponised, employing the rhetoric of war and conflict rather than recognising that the situation is simply one to be faced or managed. For Iain Scobbie, this raises the question of when and how should international lawyers respond to these pretensions. He argues that there is frequently a pressure, whether self – imposed or external, to succumb to the curse of providing an instant reaction, exacerbated by (social) media and a propensity for tabloid scholarship, which ignores the wider systemic ramifications of proposed 'solutions'.

For her part, Hélène Ruiz-Fabri wonders about the state of mind of those using the qualification of crisis and developing crisis narratives. She posits that crisis narratives can be used to study crises through the lens of international law, in which case crisis is, on the legal scale of words, one which leads to at least two questions: that of the justification for exceptional measures and that of change. Alternatively, she argues, crisis narratives can also be deployed to analyse international law through the lens of crisis, which leads to consider the possibility not only of a technological crisis but also of an epistemological crisis.

In his chapter, B.S. Chimni reflects on the theme of 'crisis and international law' from a third world approaches to international law (TWAIL) perspective. His chapter begins by advancing a typology of material crisis, distinguishing between four kinds of crisis: episodic, regional, structural and originary crisis. It follows up by touching on the accompanying epistemic crisis, including the significance of framing a crisis for identifying suitable responses. The chapter goes on to discuss the impending crisis of international law and institutions in the post pandemic era and its consequences for addressing the ecological crisis and growing poverty and inequalities in the world. The chapter finally touches on the role of resistance at times of crisis in bringing about change in the international legal order. It concludes with some final reflections.

Drawing on the work of Hillary Charlesworth, Frédéric Mégret's chapter reflects on what it describes as the « crisis mode in international legal scholarship," a way of doing research that is largely constrained by the exigencies of the moment to which international lawyers must attend urgently. For Frédéric Mégret, COVID provides just such a crisis, one that reveals much about the nature of international legal scholarship. For him, the question in this context is less "what can international law do to alleviate the COVID crisis?" but "what does the COVID crisis say about our modes of knowledge production?"

Makane Moïse Mbengue claims in his chapter that the COVID-19 crisis offers an opportunity to shape new narratives of solidarity. Africa has been at the forefront of such revisited narratives on solidarity. His chapter explores, in particular, the narrative developed by President Macky Sall of Senegal which highlights two facets of crises narratives: narratives *on* the crisis and narratives *of* the crisis. In Makane Mbengue's view, the COVID-19 might serve as a momentum to build a new international order. However, the new international order should not be based on a hegemonic perspective; it must be inclusive and allow to rebuild a new global partnership within the international community that takes into account the needs of both developed and developing nations.

For Jean d'Aspremont, international law lives off crises, lives its crises, and lives in crisis. International law is a discourse for crisis, about crisis, and in crisis. In short, international law is a crisis discourse. In that sense, engaging with international law from the vantage point of crisis hardly adds anything, let alone proves novel. International lawyers are the masters of a discourse that is all about containing, making, and surviving crises in an interventionist, and managerial spirit. Against this backdrop, the very extensive literature that burgeoned following the outbreak of the COVID-19 pandemic is nothing but business as usual for a crisis discourse like international law. And yet, as this paper tries to demonstrate, should international law let the looming climate catastrophe – as well as the calamitous consequences of the measures necessary to avert it entail – be absorbed in its crisis narratives and in what is called here its 'normally abnormal normality', international law would be condemned to wordlessness.

Anne Peters begins her chapter by recalling that an infectious disease such as Covid-19 hits with disproportionate negative effects the poorer populations and thus exacerbates the wealth and income gap inside and across states. As previous diseases, she argues, the pandemic is both a driver and an outcome of international relations. Against the background that the foundations of international law have been laid by infecting the "others", and that notably zoonoses have stimulated institution-building on the international plane, it is not out of the question that the Covid-19 pandemic will trigger developments in international law. The normative proposal that comes with her chapter is to modify and operationalise the so-far underdeveloped One Health approach, informed by the international constitutional principle of solidarity.

In his chapter, Yuval Shani wonders whether the COVID-19 crisis has the potential for generating a "constitutional moment" or a "tipping point" for the development of international law separating between epochs or significantly accelerating already-occurring trends. Discounting serendipitous changes in the course of history (the 'unknown unknowns' of historical change), such a question, according to the author of that chapter, invites an assessment of whether a structural change in international law can be envisioned or required in the near future, or whether the current crisis might facilitate such a change or accelerate existing trends going in this or the other direction. For Yuval Shani, if the answers to these questions are in the negative, then the reaction to the COVID crisis is likely to showcase 'more of the same' for international law. Building on works by Yuval Noah Harari and Yaron Ezrahi, this chapter suggests that the pandemic and the response to it may help to renew and reorient efforts to base the national and international policies aimed to tackle the major challenges confronting the world in the 21st century on science.

In her chapter, Eliana Cusato considers some implications of the narrative framing the COVID-19 pandemic as an international peace and security issue, which can be seen as the epitome of crisis narratives. If 'war talk', as other crisis discourses, allows for a simplified normative agenda, she wonders, what gets elided in such accounts of the pandemic? What does this exclusion tell us about international law and lawyers? Using the concept of structural violence, her chapter sheds light on the socio-economic-ecologic violence that pre-exist and persist beyond the COVID-19 'crisis' and that the vocabulary of war/insecurity conceals. The chapter also argues that the narrative framing the virus as the 'enemy', obscures the complex interconnection between humanity, economy, and ecology. In reproducing this separation, international law, she seeks to demonstrate, shows a myopic attitude to the root causes of the pandemic, which are the same of the ecological breakdown: exploitation of fellow humans and nature.

Christian Tams' chapter formulates two wishes for the international legal debate post-Covid. The first wish is for an expanded canon of international law in which basic aspects of global health law form part of the standard curriculum. The second is that international lawyers be able to resist the temptation of reducing the international law of 2020–21 to questions of Covid: there is so much more that has been done with, and to, international law. Both wishes are purposefully understated in an attempt to avoid the all-too-predictable attempts to present Covid as a dramatic turning point in international legal discourse.

In her chapter, Catherine Kessedjian makes the point that there is no before or after, but that we have to learn to live with viruses. In her view, surveillance of the population may not be organised to the detriment of civil liberties and strict proportionality should be observed. Mobility, globalisation and governance must be reformed.

For Laurence Boisson de Chazournes, the response to Covid-19 has highlighted weaknesses in the rules, principles and institutions of the international legal order. In the wake of this realisation, international lawyers are rightly turning their attention to reform of the International Health Regulations. But, in her view, questions should also be asked about the broader governance context in which these regulations operate. She argues that, in order to avoid the failings that Covid-19 has exposed from happening again in the future, a legal approach that prevents fragmentation trends, allows for a comprehensive rule of law response to such issues and places human dignity and fundamental rights at the forefront is needed. Her chapter aims to begin a conversation about reform of international law and organizations viewed through this lens. For her, international law needs to rise to this challenge and make solidarity a key concept.

Edith Brown Weiss makes the point that the COVID-19 crisis illustrates the workings of a kaleidoscopic world, in which patterns rapidly change, many actors beyond States are critical, flexible instruments are imperative, and scientific knowledge is evolving. In her view, the kaleidoscopic world sharply contrasts with the traditional view of an international system dominated by States in a rather static order in which States negotiate and implement binding agreements. She goes on to argue that controlling the virus is a public goods problem that shows the need for rapid and flexible responses by governments and others and collective actions at the local, regional, and global levels. At the same time, she claims, it is a private goods problem, as in development of a vaccine by private companies, which calls for public-private collaboration. According to her argument, the COVID-19 crisis reveals the need to reconceptualize public international law to broaden its scope, to include relevant actors beyond States, to encompass many kinds of legal instruments, and to recognize the imperative need for shared norms.

In her chapter, Mónica Pinto points to some of the features of States' reactions to the crisis. For her, neither the level of development nor the democratic traditions of States have made a great difference to the almost generalized authoritarian approaches to the crisis. In some scenarios the pandemic and the confinement diverged in their goals. Science driven decisions did not necessarily meet human rights criteria. The confinement highlighted discrimination, violence and, once again, the role of women as unpaid care workers. Structural inequality, underdevelopment, poverty aggravated the vulnerability of the situation of many groups. Mónica Pinto claims that the global nature of the pandemic requires effective and sustainable policy responses, involving public and private sectors as main actors of a prevention which includes universal access to vaccines and medical treatment but also to tap water and sewerage. She argues that, as lessons learned from the ongoing crisis, both the rule of law and human rights should lead to the wisest decisions.

The chapter by Benedict Kingsbury starts with a reference to the frontispiece to Hobbes' *Leviathan* (1651) which features two specially-garbed plague doctors standing together within the walls of the almost empty city. Benedict Kingsbury argues that, in conventional terms, they might symbolize one of the sovereign's greatest duties, or they may remain outside the body politic because they are hired-in only during the emergency. Benedict Kingsbury's chapter however reflects from a different thought, that the itinerant plague doctors might be emblematic of transnational knowledge circulation, and located in the complex history of science-experts (and medical experts) in relation to formalized ruling power. It builds from Thucydides, Hobbes and Foucault to argue that the courage and special status of front-line health professionals, fearless also in speaking out against political pressures, might desirably be instantiated in bodies such as the World Health Organization, and can also be an inspiration for lawyers in troubling times.

Malgosia Fitzmaurice starts her chapter by claiming that one of the most disadvantage groups in relation to pandemic crisis are indigenous peoples. The latter's vulnerabilities are placing them in a particularly sensitive as exposure to the disease appears to be situating them at risk of increased mortality, as well as more severe symptoms. Indeed, in her view, indigenous groups appear to specially vulnerable, and scholars have raised the alarm over the need to take special mitigating measures with regard to the impact of the pandemic on specific communities. Diverse but often compounding factors appear to be relevant in driving this undesirable outcome for many communities. Biological characteristics appear to play a part, although they are not always the key factor, with socio-economic causes also driving this trend. Elevated rates of transmission are also due to conditions of poverty in which many of these communities are forced to live. Poor housing quality and sanitation, crowding, weaker infrastructures, and other effects of reduced economic security result in a diminished capacity for adaptability when confronted with the social and economic restrictions typically imposed as part of official responses to coronavirus. Malgosia Fitzmaurice claims that there is evidence that Covid-19 has had a particularly negative impact in regions predominantly inhabited by indigenous populations, where health systems were fragile and may have collapsed, leaving vulnerable populations in unprecedented state of exposure and risk.

In his chapter, Fuad Zarbiyev makes the claim that international legal scholarship dedicated to COVID-19 has been largely limited to descriptions of relevant legal instruments and possible remedies offered by the latter. A characteristic common to most contributions has been the remarkable lack of anything that could be described as 'intellectual' if one means by 'intellectual' the quality of a work that furthers one's understanding beyond what should be obvious to any decently trained international legal professional capable of competently reading and interpreting legal materials. The chapter of Fuad Zarbiyev reflects on some conditions that make this reality possible or even unavoidable and conclude with a proposition.

In what constitutes the last chapter of the volume, Iga Joanna Józefiak argues that crises are inherent part of our present world, and it is even expected that in the next decades, the Earth will be increasingly subject to a variety of disasters. Her chapter looks at the recent coronavirus pandemic, analyzing the constraints of the international law. By evaluating real-life examples, it identifies the main weaknesses of crises management, such as the poor relationship between international law and science, clear primacy of politics and economics over scientific research, and failure in educating an aware and responsible society. Pandemic, as well as climate change or terrorism, she argues, is a global problem against which it is impossible to win alone. Particularly the young generation with its all determination should constitute a source of inspiration in joining international efforts. Paraphrasing Thomas Reid, she claims that the international system is only as strong as its weakest link, hence the necessity of appropriate cooperation between states, transfer of knowledge, and mutual support.

Paris and Geneva
2 July 2021

CHAPTER 1

The Love of Crisis

Jan Klabbers

An idea is 'true' so long as to believe it is profitable to our lives.[1]

∴

1 On Change and Crisis

It is one of the standard *topoi* of contemporary social and political thought that change is a good thing. Political movements, whether #MeToo or Black Lives Matter, whether pro-life or pro-choice, typically go to the streets to achieve change: if not a change in legislation, as is usually the case,[2] then at least a change in people's hearts and minds. Politicians invariably campaign on a ticket advocating change, even those who think of themselves as conservative. They may campaign by pointing to a glorious past which needs to be rekindled ('Make America Great Again') or a brave new world waiting just around the corner (whether socialist, fascist or neo-liberal), but either way, they campaign for change. And understandably so: the politician who campaigns on a theme of keeping things as they are, who merely wishes things to remain as they are, will be portrayed as boring in the press, will not raise many funds, and will not attract many votes. She will be seen as privileged (why else would she resist change?), or as deluded, or both, and be kept far from elected office. Differences of opinion amongst contenders and activists may exist with respect to the proposed pace of change, separating the revolutionaries from the others, but either way: change is the key word.

Consequently, in order to make change attractive, the existing situation must be depicted in terms of crisis, and again, this applies to politics regardless of precise orientation. Making America Great Again suggests a country that had

---

1 William James, *Pragmatism* (Bruce Kulick ed, Hackett Publishing Co 1981) 36.

2 This is bafflingly ignored by most political thinkers: political action tends to be oriented to affecting the law, but political scientists of many stripes tend to treat law as irrelevant, as merely epiphenomenal.

temporarily lost its greatness, due to the work of the 'other side' or, more sinister, as the result of dark forces or conspiracies – and it helps if the opposition can be depicted as evil and in conspiracy terms. A century or so ago, Spengler's diagnosed decline of the West and Nietzsche's diatribes against modern man suggested a civilization in crisis. Half a century or so ago, Habermas pointed to the legitimation crisis of the modern State, and on a smaller scale many have been the complaints about systems in crisis. It is, in other words, not hard to find reports about situations of crisis. By contrast, it is far more difficult to find reports about social, political, legal, or economic systems being in good shape, and where those exist, they tend to be written as responses to earlier reports about crisis. If the death of article 2(4) of the UN Charter had not been proclaimed, Louis Henkin is unlikely to have written, with a wink and a nod to Mark Twain, that reports of the death of the prohibition of the use of force were greatly exaggerated.[3]

The emphasis on crisis talk is no surprise, and stems in large measure from the commodification of information. As the old newspaper editor's quip goes: 'dog bites man' is not a story; 'man bites dog', however, might be interesting. Reporting on the normal, the quotidian, on what works, is not considered appealing. It will not sell newspapers, and it will not win its authors any awards, to propose that all is well with the world. Tabloid editors either depict famous people in relationship crisis, yearning for a break-up, or depict them as yearning for a family. In both cases, change is again the key word, and the need for change is most easily made visible if a crisis can be observed.

Likewise, the international law scholar proposing to investigate the mundane will be shrugged off as, well, mundane. Try and imagine submitting a research grant proposal that does not promise a paradigm shift, and the point will become clear. Try and imagine submitting a paper to a learned journal that suggests that the topic under review works just fine, a paper that does not offer a critique, and the point will become clear. The house that is not on fire will not attract reporters; the house on fire, however, will. Crisis takes epistemic priority, with change following in its wake.

In this light, the call by the editors of this volume for papers on crisis narratives must be seen for what it is, a clever appeal to the general affection for thinking in terms of crisis and possibly change. A call for papers on 'the current crisis' does not convey whether there truly is a crisis, regardless even of

---

3   Louis Henkin, 'The Reports of the Death of Article 2(4) are Greatly Exaggerated' (1971) 65 AJIL 544. True to form, this responded to an earlier observation about the death of Article 2(4) – the other way around is highly unlikely to happen.

questions of definition and conceptualization. Instead, it appeals to a classic, standard *topos*.

2   On International Lawyers in Crisis

Still, there might be good reason to speak of crisis narratives: the fact that it taps into a standard *topos* does not render it false in and of itself.[4] But realizing that a *topos* is being utilised suggests that there might be something about the utilisers that is worthy of exploration: if not a crisis of international law, then perhaps there is a crisis of international lawyers. That international law is in crisis is both accurate in some way (it always is) and not very interesting: international law is always said to be in crisis, and can be said always to have been in crisis, ever since day one, regardless of when exactly 'day one' is located. If located in the writings of the Spanish theologians, then the crisis, with hindsight, is a moral one: international law enabled colonialism and imperialism. If located in the Westphalian peace with its emphasis on sovereignty, then the crisis is both moral (sovereignty is often considered a bad word) and conceptual (States may be sovereign in name, but this merely covers up immense power differences: organized hypocrisy, one might say). If located in the professionalisation of the late nineteenth century, then the crisis is an epistemic one, turning international law into bureaucratic structures with their own bureaucratic interests and turf wars and accompanying structural and institutional biases. And if located in the interbellum, it failed to prevent World War II and the Holocaust – all good intentions of Wilson, Briand, Kellogg, and others notwithstanding.

International law is in a state of perennial crisis, and at best displays the workings of an accordion: when some parts seem to be going right (whatever that may entail), other parts will not – some parts inflate while others deflate. To put it bluntly: the establishment of the World Trade Organization and the creation of the International Criminal Court, both once heralded as marking the progress of international law, as manifesting the 'legalization' of world politics,[5] are now considered flawed achievements, with the WTO being paralyzed and possibly moribund, and the ICC having become the thinking world's laughing stock. And lest we forget, the New International Economic Order, that earlier hallmark of the progress of international law, died a painful death at

---

4   The role of *topoi* in thinking about international affairs is extensively discussed in Friedrich Kratochwil, *Rules, Norms, and Decisions* (CUP 1989).
5   See Judith Goldstein and others (eds), *Legalization and World Politics* (MIT Press 2001).

roughly the same time the WTO was created, and that was possibly no coincidence. The ICC was purposively limited to elusive political crime, leaving the structural crime of exploitation of individuals, and even transboundary common crime, unaffected. And that too was probably no coincidence.

So, the international legal order is said to be in crisis also around the year 2020, and indeed, plenty of evidence suggests this is the case. States that used to be important are leaving behind cooperative schemes, whether it is the momentous stupidity of Brexit or the irresponsible moves of the 'stable genius' occupying the White House in Washington, DC. The ICC has done little of note and yet still manages to tick off the US, most of Africa, and many well-meaning people who balk at the levels of incompetence, judges doubling as ambassadors, and the regular hanging out of dry laundry from the bench – and its judges nevertheless feel entitled to a significant salary boost. The jewel in the WTO's crown, the Appellate Body, is treading water to survive and temporarily (... ?) replaced by a stop-gap mechanism. And tin pot European dictators dream of endless terms in office for sitting presidents, ending the independence of the judiciary, and similar illiberal moves. Come to think of it, this points less to a crisis of international law, and more perhaps to a crisis of liberal democracy – see below.

And yet at the same time, governments join international regimes (sometimes conveniently left out of the crisis narratives):[6] the US decided to join the International Exhibition Bureau, has been seriously contemplating joining the UN World Tourism Organization and made a U-turn with respect to the venerable Universal Postal Union, which it had earlier threatened to withdraw from. North Macedonia not only settled its long-standing dispute with Greece in a peaceful manner, but also wants to join the EU, as does Albania. On some level, the 'normalization' of relations – if that's what it is – between Israel, the United Arab Emirates and Bahrain can no doubt be spun as a victory for international law. States keep concluding investment treaties and producing model investment treaties, signifying on some level a belief in some version of international law. The OECD is creatively trying to combat tax evasion through international law, while UNCTAD is busy regulating debt relief, and even if NAFTA disappeared, it was replaced by a different agreement. While some leaders in their infinite wisdom feel the need to withdraw from the World Health Organization in times of a global pandemic (possibly to cover for their own incompetence), others have realized that during a global pandemic global

---

6 As becomes evident from Stefan Talmon, 'The United States under President Trump: Gravedigger of International Law' (2019) 18 Chinese JIL 645. One also cannot help but wonder why exactly his article was published in the Chinese Journal of International Law.

cooperation, i.e., international law and international institutions, might actually be a decent idea.

In other words, to diagnose a crisis of international law typically depends on one's underlying set of values, and is often based on underlying and unspoken epistemic assumptions, such as the mistaken idea that international law is by definition a force for good. This is a mistake, obviously: multilateralism, cooperation, and international law are neither inherently good nor bad – as a moment's thought will reveal. The mistake is understandable though: generations of international lawyers have told themselves and their students (and whoever wanted to listen) that international law is inherently a force for good, mostly because the extreme alternative (unbridled anarchy) will mean a world where life is nasty, brutish, and short. And if you are often enough told that international law is inherently benign, then sooner or later this becomes its own truth.

3   On Accountability as Crisis

This suggests that the crisis is not so much a crisis of international law, but a crisis of international lawyers. The problem is not that States are suddenly 'against international law' (as if that is a credible political position to take in isolation from what specific international legal regimes demand and offer), but rather that the *praxis* of international law[7] reveals some untenable facets. The most obvious signifier is the apparent importance, highly popular for some two decades now, of accountability, of 'ending the culture of impunity'. The international law blogs, which have become useful barometers of fashion, are filled with calls for accountability. Typical contributions advocate the need for strong Security Council Resolutions against States such as Myanmar, or discuss many of the niceties of international criminal law in quite some detail and often on the level of hypothesis (as in: should individual X ever be indicted, and should he be arrested and arraigned, and should his State of nationality ratify the ICC Statute, what then would be the legal situation?). There is even much discussion of the possibilities of holding someone, anyone, accountable for the outbreak of COVID-19, or for its consequences, or the costs it has generated, or all of the above: the wars on drugs and terror are superseded by the war

---

7   This does not refer to specific practices or to practitioners, but rather to the way the discourse around international law is shaped, by academics and (some) practitioners alike. On praxis, see generally Friedrich Kratochwil, *Praxis: On Acting and Knowing* (CUP 2018).

on COVID-19. International lawyers, in other words, are terribly busy finding ways to hold others to account.

Doing so, however, reveals both a moral and an intellectual crisis, if nothing else. The moral crisis (if crisis talk is appropriate here), entails that the drive towards accountability is a manifestation of an urge to punish – a primitive urge dressed up in the respectable language of accountability, responsibility, or the unimpeachable desire to bring an end to the culture of impunity. The language is respectable; the urge less so, if only because punishment (*excusez*: accountability) tends to harden political positions. This is well-known: many have realized that starting war crimes proceedings against political leaders will drive those leaders away from the negotiating tables. But no worries, because for this as well a glorious *topos* is available: 'no peace without justice', which seems plausible, but only as long as justice is somehow reduced to punishment – and that is a position few political philosophers would find compelling, but which nonetheless passes for deep wisdom in international legal circles.

What is more, often a drive to hold someone accountable is a drive to impose one's own values. Admittedly, war crimes and the like are formulated in positive international law, and thus capable of being applied by a court, but in the international legal order as we know it, there are many situations where it is less obvious that someone has actually done something really wrong. Surely, the World Bank may act callously when suggesting that a group of people should not complain when being displaced so as to allow for the building of a dam, but there is little law to be found which could be applied as standards for accountability. Moreover, such international legal rules as do exist may point in different directions, in that the Bank is expected to behave in a certain manner under its Articles of Agreement, and in different manner under customary international human rights law – presuming the latter applies to the Bank to begin with. Callousness is not illegal (if only ...), and neither is the building of dams, even less so if done in the sincere expectation that doing so would contribute to the common good of those same people. In such circumstances, claiming that the Bank should be held accountable sounds hollow: accountable for what, exactly? There may be (no, there is) a lot wrong with the World Bank, but invoking international law to stop the construction of a dam (or infrastructure, or other projects) mostly smacks of substituting one's own value system for that of the Bank. Again, this is not to deny that there may be a lot about the activities of international organizations and other actors that is wrong, but punishing them for doing their job is not the way to go about it – there will be considerably more merit and mileage in changing their job descriptions. That, though, is much harder work, and much less visible; it will be hard to mobilize activists and donors for trying to change the Bank's mandate.

Insisting on punishment (sorry: accountability – doing it again ...) has the additional drawback that it serves to keep in place highly problematic ideas about international law. International law (law in general), after all, is not only relevant if it can contribute to punishment – that is an early nineteenth century sentiment that is no longer tenable and has been discarded by most observers.[8] Instead, the main relevance of law, including international law, lies elsewhere: in weaving the fabric of international society. Law facilitates every social action, whether people are aware of it or not. Contract law facilitates commercial transactions, and does so not by insisting on punishment, but by making clear what is expected once a contract is concluded and what exactly constitutes a contract, when a contract is valid, how it should be understood, and how it can be terminated. Any system of contract law will devote a few words to what happens when a contract is breached, but this is only a small part: contract law is not about punishment for breach, but is about facilitating social action in all walks of life. One might rebut that it supports an unfair capitalist economy, and that would be on target, but against the background of such an economy, it is clear that contract law (or private law generally) facilitates social action and interaction, and is considerably less interested in constraining action. Likewise, administrative law facilitates and controls executive action; family law makes family life possible, et cetera. All those branches contain structural biases and leave some worse off and others better off (and are thus susceptible to critique), but none of them can be equated with punishment alone. The rules of the road are not about punishing those who drive over the speed limit; instead, these rules make it possible for people to move from one place to another without lapsing into chaos and constant accidents.

The contrast with the punishment drive endorsed by international lawyers is striking. The punishment drive suggests that international law is mostly about constraining action – otherwise it is thought to be useless. International lawyers are not alone in this crude sentiment: so-called 'realist' international relations (IR) scholars think much the same, and sadly, many international lawyers take their cues from such impoverished IR thinking. But the thought that law is only relevant when it constrains action reveals intellectual poverty – perhaps even an intellectual crisis.

---

8   John Austin, *The Province of Jurisprudence Determined* (Wilfred Rumble ed, CUP 1995).

4   On Crisis Talk

A good crisis also calls for attention and action, and there is thus a premium on framing issues as "crises" rather than "problems" or "challenges". A "problem" can be met, so it is typically presumed, by working a little harder, or thinking a little deeper, or being a little smarter. "Challenges", likewise, do not disturb the status quo ante: some creative tinkering may be sufficient; some reshuffling of staff or attention will be considered an apt response to most challenges.

But a proper crisis probes deeper, and does so in pretty much all walks of life. A football club losing three games in a row may have a problem, which perhaps can be solved by replacing the central midfielder by a younger player from the academy, or by tweaking the tactics during games a little. The same club playing against a better team faces a challenge, which may call for a twist in the starting formation, or the adoption of a more cautious attitude. But proclaiming that the club is in crisis provides an excuse for buying a new player or two, or sacking the coach. The crisis narrative, in other words, provides a ready-made excuse for drastic action.

This holds true not just for football clubs, but across the board. The crisis narrative is, paradoxically perhaps, a winner. Authors predicting or diagnosing a crisis sells books. And scholars are awarded large research grants on the promise of either diagnosing a crisis or solving a crisis – any crisis. The very term 'crisis' carries an association with urgency, with emergency, with the need for a radical response, far more than the same story would if and when cast in terms of 'challenge' or 'problem'.

The same applies ultimately in politics. The political leader confronted with a refugee 'problem' or 'challenge' may be tempted to just re-arrange how the migration authority works or free up additional funds, but refer to the situation as a 'crisis' and all of a sudden it seems justifiable to make shady deals with untrustworthy but necessary partners, or even close the borders altogether. The crisis narrative is a potent political weapon. Our political culture puts a premium on the identification of crises; it is only the crisis which justifies immediate and strong political action.

Whether the crisis actually is a full-blown crisis is often difficult to verify and, in an important sense, beside the point. In our socially constructed world, what matters is not whether the labels are true or false, but whether they come to be accepted or not. Whether the crisis is 'real' or 'manufactured', assuming the difference can be spotted to begin with, is irrelevant. Likewise, whether a proposed solution actually works is irrelevant, for it can always be embedded in a narrative of success. Half a century of austerity policy in western Europe provides an educational example. Austerity has always been sold as necessary, in order to stave off a coming economic crisis, and true to form, the impending economic crisis that spurred on the policies has yet to materialize. Whether this is the result of those policies is anyone's guess; one might as well adopt the narrative that since the same policies need be invoked time and again, they signify a constant failure. And one might as well suggest that the one truly major crisis that hit (the 2008 financial crisis) owed much to those same austerity policies, but that too would be beside the point: a good crisis, one might say, is its own reward – at least for those who gain something, whether material gain or gain in the form of re-election or some immaterial benefit. And indeed, the 2008 financial crisis shows the mechanism at its most glorious: those mostly responsible for the crisis (the irresponsible parts of the banking world) came out best, having been bailed out after making indecent profits.

Since crisis talk sells and can be hugely profitable, it should come as no surprise that crisis talk is endemic. One important ramification though, and one that is insufficiently examined, is that crisis talk thus also comes with winners and losers. Someone gains from referring to a situation as a crisis: that someone can justifiably claim more funds, or will sell more books, or will generate more retweets or Facebook likes and thus potentially attract greater revenue, than those of us who do not immediately grasp for the c-word. No one donates money to an NGO that is merely out to contribute to solving a problem, let alone an NGO that wants to leave things as they are; ending a minor crisis is the least that the NGO should aspire to (and if the crisis is not acute but chronic, it may be called a 'culture', as in 'ending the culture of impunity'). These things are related, of course: change is costly, and thus requires a crisis to be justified. Not changing things, by contrast, is perceived (often wrongly) as cost-free. Like political activists looking for NGOs to sponsor, no research funder is going to provide a grant to someone merely promising an incremental increase in knowledge to solve what is presented as at best a challenge; instead, the promise must involve solving, or at least managing, a crisis, and preferably in one fell swoop, through a paradigm shift rather than an incremental increase. And no statesman (sticking to the masculine pronoun seems reasonably appropriate here) will benefit from downplaying a crisis – unless he is hopelessly incompetent, and unable to handle a crisis. In that case, crisis language is best avoided (current occupants of the White House and 10 Downing Street need not respond). The sheer inevitability of crisis talk in politics owes much to the strong and deep cultural appeal of the crisis.

5   On Crisis Culture

For it is not just the case that we talk of crisis because we want to make a buck, or because bureaucrats wish to earmark additional funds, NGOs wish to attract donations, and politicians wish to get re-elected – or even because we don't really give it much thought and the crisis talk comes naturally. None of this would be effective without the deep-seated cultural appeal of the crisis. For a good crisis, properly understood, promises authenticity,[9] promises truthfulness; it separates the men from the boys, so to speak. It is arguable, at the very least, that the crisis that was World War II catapulted Churchill, and to a lesser extent Roosevelt perhaps, to eternal fame. It is only during a crisis that people can become heroes; it is during a crisis that true characters are revealed. And thus some aspiring political leaders cannot help but manufacture a crisis, which then calls for their leadership.[10] US President Trump invented an immigration crisis, without any provocation; UK Prime Minister Johnson, in his bid to become Churchill 2.0, helped to generate his own so-called crisis, in which Britain is being enslaved by the EU.

Hollywood delivers the archetype cultural referent, whether in western movies (where the settlers are invariably attacked by wild natives and need to circle the wagons in order to survive) or gangster movies (where rival families fight it out). Even in romantic comedies, the impending romance first needs to survive a misunderstanding or two, a crisis of sorts, before catharsis is possible and Bridget can get together with (no coincidence) her human rights lawyer boyfriend. In all those cases, it is during the crisis that authentic character is revealed. Some, like Michael Corleone, become leaders; others remain followers. Some, like Fredo Corleone, will commit treason for personal gain; others will display loyalty to their families, romantic partners, or groups. Some will show courage in the face of danger and adversity, others will run away, proverbial tail between their legs. Either way, character traits that remain hidden in mundane, non-crisis times, will come to the fore in a crisis. We live, as someone once said, through the stories we tell, and any decent story needs some drama – any decent story needs a crisis of sorts; otherwise there can be no happy ending.

---

9   This is itself a strange cultural phenomenon: we seem to strive for authenticity, but only in a stylized manner: faux authenticity, so to speak. But that's a story for another day.

10   There is, sadly perhaps, little unusual about this – politics and manipulation have long gone hand in hand. "Traditions" are often invented; communities likewise are often "imagined". See e.g., Benedict Anderson, *Imagined Communities* (first published 1983, Verso 1998).

As a result, in times of crisis, we are culturally programmed to seek out leaders. In times of crisis there is no Habermasian ideal speech situation thinkable; deliberation and compromise seem luxuries we can ill afford under siege. Hence, the conception of politics as inherently involving crises has an equally inherent, built-in, flaw: sooner or later, the crisis will engender a call for strong leadership, and during such times, all non-essentials are suspended. When the wagons are circled, most ordinary activities will seem folly. Likewise, dancing on the volcano is strongly dissuaded, as is fiddling while Rome burns, or rearranging the deck chairs aboard the Titanic. All of these are expressions of the same underlying trope: in times of crisis, one should act with a sense of purpose, one should act decisively.

The absence of the ideal speech situation associated with crisis talk is difficult to reconcile with liberal democracy. It is no coincidence that human rights conventions typically contain clauses which make it possible to suspend liberal democracy in times of crisis – article 4 ICCPR and article 15 ECHR are the best-known examples. The underlying rationale is clear: there is a threat (a crisis, an emergency) which justifies the suspension, in order for the crisis to be staved off and normality to be restored, at which point the suspension should be lifted and liberal democracy can resume.

This suspension works as long as the crisis is temporary, or perceived to be temporary. But where a crisis is perceived to be of longer duration, liberal democracy becomes a luxury. Whether the crisis stems from refugee flows or global pandemics, domestic or foreign terrorists or the so-called 'deep state', or even a pending economic catastrophe, there will be a call, in liberal democracies too, for strong leadership. Whether that leadership is really strong (or really leadership) is, again, beside the point: Trump, Erdogan, Bolsonaro, Orban, Duterte, Putin – all have been democratically elected, as was Hitler less than a century ago. Liberal democracies in the eastern part of Europe have stopped being very liberal and very democratic, and established democracies in the western world, with a longer democratic tradition, have nonetheless succumbed to electing autocrats to high office, and have typically done so amidst much crisis talk, invariably manufactured.

6   On Moral Holidays

All this points to an inevitable and hugely ironic conclusion: if it is plausible to say that international law is in a state of crisis because autocrats left, right and centre play fast and loose with treaties and other commitments, it is precisely this kind of crisis talk that has facilitated the emergence of autocratic leaders playing fast and loose with treaties and other commitments. If it is plausible to suggest that talk of crisis engenders responses appropriate to crisis, then the only remedy is to put a stop to the crisis talk. Our political leaders cannot be counted upon to tone down their rhetoric: they have too much at stake. But the praxis of international law might be able to just about afford some responsibility – tone down the crisis talk and reserve it for really catastrophic developments. The US leaving a handful of multilateral regimes is silly and will cost it dearly, but this does not mean that international law's grave must be dug. Duterte may be committing a crime against humanity, but legal rules have rarely, if ever, stopped atrocities, as the citizens of Rwanda know all too well – and that might be a useful thing to realize. Duterte's conduct can justifiably be called a crisis for the Philippines, but it is not a crisis of or for international law. Brexit is mostly thoughtless, and harmful to the British population, but does not mean that international law is in crisis. Boris Johnson sponsoring a bill that authorizes the breach of treaty is not a glorious moment for international law, but it is nothing new, really: irresponsible politicians (and some responsible ones perhaps as well) have suggested similar moves for centuries. The point is not to close our eyes to these and similar developments, but quite the opposite – there is nothing wrong with insisting that, generally speaking, legal rules should be respected – call this a culture of formalism, if you will. The point is, rather, to stop calling everything a 'crisis', because the concept of a crisis calls for desperate measures and gives cynical autocrats the language that they need to justify their bullying.

In the end, it is not so much international law that is in crisis, but liberal democracy. This has been propped up for 75 years by parts of international law, but they are not identical – international law is just as easily capable of propping up colonial exploitation or the vagaries of neo-liberalism. It has done so in the past, and will do so in the future, if only because international regimes are always someone's project and cannot be well-understood in the absence of its political and economic drivers and effects. But if there is a crisis at present, it is a crisis of liberal democracy, exemplified by Orban's explicit philosophy of 'illiberal democracy' formulated a decade ago, or the indecent haste in which elite politicians in the banana republic formerly known as the USA have responded to the death of a Supreme Court Justice. And this, in turn, suggests that liberal democracy carries the seeds of its own demise within it. International law is incapable of doing much about it. Individual international lawyers, however, may do something, however minimal perhaps: by refusing to let power alone triumph, by keeping a standard of decency alive, by thinking of alternative designs and regimes. This is difficult, far more difficult than embracing lazy slogans about 'crisis' and prevailing 'cultures' or proposing to resort to punishment and does not allow anyone to take a 'moral holiday'.[11] Crisis talk is perennial and not always appropriate. But if we insist on there being a crisis of international law, then this is the time to work towards a better international law. Liberal democracy is hard work, placing serious intellectual and mental demands on the electorate. If international lawyers are to assist liberal democracy, they cannot insist on accountability and punishment and cry 'crisis' every other week, but rather they must vigilantly patrol the borderline between decent and indecent uses of power, between just and unjust manifestations of authority.

---

11   The idea was developed more than a century ago by pragmatist philosopher William James and elaborated on in the international law setting in Jan Klabbers, 'On Epistemic Universalism and the Melancholy of International Law' (2018) 29 EJIL 1057.

CHAPTER 2

Crisis? What Damned Crisis?

Iain Scobbie

It's not the bullet that kills you, it's the hole.[1]

.·.

Catherine Parr Traill,[2] an early English colonist in Canada, was of the opinion that, 'In cases of emergency, it is folly to fold one's hands and sit down to bewail in abject terror: it is better to be up and doing'.[3] But faced with crises, whether international *per se* or where the international impinges upon the domestic sphere, what do international lawyers do? What should they, or rather we, do?

In 2004, Paul Romer, then a professor at Stanford University and subsequently a Nobel Prize Winner in Economic Science, when discussing the increasing competition that US industry faced from rising educational levels abroad, observed that 'A crisis is a terrible thing to waste'.[4] This was not a negative comment, but more a call to arms, a call to address an emerging and potentially challenging and possibly detrimental state of affairs. It has an affinity with Hilary Charlesworth's adage that:

> International lawyers revel in a good crisis. A crisis provides a focus for the development of the discipline and it also allows international lawyers the sense that their work is of immediate, intense relevance.[5]

---

1 Laurie Anderson (1977)

2 See Charlotte Gray, *Sisters in the Wilderness: The Lives of Suzanna Moodie and Catherine Parr Traill* (Penguin 2000). It must be admitted that neither Mrs Moodie nor Mrs Traill would have approved of the original title of this chapter which was somewhat more emphatic.

3 Catherine Parr Traill, *The Canadian Settler's Guide*, chapter titled 'Fire' (first published 1855, 7th edn, Toronto, 1857) 194, 196.

4 See Jack Rosenthal, 'A Terrible Thing to Waste' *New York Times* (New York, 31 July 2009) <https://www.nytimes.com/2009/08/02/magazine/02FOB-onlanguage-t.html> accessed 23 March 2021.

5 Hilary Charlesworth, 'International Law: A Discipline of Crisis' (2002) 65 MLR 377; compare Rebecca Ingber, 'Interpretation Catalysts and Executive Branch Legal Decisionmaking' (2013) 38 Yale J Int'l L 359.

Another way to perceive the law–generative capability of a crisis might be to classify it as a 'Grotian moment' – 'a transformative development in which new rules and doctrines of customary international law emerge with unusual rapidity and acceptance'.[6]

But is this a correct or an appropriate way for us, as international lawyers, to react to a 'crisis'? The initial question that must be addressed is not 'what is a crisis?', but to go one step further than that to ask who decides when a 'crisis' exists? Who controls the narrative? This question has become more acute given the blossoming of the phenomenon of 'fake news', which always was there, but which has been magnified by pernicious social media accounts which frequently target conspiracies and allegations to recipients who are thought to be susceptible. Legally this can be mirrored by the knee–jerk generation of 'tabloid scholarship',[7] which all too instantaneously offers up clear–cut analyses and solutions in (social) media and blogs, without pause for reflection or consideration of their wider systemic implications. And all the time this can be augmented by conscious and deliberate misdirection by political élites who, like magicians, distract their audience to get it to focus on some unimportant object instead of where the sleight of hand is actually happening, away from their mis–governance, mis–management, or sheer incompetence in the conduct of public affairs.

Just like Hilary Charlesworth's international lawyers, politicians also thrive on 'crises'. As a professional class, they need to be seen to be doing 'something', characteristically passing yet more laws domestically while talking externally to other governments and politicians, or at international fora such as summits or within intergovernmental organisations, conspicuously governing, dealing with 'crises', whether real or manufactured, in order to justify their continued existence, power, and influence. Much political discourse has degenerated into a 'war' on everything – the war on COVID, the war on drugs, the war on terrorism, the war on the 'other' however the 'other' is defined. The rhetorical trope is not one of challenges to be faced, but rather one of conflict. The notion of 'crisis' has been weaponised to achieve political ends, all too often at the expense of civil liberties and human rights, in which law is expected to play the role of handmaiden and facilitator. Should we, us international lawyers and as international lawyers, be complicit in this process?

It is manifestly obvious that the COVID pandemic constitutes a crisis, regardless of how one defines a 'crisis', but would an appropriate response be

---

6   Michael P Scharf, *Customary International Law in Times of Fundamental Change: Recognizing Grotian Moments* (CUP 2013) 5.

7   I owe this term to Joe Powderly of the University of Leiden.

the generation of new 'law' or should it rather be a question of the adoption of a new and appropriate regulatory regime, or a more assiduous implementation of existing regulations, rather than a change in the 'law' as such? Further, even if additional measures were to be adopted, it seems likely that these would be embodied in written instruments rather than through the emergence of new customary law, and one might even question if these could embody propositions of a 'fundamentally norm– creating character such as could be regarded as forming the basis of a general rule of law'.[8]

There should be reservations about the desirability of international lawyers advocating for the deviation from or replacement of established doctrine, either by the generation of new custom or through the radically different interpretation of settled propositions, when faced with a 'crisis'. It can be understood why politicians might want to do this, in order to pursue or consolidate their quest for power and not infrequently material gain, but why should lawyers? In the interests of honesty, I should admit that I generally subscribe to e. e. cummings' poetic definition of a politician which has an added force in these apparently 'post– truth' times where 'alternative facts' are given gospel credence–'a politician is an arse upon which everyone has sat except a man'[9] or, for that matter, a woman. I must concede that there are some exceptions to this rule, but we shall get to exceptions to rules later.

But what is a 'crisis'? Apart from physically material episodes such as a pandemic, natural disasters like earthquakes or tsunamis, famines or drought, situations which insurers might term 'acts of God', 'crises' tend to be situations which are dependent upon, are engineered by, or involve human agency in some significant if not critical way.[10] These are different types of 'facts'. The former can be classified as 'brute' facts, simply physical or material phenomena, but the latter depend on the application of an interpretative schema which identify them as 'crises' and thus may be classified as institutional facts:[11]

---

8   *North Sea Continental Shelf case (Federal Republic of Germany v the Netherlands)* [1969] ICJ Rep 3, 42, para 72.

9   e. e. cummings, *1 x 1*, 'No. 10' (Henry Holt 1944).

10   I am well aware that some famines result from direct human agency, whether politically motivated or as the result of armed conflict, such as the Povolzhye famine in the Soviet Union in 1921–22, or that in 1932–33 in which the forced collectivisation of agriculture was a significant contributing factor, or the Great Chinese Famine of 1959–61 in which the Communist Party's Great Leap Forward policy was closely implicated, or the 2017 famine in Sudan and the current crisis in Yemen which have been exacerbated by armed conflict, but others are predominantly 'natural'.

11   For an account of the notion of brute and institutional facts, see, e.g., Neil MacCormick, *Institutions of Law: An Essay in Legal Theory* (OUP 2007); and Neil MacCormick, *Rhetoric and the Rule of Law: A Theory of Legal Reasoning* (OUP 2005) especially ch. 1; and also

those facts that depend not only on some physical events and occurrences which are supposed to have taken place, but also on an interpretation of these (and/ or other) events or occurrences in terms of some stable set of norms (either institutional or conventional norms) of conduct
or of discourse.[12]

In short, when faced with a situation which is not a mere material brute fact,
identifying a situation as a 'crisis' depends on interpretation, but who makes
this decision, who controls the narrative?

It could often be that this determination is made from a relatively detached
and objective standpoint by recognised experts using quantifiable or statistical
criteria, for example, the claim that there has been a crisis in opioid prescrip-
tion drug abuse in certain areas of the United States, but when we are dealing with international affairs this type of metric is often lacking and claims
of 'crises' all too often impinge on matters of 'politics' and/or 'security' in one
way or another. This type of claim depends inexorably on presentation and
the selection of facts, issues, and arguments, all of which involve the rhetorical
technique of 'presence', the argumentative concentration on particular factors
in order to stress their importance while discounting or de-emphasising other
factors. The selection of data, topics, and modes of argument is inevitable in
the construction of any narrative:

> choice is ... a dominant factor in scientific debates: choice of the facts
> deemed relevant, choice of hypotheses, choice of the theories that should
> be confronted with the facts, choice of the actual elements that consti-
> tute facts. The method of each science implies such a choice, which is
> relatively stable in the natural sciences, but is much more variable in the
> social sciences.
>
> By the very fact of selecting certain elements and presenting them
> to the audience, their importance and pertinency to the discussion are
> implied. Indeed, such a choice endows those elements with a presence,
> which is an essential factor in argumentation.[13]

Iain Scobbie, 'Legal Theory as a Source of International Law: Institutional Facts and the
Identification of International Law' in Samantha Besson and Jean d'Aspremont (eds), *The
Oxford Handbook on the Sources of International Law* (OUP 2017) 493.

12   MacCormick, *Rhetoric and the Rule of Law* (n 10) 65.

13   Chaïm Perelman and Lucie Olbrechts–Tyteca, *The New Rhetoric: A Treatise on
Argumentation* (John Wilkinson and Purcell Weaver trs, University of Notre Dame Press
1969) 29, 116: originally published as *La Nouvelle Rhétorique: Traité de l'Argumentation*
(Presses Universitaires de France 1958).

The content of any argument is simply selective, emphasising some factors while ignoring others, and this is never disinterested but is geared towards the picture its author wishes to present, and to present persuasively, in order to justify action in response to the perceived 'crisis'. But it is equally inexorable that different interpretations may be constructed of the same 'crisis', and that a response justified by one party may be contested and perhaps even seen as manifestly unlawful by another. How should we international lawyers react to these competing claims?

Martti Koskenniemi has observed that when he worked for the Finnish foreign ministry, politicians seeking international legal advice saw every situation as a 'new, exceptional, crisis'. The legal adviser's function was to link this back to precedents, to 'tell it as part of a history', and thus to present it as meshed in 'narratives in which it received a generalizable meaning' in order that the politician 'could see what to do with it'.[14] But is this always possible? Faced with demands that some new 'crisis' exists, whether emanating from politicians or from traditional or social media which claim to reflect 'public opinion', pressure might build on lawyers to proffer novel 'legal solutions'. The claim that an international 'crisis' exists can all too often give rise to an existential dread on the part of international lawyers which causes us to question whether our professional lives, if not that of the very profession itself, have meaning, purpose, or indeed any value at all apart from keeping ourselves in a job.

This can lead to a normative panic, as these 'crises' almost seem to require some proactive reaction by lawyers, some attempt to meet the perceived exigencies of the situation which aims at providing a 'solution'. This may often involve norm entrepreneurship, where novel interpretations of existing norms are proposed or claims are made that the existing normative framework is inadequate and must be replaced. Frequently these proposals entail a plea to exceptionalism in one form or another – that the situation is completely unprecedented; that the State concerned is facing threats which are unique to it and to no other; or that the circumstances demand that an exception be made to existing doctrine.

During a 'crisis', we international lawyers face the peril of succumbing to the accommodation of political pretensions, descending into the apologetic justification of State behaviour: courting patronage, international lawyers all too often applaud the emperor's new clothes. As Philip Allott has observed,

---

14   Martti Koskenniemi, 'International Law in Europe: Between Tradition and Renewal' (2005) 16 EJIL 113, 120.

"international law is left speaking to governments the words that governments want to hear",[15] and thus remains marginal in the international system:

> International law has been neither very threatening nor very useful to the politicians and the diplomats".[16]

Examples of international lawyers facilitating the legal justification of States' desires and bending to political winds are not lacking, especially in times of perceived 'crisis'. For example, Richard Falk has observed that, although not inevitable, the outcome of the application of New Haven analysis to a given issue 'had an uncomfortable tendency to coincide with the outlook of the US government and to seem more polemically driven than scientifically demonstrated'[17] – exhibiting a 'penchant for applying their theory in justification of U.S. foreign policy'.[18]

This should not be surprising given the foundational objectives of the New Haven School. Its genesis lay in the Second World War and the emergence of communism as an international political force. In launching their project at the height of the war, New Haven's founding fathers, Harold Lasswell and Myres McDougal, argued that, when law schools in the United States reopened after hostilities ended, they should be 'a place where people who have risked their lives can wisely risk their minds'.[19] Their aim for legal education was to provide systematic training for policy–makers attuned to 'the needs of a free and productive commonwealth':

---

15   Philip Allott, *Eunomia: New Order for a New World* (OUP 1990, reprinted 2001) 296, 16.1. The text of the reprint usefully retains the pagination of the first edition, but is augmented by a lengthy new preface which summarises the core ideas of Allott's thought and replies to the principal criticisms made to *Eunomia* on its first appearance. For commentaries on Allott's work, see the symposium 'Philip Allott's "Eunomia" and "The Health of Nations", Thinking Another World: "This cannot be how the world was meant to be" ' (2005) 16 EJIL 255; and Iain Scobbie, ' "The holiness of the heart's affection": Philip Allott's Theory of Social Idealism' in Alexander Orakhelashvili (ed), *Research Handbook on the Theory and History of International Law* (Edward Elgar 2011) 168.

16   Allott, *Eunomia* (n 14) 297, 16.3.

17   Richard Falk, 'Casting the Spell: the New Haven School of International Law', (1995) 104 Yale LJ 1991, 2001; and Harold H Koh, 'Is There a "New" New Haven School of International Law?', (2007) 32 Yale J Int'l L 559, 563.

18   Falk (n 16) 1997.

19   Harold D Lasswell and Myres S McDougal, 'Legal Education and Public Policy: Professional Training in the Public Interest' (1943) 52 Yale LJ 203, 292.

The proper function of our law schools is, in short, to contribute to the training of policy-makers for the ever more complete achievement of the democratic values that constitute the professed ends of American polity.[20]

On the other hand, the ideologically competing pre-perestroika Cold War Soviet theory of international law, as exemplified in the writings of Grigorii Tunkin,[21] was so firmly rooted in Marxist-Leninist doctrine that, at times, it seemed simply to amount to taking the dogma for a walk.

But this malleability to the pressures of political exigencies need not always be the case. Take the example of Gerald Fitzmaurice in relation to the Suez Crisis of 1956.[22] Following Egypt's nationalisation of the Suez Canal, the United Kingdom government wanted to take action to assert control over the canal through the use of armed force. Fitzmaurice was then legal adviser to the Foreign Office and strenuously denied that a lawful response to nationalisation could lie in the use of force. His lines of communication to political decision makers were impeded and blocked, and his advice ignored:

when the Minister of State at the Foreign Office, Sir Anthony Nutting, recommended that Fitzmaurice should be brought in 'on a matter which involved taking the law into our own hands', [Prime Minister] Eden's response was that 'Fitz is the last person I want consulted. The lawyers are always against our doing anything. For God's sake, keep them out of it. This is a political affair'.[23]

It is perhaps not a coincidence that Fitzmaurice was dismissive of the approach to international law adopted by the New Haven School – 'Aiming at order and

---

20   Lasswell and McDougal (n 18) 206; see also Falk (n 16) 1993.

21   See, eg Grigorii I Tunkin, *Theory of International Law* (William E Butler tr, Allen and Unwin 1974); and Grigorii I Tunkin, *The Tunkin Diary and Lectures* (William E Butler and Vladimir G Tunkin ed and tr, Eleven 2012).

22   See Lewis Johnman, 'Playing the Role of a Cassandra: Sir Gerald Fitzmaurice, Senior Legal Adviser to the Foreign Office' (1999) 13 Contemporary British History 46; Geoffrey Marston, 'Armed Intervention in the 1956 Suez Crisis: the Legal Advice Tendered to the British Government' (1988) 37 ICLQ 773.

23   Quoted Johnman (n 21) 56. Lord McNair, former President of the International Court, was equally scathing of the legal position adopted by the UK government, see Johnman (n 21) 59–60; and Marston (n 21) 812–814.

liberality, its concepts, by their very breadth, open the door to anarchy and abuse'.[24]

These differences of approach highlight the question of the correct or appropriate relationship between the lawyer and the law, if this is perceived as a set of reasonably discernible principles to guide and evaluate behaviour, and the relationship between the lawyer and his or her client. How much strength does it take for lawyers to say 'no' to a client who is hellbent on setting in motion a manifestly unlawful train of events or, like Fitzmaurice, if they make their views known, will they simply be sidelined?

There is always the risk that lawyers may too easily identify with their client and the client's interests: this is an inherent danger in law which is an instrumental practice aimed at justifying claims and justifying action. It would be stupid to claim that us, we international lawyers, are apolitical, but as a class we must examine and take responsibility for our politics and for the consequences of our choices. The issue is one of integrity, both personal and professional, what I have called elsewhere 'Tom Franck's moral compass',[25] as although law is instrumental, it should contain a vector of constraint as well as enablement. It does us no good and denies us credibility if we simply become lackeys to politics, swaying uncertainly as its winds blow hither and thither.

'Be careful what you wish for' should be our governing maxim. Lawyers' reasoning can too easily switch between advocacy in aid of a client and recourse to a more disinterested authoritative account of the 'law'. In times of 'crisis' the former can lead to argumentation which is atomised and asystematic, focusing on the particular issue while failing to consider the wider, and future, normative implications that an immediate reaction might entail. A descent into apology, proffering normative support to novel State conduct, too easily suggests that all State practice becomes relevant to some normative realignment, where the measures adopted in an 'emergency' become the new 'normal', in which every action or reaction is somehow thought to be relevant to a calculation of change.

We can, however, learn from 'crises'. They can demonstrate that the existing normative structure is inadequate to provide a robust answer or reaction to a

---

24   Gerald G Fitzmaurice, 'Vae Victis or Woe to the Negotiators! Your Treaty or 'Our' Interpretation of It?' (1971) 65 AJIL 358, 373.

25   See Iain Scobbie, 'Wicked Heresies or Legitimate Perspectives? Theory and International Law' in Malcolm Evans (ed), International Law, (3rd edn, OUP 2010), Section V, 'The Decadence of Hegemonic Instrumentalism', referring to Thomas M Franck, 'Raising the Hoe: the New Clientage: Andy and Me at Vanderbilt Hall' (2009) 42 NYU J Int'l Law and Pol 11.

given situation. There are two competing issues at place here: the notion of negative feedback and the doctrine of inertia. Negative feedback lies in the realisation that existing normative propositions are lacking in perspective or efficacy which can then lead to a search for a better crafted and more appropriate or desirable solution.[26] The doctrine of inertia refers to the presumption that, failing contrary proof, an attitude adopted in the past should subsist and may be relied upon, because change requires justification.[27] This was one of the major contributions to argumentation theory by Chaïm Perelman which provides a foundation for the ascription of the burden of proof in practical discourse,[28] and which he argues underlies the rule of formal justice that what has been considered as valid in one situation will be considered valid in all similar situations. These two vectors, the opposition of stability and change, must be balanced and handled with discernment. The time to make lasting decisions is not at the height of a 'crisis' when a detached evaluation of which changes, if any, should be made can too easily be blunted by a kaleidoscopic blizzard of changing and mutating factors and immediate concerns. We need to take a step back, take a breath, take time to think, and not simply blindly react.

There needs to be a systemic analysis of the implications of any proposed changes; for instance, consider some relatively recent attempts to reformulate and widen the parameters of self–defence, ostensibly under the guise of the so–called crisis labelled the 'war on terror'.[29] These involve a number of inter–twined strands of argument on the part of States, politicians, and lawyers who advocate for change, such as norm entrepreneurship; a desire to have or to

---

26   On negative feedback see, eg, FA von Hayek, *Law, Legislation and Liberty* (Routledge and Kegan Paul 1973–1979), especially Volume 1, *Rules and Order* (1973).

27   See Perelman and Olbrechts–Tyteca (n 12) s 27, 104–110, and s 52, 218–220; also Chaïm Perelman, *Justice, Law, and Argument: Essays on Moral and Legal Reasoning* (Reidel: Dordrecht: 1980) 27–28, 169 *et seq*. Perelman sees inertia as allowing the transition from normal to norm by way of argumentative justification, although he concedes that Hume's view that this is a logically illicit transition is valid (for instance at *Justice, Law, and Argument* (n 12) 28). Hume's argument is in David Hume, *A Treatise on Human Nature* (Clarendon Press 1739) §III.i.1. On Hume's argument, see John L Mackie, *Hume's Moral Theory* (Routledge and Kegan Paul 1980) Chapter Four; and also Chaïm Perelman, *Logique Juridique: Nouvelle Rhétorique* (Dalloz 1976) paras 49, 99–101.

28   See Robert Alexy, *A Theory of Legal Argumentation: The Theory of Rational Discourse as Theory of Legal Justification* (Ruth Adler and Neil MacCormick trs, Clarendon Press 1989) ch. 4.

29   For a more detailed examination of some of these issues regarding self–defence, see Iain Scobbie, 'Exceptions: Self–defence as an Exception to the Prohibition of the Use of Force' in Lorand Bartels and Federica Paddeu (eds), *Exceptions in International Law* (OUP 2020) 150. This volume contains a useful survey of both conceptual and substantive issues.

create a normative framework which is meant to address perceived problems States argue are raised by non–State actors or armed groups; feelings of uncertainty and inadequacy in dealing with possible threats formulated abroad; and a confusion, which might be conscious, of legal categories which otherwise might be seen as distinct. Some of these attempts have been criticised and dismissed by doctrinal writings, such as the unreconstructed Bush doctrine of pre–emptive self–defence even in the absence of an imminent threat,[30] while others have gained more traction, even though they might simply present discredited arguments anew.

One of the principal areas of controversy is that of self–defence against non–State armed groups which are located abroad. While a State taking action against a non–State armed group within its own territory might raise human rights questions, it does not raise issues related to the international law governing self–defence. Key questions here include whether a State may lawfully take armed action against a non–State armed group located within another State in the absence of invitation or consent when it deems that the latter is unable or unwilling to take effective or repressive action against that armed group to contain or end actual or threatened attacks planned or perpetrated by it; and what constitutes 'imminence' in relation to an anticipated attack. The latter might simply be the Bush doctrine revived.

Proposals of this type, such as the principles proposed by Daniel Bethlehem in 2012, are avowed attempts at norm entrepreneurship. He noted that much doctrinal commentary has discussed the question of resort to self–defence by States against imminent and actual armed attacks by non–State actors, but this has had little impact on governmental and military decision–makers as '[t]here is little intersection between the academic debate and the operational realities'. In contrast, his principles were 'informed by detailed discussions over recent years with foreign ministry, defense ministry, and military legal advisers from a number of States who have operational experience in these matters'.[31] In 2017, in expounding the United Kingdom government's understanding of 'imminence' in relation to invoking self–defence in relation to threats posed by non–State armed groups, the then UK Attorney General, Jeremy Wright, expressly endorsed the Bethlehem Principles, reiterating that these had been

---

30   See, eg, Christine Gray, *International Law and the Use of Force* (3rd edn, OUP 2008) 209–216, and also 4th edn (OUP 2018) 248-253; and Christine Gray, 'The Bush Doctrine Revisited: the 2006 National Security Strategy of the USA' (2006) 5 Chinese JIL 555.

31   Daniel Bethlehem, 'Self–Defense Against an Imminent or Actual Armed Attack by Non–State Actors' (2012) 106 AJIL 770, 773.

informed by 'detailed official–level discussions'.[32] The non–disinterested origin of these principles has attracted comment and criticism in scholarly reaction – for example, by two former legal advisers to the UK Foreign Office who stated that 'it was no doubt anticipated that a select group of governmental representatives might reach agreement among themselves when the UN membership as a whole could not'.[33]

One prominent aspect of this attempt to expand the parameters of self–defence is the use of targeted killings by drones against specific individuals, the notion of 'personality strikes', who may be nationals of the State concerned, as opposed to 'signature strikes' which are employed against those who display alleged characteristics of terrorist activity or involvement.[34] This seems to be an exercise in collapsing categories. The recourse to self–defence as a justification for engaging in targeted killings is ambivalent, blurring the borders between the *ius ad bellum*, the *ius in bello* through the invocation of the direct participation in hostilities by civilians who are members of non-State armed groups, and international human rights law, making issues liminal, as they exist neither here nor there.

Consider this statement made by then UK Prime Minister David Cameron in the House of Commons on 7 September 2015 regarding the targeted killing by a Royal Air Force drone of United Kingdom nationals, alleged to be members of the Islamic State armed group, and who were alleged to be involved in plotting terrorist attacks in the United Kingdom and other States. He said that as 'their intention was the murder of British citizens':

> We took this action because there was no alternative. In this area, there is no Government we can work with; we have no military on the ground to detain those preparing plots; ... we had no way of preventing his planned

---

32   Jeremy Wright, 'The Modern Law of Self–Defence', (Speech at International Institute for Strategic Studies, London, 11 January 2017) 15 <https://assets.publishing.service.gov.uk/government/uploads/system/uploads/attachment_data/file/583171/170111_Imminence_Speech_.pdf> accessed 23 March 2021.

33   Elizabeth Wilmshurst and Michael Wood, 'Self–Defence Against Non–State Actors: Reflections on the "Bethlehem Principles"' (2013) 107 AJIL 390, 391: see also, eg, Michael Glennon, 'Law, Power, and Principles' (2013) 107 AJIL 378; Mary Ellen O'Connell, 'Dangerous Departures' (2013) 107 AJIL 380, 384–385; and Victor Kattan, 'Furthering the "War on Terrorism" Through International Law: How the United States and the United Kingdom Resurrected the Bush Doctrine on Using Preventative Military Force to Combat Terrorism' (2018) 5 Journal on the Use of Force and International Law 97, 112–123.

34   For a critical analysis of this distinction, see Kevin Jon Heller, ' "One Hell of a Killing Machine": Signature Strikes and International Law' (2013) 11 JICJ 89.

attacks on our country without taking direct action ... We were exercising the UK's inherent right to self–defence. There was clear evidence of these individuals planning and directing armed attacks against the UK ... given the prevailing circumstances in Syria, the airstrike was the only feasible means of effectively disrupting the attacks that had been planned and directed. It was therefore necessary and proportionate for the individual self–defence of the United Kingdom.[35]

Self–defence – *ius ad bellum*; planned attacks – *ius in bello*, under the rubric of direct participation in hostilities; inability to detain – human rights law; but which should be predominant? It is commonplace that legal reasoning is cumulative, but surely all the reasons should point in the same direction?

Targeted killings are only lawful within the context of an armed conflict, whether international or non–international,[36] otherwise they are unlawful extra–judicial executions. There are two pertinent issues here. Does a claim of recourse to self–defence by a State against a purported non–State armed group automatically entail the existence of an armed conflict between them? If a claim of self–defence is being made by a State is there a sufficient intensity of conflict to determine that an armed conflict exists, or that its adversary is actually an organised armed group which is capable of being classified as a party to a conflict?[37] If incidents perpetrated by a suitably organised group are sporadic and episodic, can the intensity of a purported conflict be hypothetical or potential where there is 'no specific evidence of where an attack will take place or of the precise nature of an attack',[38] or even that such an attack might take place?

Let us suppose that, despite these reservations, an armed conflict may exist between a State and a non–State armed group and that the State conducts targeted killings extra–territorially under the rubric of self–defence. This entails conflict beyond and without borders, ripping off the territorial constraints identified by distinguished commentators such as Christopher Greenwood

---

35   House of Commons Debates, 7 September 2015, Vol. 599, Columns 25–26: see also the House of Lords and House of Commons Joint Committee on Human Rights Second Report of Session 2015–16, *The Government's Policy on the Use of Drones for Targeted Killing*, HL Paper 141/HC 574 (10 May 2016), Chapters 3 and 5; and Intelligence and Security Committee of Parliament, UK *Lethal Drone Strikes in Syria*, HC 1152 (26 April 2017).

36   On classification of conflicts, the leading work is Elizabeth Wilmshurst (ed), *International law and the Classification of Conflicts* (OUP 2012).

37   See Noam Lubell, 'The War (?) Against Al-Qaeda' in Wilmshurst (n 35), 421, 434–437.

38   Bethlehem (n 30) 776: quoted and endorsed in Wright (n 31) 17.

and Daniel O'Connell.[39] Law, however, is reflexive: normative proposals and classifications made to govern others equally govern you. If a conflict can legitimately be taken abroad by the State, then can it not equally legitimately be brought home by the non–State armed group, making acts generally denounced as 'terrorism' be reclassified as acts of 'war'? During an apparently never–ending 'war on terror' are, for instance, civilian operators of weaponised drones legitimate targets, and their families and possibly neighbours collateral damage? Would such a reclassification make (civilian) populations think about what their politicians have wrought ostensibly in their name, and reflect upon the effects these decisions have had on people far away? We have to be careful what we wish for because it can bite back.

As international lawyers we must be rational and clear–sighted. In times of 'crisis' a seductive argument can too easily be made that because these are exceptional times or present exceptional challenges, exceptions or reclassifications or changes should be made to established doctrine or interpretation. International lawyers should tread cautiously and carefully weigh arguments in favour of these temptations and pressures which can all too easily become embedded in doctrine and unshackle States and politicians from normative restraints. All too often these claims are normatively localised, focusing on a narrow issue without regard to its systemic ramifications. We must be disciplined in our approach to our discipline in order to guard against a:

> lawless science of our law,
> that codeless myriad of precedent,
> that wilderness of single instances ...[40]

Would it not be more honest for us international lawyers to acknowledge that State action in response to a given 'crisis' might be illegal rather to than dress it up in a spurious legal tinsel which glitters and whose only function is to distract us and others from the politicians' sleight of hand? When do we embrace responsibility for our discipline?

---

39 See Christopher Greenwood, 'The Relationship between *ius ad bellum* and *ius in bello*' (1983) 9 Review of International Studies 221; Daniel O'Connell, *The Influence of Law on Sea Power* (Manchester University Press 1975) ch. 9.

40 Alfred, Lord Tennyson, *Aylmer's Field* (first published 1864, MacMillan and Co 1891) 14.

CHAPTER 3

Crisis Narratives and the Tale of Our Anxieties

Hélène Ruiz Fabri

Un sage oriental demandait toujours, dans ses prières, que la divinité voulût bien lui épargner de vivre une époque intéressante. Comme nous ne sommes pas sages, la divinité ne nous a pas épargnés et nous vivons une époque intéressante. En tout cas, elle n'admet pas que nous puissions nous désintéresser d'elle. Les écrivains d'aujourd'hui savent cela. S'ils parlent, les voilà critiques et attaques. Si, devenus modestes, ils se taisent, on ne leur parlera plus que de leur silence, pour le leur reprocher bruyamment.[1]

∴

While I was struggling with the few lines below, Oscar Wilde's famous quote "the only thing worse than being talked about is not being talked about" came to my mind, and I briefly thought that the only thing worse than having nothing to say about crisis narratives was having to write about crisis narratives. After one pandemic year, and as a recently published comic showed accurately, I was a researcher looking for meaning in what she was doing. Indeed, was it possible to do something meaningful in research, except speaking of COVID-19? The big global pandemic crisis was probably covering millions of tiny individual crises like mine, each of us in our bubble. However, silence was not an option.

At first, the invitation to write about crisis narratives had thrilled me as it had immediately rung a bell. It made me feel young. Indeed, I had begun to struggle with the subject-matter of my doctoral thesis, customary international law, in a context where, if I were to believe the literature, the crisis was a core issue – the crisis of international law or the international legal system, crisis of customary international law, veering between instant and long term, wisdom and wildness (to borrow the words of René-Jean Dupuy opposing *coutume sage* et *coutume sauvage*). Said crisis played a significant part in the attraction

---

1 Albert Camus, Conférence d'Upsala, 14 décembre 1957, A. Camus, *Essais*, Bibliothèque de la Pléiade (Gallimard, 1965), p. 1079.

to the topic as, where there is a crisis – or it is said so, there is certainly something new to say. Without that trigger, what could a young scholar bring to an eternal topic on which so much literature had already been published? The crisis had opened a window of opportunity, including to reflect on what allowed speaking of a crisis? About which crisis were people speaking?

Indeed, such vocabulary sounds quite dramatic and suggests something serious. However, it does not mean that there is consensus in all definitions that dictionaries provide for the term crisis. Some sources define a crisis as "a time of great danger, difficulty or confusion when problems must be solved, or important decisions must be made" (Oxford English Dictionary) or "a time when a problem, a bad situation or an illness is at its worst point" (Oxford Advanced American Dictionary). Other sources like the *Trésor de la langue française* propose a more sophisticated definition offering to stress the idea either of "sudden and intense manifestation of certain phenomena, marking a rupture", or of "a troubled situation, due to a loss of balance and the outcome of which is decisive for the individual or society, giving rise to fear or hope for a profound change" (translation of the author). The common trend is the drama reaching an apex; the differences are the connotations. A crisis is not necessarily dire and does not necessarily involve changes. One can wonder whether the more intense the drama, the more ineluctable the changes. Discourses may swing between the return to normal and prediction of a "new normal". Nevertheless, more than that, one can wonder about the state of mind of those using the qualification of crisis, either to study crises through the lens of international law or to study international law through the lens of crisis.

1/ To analyse crises through the lens of international law is incredibly banal. Each discipline, including international law, crosses fashions. Some words then become more common. Lately, international lawyers heard – and wrote – a lot about empire and decolonisation. However, "crisis" is a word which seems to escape all fashions and never looks outdated, quite the opposite, always at hand to help approach and narrate a situation of broken balance. Whether this balance was satisfactory may be another issue. Notwithstanding, the corresponding underlying value judgement plays a role in the crisis narrative.

When I was drawn to the analysis of the concept of crisis, I could see crises everywhere. Indeed, the 1980s were a period of crisis. The new international economic order had aborted, just as the new international information order, the monetarist school was taking over Keynesianism, the contestation of the international legal order fizzled out, AIDS spread, famines tormented Ethiopia. Was it the 1970s which were a period of crisis in which the 1980s were receiving the effects and consequences? Oil shocks, the fall of the golden standard, a swarm of *"nations prolétaires"*, in Franz Fanon's words, which were claiming their majority to put international law upside down. Nevertheless, weren't these the effects of the crisis/crises of the 1960s? Decolonisation, the Vietnam war among many other national liberation wars, the South-West Africa case, the right of self-determination, Russian missiles in Cuba. Or maybe, these were the consequences of the 1950s? And so on back in time. The listed examples are necessarily subject to criticisms if one does not consider them as somehow randomly picked examples. They have in common to have at some point given way to an analysis, or a diagnosis, in terms of crisis. However, it shows how relativistic and flexible the term is, as a temporal and spatial perspective quickly shows.

Generally, crisis narratives are dated. What is seen as a crisis at some point may last in memories as a historical event but not as a "crisis" in most cases. That a situation or an event remains named a crisis does not even mean that it was more outstanding than others that lost such qualification through time, nor that it lasted longer. It might merely be that it has become part of its familiar name like "the Cuban Missile Crisis". In other words, the closer to an event or a situation, the greater the tendency to qualify it as a crisis, whereas such qualification might vanish through time. Crises are also located. The spatial scope can vary from global to local (which tells nothing about their intensity). Events or situations lived or seen as a crisis somewhere may not be seen as such elsewhere. There is no authority to tell us that the use of the word is more or less legitimate in one case than in another, even if everyone knows that it is part of a rhetoric which can be abused. Where is the term "crisis" located on the scale of our words? Does the question have a special bearing for lawyers, even more for international lawyers?

Having had to sit on a multidisciplinary body, I had the good fortune to meet with a physicist whose speciality was tribology. Simply put, it is the science of friction. A thousand images of various and varied frictions crossed my mind, making me laugh at first. Don't we spend a good part of our life scratching against one another, both literally and figuratively? I perceived the factual reality, but it took some explanation, and, as often for beginners, an excellent example to understand the scientific issue. Thus, I was told about the design of the tiles forming the envelope of a space shuttle. The latter rubs against the air when it takes off, then against something else (do not ask me) when it leaves the atmosphere. The nature and intensity of this friction – and the wear and tear it can generate – must be taken into account for the shuttle to resist and return. It was simple and obvious. It was also evident that it involved calculations that I could not understand, but the idea was there. Isn't law, or the discourse on law, itself a science and engineering of friction? Suffices to admit that relationships between physical and/or legal entities can be seen as frictions. Not any friction is unpleasant or damaging, but some may be. The rules surrounding our relationships may be aimed at preventing them from becoming unpleasant (prevention or lubrication) or helping to remedy the possible inconvenience (redress or redesign). What is a crisis from such a functional perspective? Is it one type of friction belonging as such to the usual business of law? Yes and no.

Indeed, there is a constant bias resulting from the fact that little is said in legal literature about what works well, which does not exclude vigilance or criticism, but because, like in newspapers, good news does not get much attention. Without a crisis, and the worry it causes, it is enough to let the law work as it is. Who cares about the rules of international air transport until a plane is shot down? In the absence of a crisis or one-off event, this remains an honourable and respected speciality but largely ignored. Perhaps if we admit that the jurist is to society what the physician is to the individual, does the tendency to be interested in pathologies more than good health make sense? It remains a bias nonetheless, and undoubtedly this bias affects academics more than practitioners. Perhaps crises help to enhance the usefulness of law – and lawyers – but also its limits?

Common wisdom wants crisis times to need rules more than ever to manage outstanding frictions that inevitably occur. Of course, there is more. "Crisis" is not only a convenient descriptor to convince of the seriousness of a situation or event without having to go into details. However, law has its language, while being itself a language. Jurists generally choose their words according to the legal consequences possibly attached to them (this is also why the word "crisis" may be avoided to prevent any idea of a pre-judgment. Thus, what is felt and/ or named a crisis in the field may become an "incident" when a case is brought before the International Court of Justice). Crisis is, on the legal scale of words, one of those which lead to at least two questions which are actually linked: the first and most immediate is that of the justification for exceptional measures; the second, which begins with the exception but extends beyond, is that of change.

These two questions have, of course, broader implications. They cover an assessment of the efficiency of the existing rules, provided one assumes law actually can play a role in solving or overcoming crises. In such a functionalist perspective, as much as rules are seen as tools to deal with crises, crisis narratives are tools to contextualise the rules. They are instrumental in explaining the existing rules' (in)adequacy and the eventual elaboration of new rules. One cannot ignore that significant changes often occur in the aftermath of crises, and it is often assumed or narrated that such changes would not have been possible without the preceding crisis. These changes are most of the time translated into legal rules which reflect the power balance then reached. That this balance is unstable is inevitable as society is a living body.

Nevertheless, law is conservative and does not move at the same pace as society. For example, it is often said that international humanitarian law is fighting the last war. More generally, law looks at life in a rear-view mirror. Not that it cannot have an anticipatory function, but the latter is closely linked to the past to which law answers and from which it was born. How do we tell this past, of which crisis narratives are part? Moreover, as mostly reflecting past times, law can play a role in triggering a crisis, when the gap between it and the facts is such that it becomes directly contested and the object of the crisis.

2/ Analysing international law through the lens of crisis leads to tackle the recurring issue of the crisis of international law itself. The literature is peppered with writings evoking the crisis of law, like the issue entitled "Crises dans le droit" (Crises within the law),[2] published in 1986, in *Droits*, the *Revue française de théorie juridique*. Although not dedicated to international law, this publication pointed to issues which have also given rise to ample literature in international law and showed that crisis narratives as part of the discourse which supports what is said about the law, also speak about the narrators. This inevitably leads to wondering if the supposed crisis of the law is not also, or even above all, a crisis of the discourse on the law.

It all starts with expression of unease with the evolution of the law, what one might call a "technological crisis" (S. Rials). Law would not be anymore what it used to be. It would have become poorly manufactured, too quickly instrumentalised with an anarchic multiplication of rules. As if we had to answer every problem by enacting new rules because the existing ones would not be enough. It is indeed a multiplication of rules that has led to fragmentation, perceived by many as a pathology where others could see it as the opportunity for anti-hegemonic struggles, one of the dominant themes of the discourse on international law for more than two decades. From then on, the question was no longer only to assess whether the rules were "good"; it was also necessary to look at their articulation. Is this possible without a sufficiently informed overview which becomes beyond the reach of an ordinary international lawyer? Is this the legal translation of the rise of intersectionality?

Also, the said technological crisis affects the content as well as the container. Both have the disease of softness, also called relative normativity or managerialism. When it comes to content, the legal discourse is invaded by lacunae's assertion, while the absence of a specific written rule does not mean the absence of general principles. There are undoubtedly internal rationalisation efforts, such as those made by the International Law Commission. However, the use of "experts" no longer conceals the political agenda driving the endeavour. It reveals more than ever the instrumental vocation of law which, as a toolbox, could legitimise any purpose, but it also

---

2   Droits. *Revue française de théorie juridique* (Presses Universitaires de France, 1986), Issue 4.

shows the increasing confrontation between the old and the new. It reflects the growing polarisation of doctrinal discourse and its welcome diversification which lets other voices be heard and opens the way to alternative crisis narratives.

As we can see, we have gradually slipped from the technological crisis to an epistemological, or even ontological, crisis. However, how do we tell the latter? Like any crisis narrative, it only makes sense if it reveals the battles of ideas and the power struggles that drive the crisis. What do we do with it? Finally, as Jan Klabbers has quite rightly said, is not there the risk that international lawyers end up speaking more of themselves than of international law? However, maybe the term of crisis is here too quickly used, as a contribution to a growing emphasis in vocabulary linked to the obligation to express oneself with slogans?

As it happens, one of the most popular these days is "Never let a good crisis go to waste". What remains at stake is our ability to talk about change and its feasibility and to use crisis narratives as a means of opening a critical discussion, not closing it. The difficulty is that our narratives are situated because we are situated. It is up to us to know how to deal with our eventual parochialism. Indeed, if international law is not international, crisis narratives can be as diverse as our visions of international law.

Concerning the relationship mentioned above between crisis and exception, the exception seems to have become the period's legal technique to address emerging concerns, not just in response to the pandemic but much more generally. The exception is schizophrenic. First of all, it claims to be provisional, but without giving up on becoming the rule. However, above all, it can contribute to putting at stake the base of values on which the provisionally waived rule relies. The emergency measures that the pandemic provokes and at the same time justifies bring back debates not only on democracy and the free will of citizens in a context of crisis (when and where they exist) but also on sovereignty, solidarity and borders. We cannot waive our values when narrating a crisis to speak of the law. The latter may be a paper tiger but can also be the watchdog of fundamental values, whether we speak of the existing law or the law we wish to happen. It is time to return to Camus' words, "Le monde serait toujours désespérant s'il n'y avait pas l'homme, mais il y a l'homme et ses passions, ses rêves et sa communauté."[3]

---

3 Albert Camus, Lecture: "La crise de l'homme" (McMillin Theater, Columbia University, New York, 28 March 1946) <https://perma.cc/JQF4-LG9X> accessed 21 March 2021.

CHAPTER 4

Crisis and International Law

A Third World Approaches to International Law Perspective

B.S. Chimni

> The crisis consists precisely in the fact that the old is dying and the new cannot be born; in this interregnum a great variety of morbid symptoms appear.[1]

∴

1 Introduction

This essay offers some reflections on the theme of 'crisis and international law' from a third world approaches to international law (TWAIL) perspective. It departs from the standpoint of mainstream international law scholarship (MILS) which uses the term "crisis" primarily for events or episodes that expose gaps and inadequacies in particular domains of international law. In so far as TWAIL is concerned the crisis of modern international law is originary, deep and enduring and can be traced to its roots in colonialism. Indeed, in as much as the phenomenon of imperialism has played a central role in the evolution and development of modern international law the narrative of crisis has been written into the very being of contemporary international law. The different perspectives on crisis is also at the root of an epistemic crisis which has seen the emergence of several critical approaches to international law (CAIL). Given the different standpoints on "crisis" the first section of this essay is devoted to offering a typology of crisis and underscoring the significance of framing a crisis. The next section discusses the impending structural crisis of international law and institutions in the post pandemic era and its consequences for addressing the growing poverty and alienation of the peoples of the Global South and the global ecological crisis. The section also touches on the role of

---

1 Antonio Gramsci, *Selections from the Prison Notebooks* (International Publishers 1971) 276.

© B.S. CHIMNI, 2022 | DOI:10.1163/9789004472365_006

resistance at times of crisis in bringing about change in the international legal order. The essay concludes with some final remarks.

2 A Typology of Crisis

In order to understand different kinds of crisis that have characterized modern international law it is useful to make a distinction between material and epistemic crisis, the former a reference to objective real world developments and the latter to the sphere of knowledge production pertaining to the condition of international law.

2.1 *Material Crisis*

In so far as material crisis of international law is concerned it is possible to speak of at least four kinds of crisis: episodic, regional, structural, and originary crisis. An *episodic* crisis is a result of a serious violation of international law (e.g., Russian occupation of Crimea or China's rejection of South China Sea arbitral award) or a flawed response to particular developments (e.g., to migration and refugee flows to Europe). A *regional* crisis occurs when an entire area of international law such as international investment law (IIL) comes to be contested. IIL is in crisis today because of the sustained and effective questioning of its normative basis and the contested outcomes of inter-State dispute settlement (ISDS) mechanisms. A *structural* crisis indicates a simultaneous crisis in many fields of international law or what may be called a generalized crisis. For instance, the two world wars, and the accompanying failure of the "Peace through Law" project, caused a structural or generalized crisis in international law.[2] A structural crisis in the international legal system was also brought about by the October Revolution as there came to exist two radically different understandings of the evolution, doctrines, rules and the role of

---

2 The Preamble to the Charter of United Nations, which states the reasons for its adoption, testifies to the crises of international law and institutions in the first half of the 20ᵗʰ century: Charter of the United Nations (adopted 26 June 1945, entered into force 24 October 1945) 1 UNTS 16, preamble:

- to save succeeding generations from the scourge of war, which twice in our lifetime has brought untold sorrow to mankind, and
- to reaffirm faith in fundamental human rights, in the dignity and worth of the human person, in the equal rights of men and women and of nations large and small, and
- to establish conditions under which justice and respect for the obligations arising from treaties and other sources of international law can be maintained, and
- to promote social progress and better standards of life in larger freedom.

international law. A contemporary instance of a structural crisis is that caused by climate change and COVID-19 pandemic which simultaneously impact international health law, international economic and trade law, and international human rights law. An *originary* crisis relates to conditions that are foundational to modern international law. It refers both to the anarchic character of international society and to the inextricable relationship of modern international law with imperialism.

Every crisis can act as a catalyst for change in international law with the scope and extent of changes depending on the type of crisis. The word "crisis" is generally confined by MILS to episodic and regional crisis, which are seen as an opportunity for the positive development of international law; the crises are viewed as moments that lends dynamism to the legal order. In order to deal with episodic or regional crisis MILS identifies and recommends an "arsenal of devices".[3] These include techniques such as identifying gaps, weighing and balancing interests, advancing innovative interpretations, proposing new concepts and rules, and promoting institutionalization. These devices do not address the relationship of the crises with deep structures viz., global capitalism, global patriarchy and global racism. Therefore, the proposed responses may further the interests of the very social forces that have caused the crisis. In the event there could even be, as Crawford notes, 'a reversal of rules'.[4] This is what is happening in the instance of ongoing deglobalization. However, generally speaking, MILS is sanguine about the role of international law in an episodic or regional crisis. In its view, such crises lead to progressive efforts to fill normative and institutional gaps.

A structural crisis can lead to more far reaching changes. Over the past centuries each structural crisis has been the basis for a range of normative and institutional developments with the aim of stabilizing and legitimizing the international legal order. The rapid development of international human rights law (IHRL) in the aftermath of the second world war, or international environmental law (IENL) in the last quarter of the last century may be cited as evidence in this regard. Even in the instance of structural crisis MILS does not tend to draw attention to its links with deep structures. In contrast TWAIL points out that the two world wars can be traced to the workings of global capitalism, more specifically to inter-imperialist competition. The ensuing institutionalization of international life in the form of League of Nations and

---

3   James Crawford, 'Reflections on Crises and International Law' in George Ulrich, Ineta Ziemele (eds), *How International Law Works in Times of Crisis* (OUP 2019) 10, 17.

4   ibid 15.

the United Nations was meant to prevent these in the future, albeit without undermining the imperialist project.[5]

Turning to originary crises MILS recognizes one dimension that flows from the anarchic nature of international society. For instance, Crawford writes that crises occur in international law because of 'the absence of any constitutional order, other than constitutional order of States'.[6] As a result national interest and nationalism trump international law (Morgenthau's "iron law of politics that international law gives way to national interest").[7] This form of originary crisis explains why the issue of compliance is seen as central to the integrity and effectiveness of international law.

But MILS does not take cognizance of the originary crisis flowing from the crisis of capitalist accumulation necessitating its universalization which has historically translated into imperialism assuming different forms in different eras. In the TWAIL view the phases of development of international law and institutions reflect the different phases of imperialism from the 17th century to the present. In other words, the story of crisis in international law is indissolubly bound to the history of imperialism.[8] It may only be added that imperialism is not simply about the exploitation and oppression of weak nations but also the rapacious exploitation of Nature with which capitalism is at war.

The TWAIL understanding of crisis is thus rooted in *deep history and deep structures*. In its view the crisis of and in modern international law will be with us as long as the phenomenon of imperialism is not addressed. The combination of anarchic nature of international society and imperialism greatly diminishes the possibility of bringing about change in the international legal system to meet the concerns of weak nations. This does not mean that international law merely advances the imperialist project. It manifests in the postcolonial era a degree of relative independence from deep structures and can tolerate reforms at times of crisis depending on the correlation of global social and political forces.

2.2 *Epistemic Crisis*

A material crisis can concurrently manifest an epistemic crisis as the two domains are intimately connected. But the dominance of positivist method in international law scholarship since the 19th century, averse as it is to

---

5 B.S. Chimni, 'Peace through Law: Lessons from 1914' (2015) 3 Lond Rev Int Law 245.

6 Crawford (n 3) 14.

7 B.S. Chimni, *International Law and World Order: A Critique of Contemporary Approaches* (2nd edn, CUP 2017) ch 2.

8 Antony Anghie, *Imperialism, Sovereignty and the Making of International Law* (CUP 2005).

inter-disciplinary analysis, has impeded the emergence of alternative legal epistemologies with distinct understanding of crisis. This has had serious implications for the progressive development of international law as scholarship plays a crucial role in both diagnosing the nature of the crisis and proposing, shaping and embedding suitable responses. Indeed, the writings of eminent scholars are treated as a subsidiary source of international law and in the absence of a global legislature help fill at times of crisis normative or institutional gaps in the international legal order.

It was the October Revolution which first introduced a rupture in the epistemic domain by speaking of international law as class law i.e., underscoring the role of classes, as against merely States, in the making of international law. The breach caused by the October revolution called forth, in the wake of the Cold War, its liberal counterpart in the form of the New Haven Approach to International Law (NHAIL) which was also critical of the positivist approach. But the latter rather than take an independent view of material and epistemological developments became too caught up in the Cold War. It therefore ended up collating social science materials to justify US foreign policies. What is more it did not seriously engage with the concerns and interests of decolonized nations.[9]

But in the post-Cold War era there have emerged, in response to the epistemic crises caused by the end of "actually existing socialism" and the absence of MILS focus on deep structures, a range of CAIL with different methodological standpoints (viz., deconstruction, feminism, historical materialism). These approaches are elaborated using varying categories (class, gender, race, caste, indigenous peoples) with implications for both identifying a crisis in international law and how it is to be addressed. But as Alvin Gouldner wrote in the *Coming Crisis of Western Sociology* the "central implication" of an epistemic crisis is not that mainstream scholarship "will die" '.[10] It only 'points to the possibility of change that may be more permanent, producing a basic metamorphosis in the total character ...'.[11] His expectation was that 'a part of sociology will become increasingly radicalized ... [and] will grow in influence, particularly among the younger, rising generation'.[12] This is an incremental process for as Gouldner pointed out with respect to western sociology '... those who supply the greatest resources for the institutional development of sociology are

---

9   For a detailed critique of the New Haven approach see Chimni (n 7) ch 3.
10   Alvin Gouldner, *The Coming Crisis of Western Sociology* (Basic Books, 1970) 341.
11   ibid 341.
12   Gouldner (n 10) 437.

precisely those who most distort its quest for knowledge'.[13] His observations are apposite to the present state of the discipline of international law.

Meanwhile, CAIL have begun to question the mainstream narrative of crises. In an important essay on the subject Hilary Charlesworth criticizes MILS for its episodic approach to crisis. She begins by pointing out that while for MILS 'crises are not ... the only catalyst for the development of international law [...] they dominate the imagination of international lawyers'.[14] Further, in approaching a crisis there is either the lack of acknowledgment that the facts assumed 'may be inaccurate or partial', or the absence of recognition of the need to build 'on past scholarship', and above all 'concentrate(s) on a single event or series of events ... to miss the larger picture'.[15] She goes on to observe that '... international lawyers tend to hone in on isolated aspects of selected crises' which '... promotes a narrow agenda for international law'.[16] Charlesworth concludes that in this way 'international law steers clear of analysis of longer-term trends and structural problems'.[17] At this point she draws on the feminist standpoint and points out that:

> One major silence is the position of women in the representation of crises. The players in international law crises are almost exclusively male. Men are the protagonists, men are at the negotiating table, men are making threats, retaliating, intervening. The lives of women are considered part of a crisis only when they are harmed in a way that is seen to demean the whole of their social group.[18]

She rightly concludes that 'forms of systemic violence, or structural discrimination against women, do not constitute a crisis for international lawyers'.[19] With the result that '... international law becomes simply a source of justification for the status quo'.[20]

But while Charlesworth is entirely right about the neglect of the "big picture" its ambit cannot be confined to the position of women. While at one point Charlesworth does speak of "non-elite groups" these are not identified

---

13   Gouldner (n 10) 498.
14   Hilary Charlesworth, 'International Law: A Discipline of Crisis' (2002) 65 MLR 377, 382.
15   ibid 384.
16   Charlesworth (n 14) 385–386.
17   Charlesworth (n 14) 389.
18   Charlesworth (n 14) 389.
19   Charlesworth (n 14) 389.
20   Charlesworth (n 14) 391.

or their concerns articulated.[21] This omission flows from a mainstream liberal rendering of feminist international law scholarship (MFILS) with the central objective of promoting the equality of sexes.[22] A TWAIL perspective would instead recommend *a class centred intersectional analyses* as it is more productive in pointing to the limits of the MILS approach to crisis. The intersectional analysis has to be explored along two axes: the history of global capitalism and imperialism on the one hand and the history of class, gender, and race on the other.

2.3 *More on Framing a Crisis*

It has been seen that the manner in which a crisis is framed often determines the nature of response. In this regard Bob Jessop helpfully suggests that a distinction be made 'between crises in a given social configuration and crises of that configuration. Crises 'in' occur within the parameters of a given set of natural and social arrangements'.[23] If for instance a structural crisis is framed as an episodic crisis it may divert attention from a deeper crisis, pre-empting a more effective response. In other words, '... crises are complex moments of indeterminacy' and the course of action taken on the basis of particular understandings 'can make a major difference to future developments'.[24]

If the interpretation of a crisis by dominant social forces, States, and scholarship is accepted it can lead to troubling consequences. Thus, for example, the episodic crisis caused by September 11 terror attack was depicted as a structural crisis which legitimized a discourse of national security that undermined democracy and human rights the world over. To be sure, the scourge of terrorism has to be fought, calling for an effective response from States. But the portrayal of terrorism as a central global issue has been used to diminish the substance and significance of the most basic rights. The COVID-19 pandemic, certainly a structural crisis, has been framed in a manner that instead of the focus being on health infrastructure or health workers or the welfare of those who have been devastated by the consequences of lockdowns the stress is on the control of the everyday life of citizens, raising concern that States have used the pandemic to avoid observing human rights obligations.

---

21 Charlesworth (n 14) 391.

22 For a detailed critique see Chimni (n 7) ch 6.

23 Bob Jessop, 'Narratives of Crisis and Crisis Response: Perspectives from North and South' in Peter Utting, Shahra Razavi, and Rebecca Varghese Buchholz (eds), *The Global Crisis and Transformative Change* (Palgrave Macmillan 2012) 3.

24 ibid 2, 3.

Further, despite impacting different fields of international law such as IHL, IIL, and ITL, the COVID-19 pandemic is not viewed by the MILS as a structural crisis in the international legal order. IHL is in crisis as the International Health Regulations, 2005 do not allow a timely and successful response to COVID-19. IIL is in crisis because foreign investors find the value of their investment and assets devalued, and host nations deprived of due benefit, without adequate remedies in sight. ITL is in crisis as WTO has been unable to effectively respond to the need of poor nations for timely access to the vaccine. The pandemic also has drawn attention to the inadequacies in the doctrines of international law. For instance, there is no easy answer to the question whether the rules of State responsibility cover the case of China omitting to inform the international community in time about COVID-19 or the case of vaccine nationalism. In short, the pandemic has exposed a structural crisis in international law. By treating it as an episodic or regional crisis MILS has avoided addressing its deep roots in the extant world order. This is a point that critics are making: that the pandemic has deepened the crisis of neoliberal capitalism caused by the 2008 financial crisis and unless structural reforms are undertaken it will not be possible to address the impending post pandemic crisis.[25]

3 International Law and the Post Pandemic Era

3.1 Deepening Crisis of Poverty

In his Nelson Mandela lecture in July 2020 the UN Secretary General (UNSG) noted that the world was facing 'the deepest global recession since World War II, and the broadest collapse in incomes since 1870'.[26] Already, as he went on to observe, 'inequality defines our time ... The 26 richest people in the world hold as much wealth as half the global population'. Indeed, 'between 1980 and 2016, the world's richest 1 per cent captured 27 per cent of the total cumulative growth in income'. He traced this outcome among other things to the fact that 'the legacy of colonialism still reverberates'. He gave the example of the

---

25   Monty Neill, 'COVID-19, Capitalist Crises, Class resistance' (*Counterpunch*, 12 June 2020) <https://www.counterpunch.org/2020/06/12/covid-19-capitalist-crises-class-resistance/> accessed 6 July 2020.

26   Antonio Guterres, 'Tackling the Inequality Pandemic: A New Social Contract for a New Era' (United Nations Secretary-General's Nelson Mandela Lecture, 18 July 2020) <https:// www.un.org/sg/en/content/sg/statement/2020-07-18/secretary-generals-nelson-mandela-lecture-%E2%80%9Ctackling-the-inequality-pandemic-new-social-contract-for-new-era%E2%80%9D-delivered> accessed 25 July 2020.

global trading system pointing out that 'economies that were colonized are at greater risk of getting locked into the production of raw materials and low-tech goods – a new form of colonialism'. Matters were compounded by 'another great source of inequality in our world: millennia of patriarchy' and continuing racial inequalities. The problems of climate change and digital inequalities did not escape him. The pandemic was only going to exacerbate these negative trends. In fact 'entire regions that were making progress on eradicating poverty and narrowing inequality' have already been 'set back years, in a matter of months'. The future looks dark for the poor as the spectre of unemployment and hunger begins to haunt them. In the view of UNSG what we need is 'a New Social Contract and a New Global Deal that create equal opportunities for all and respect the rights and freedoms of all'.

> A New Global Deal, based on a fair globalization, on the rights and dignity of every human being, on living in balance with nature, on taking account of the rights of future generations, and on success measured in human rather than economic terms, is the best way to change this.

If the new global social contract and global deal is to become a reality the developing world must have, he emphasized, 'a far stronger voice in global decision-making'.

The UNSG is not alone in pointing to the economic and social crisis that is visiting the world. The World Social Report, 2020 also reported the growth of global inequalities:

> Despite progress in some countries, income and wealth are increasingly concentrated at the top. The share of income going to the richest 1 per cent of the population increased in 59 out of 100 countries with data from 1990 to 2015. Meanwhile, the poorest 40 per cent earned less than 25 per cent of income in all 92 countries with data.[27]

A report of the Special Rapporteur on extreme poverty and human rights also portrays a dismal picture.[28] In short, the post pandemic world will see the current crisis of poverty and inequality exacerbated impacting nearly 75

---

27   United Nations Department of Economic and Social Affairs, *Inequality in a Rapidly Changing World* (World Social Order Report, 2020) 3.

28   Phillip Alston, *The parlous state of poverty eradication* (Report of the Special Rapporteur on Extreme Poverty and Human Rights, 2 July 2020).

per cent of the world.[29] In the circumstances the poor and oppressed in the Global South are coming to feel a deep sense of alienation from international law and institutions as these cannot protect their dignity.[30] Yet the all affected and all subjected principles are rarely adhered to while taking decisions in international forums.[31] There is something about modern international law that it facilitates and tolerates inhumane outcomes. Even the fate of asylum seekers and refugees does not move many; thousands of them can drown in the Mediterranean without necessitating a call for the structural reform of International refugee law (IRL). It would appear that the haunting realities of the contemporary world which tolerates endless violence on people is still not a sufficiently grave crisis for the mainstream practitioners of the discipline to call for the overhaul of international law and institutions.

3.2 Accelerating Ecological Crisis

A silver lining of the pandemic is that the precipitous decline in economic activity has meant a pause in the growing deterioration of the global environment. It implies that unless different production and distribution systems are adopted the restoration of economic activity will bring back the problem of environmental degradation, accentuating in particular climate change. But there is a lack of appreciation among segments of the powerful global elite that climate change can cause far greater disruption than a pandemic. As has been pointed out, 'the timescales of both the occurrence and the resolution of pandemics and climate hazards are different. The former are often measured in weeks, months, and years; the latter are measured in years, decades, and centuries'.[32] What this means is that 'a global climate crisis, if and when ushered in, could prove far lengthier and far more disruptive than what we currently see with the coronavirus (if that

---

29 The Special Rapporteur on extreme poverty and human rights calls for a range of measures to address the problem of poverty: 'reconceiving the relationship between growth and poverty elimination; (ii) tackling inequality and embracing redistribution; (iii) promoting tax justice; (iv) implementing universal social protection; (v) centering the role of government; (vi) embracing participatory governance; and (vii) adapting international poverty measurement'; ibid 1.

30 B.S. Chimni, 'The Past, Present and Future of International Law: A Critical Third World Approach' (2007) 8(2) Melbourne Journal of International Law 499.

31 B.S. Chimni, 'The limits of the all affected principle: attending to deep structures' (2018) 3 Third World Thematics: A Third World Quarterly Journal 807.

32 Dickon Pinner, Matt Rogers, and Hamid Samandari 'Addressing climate change in a post-pandemic world' (2020) McKinsey Quarterly 1, 3 <https://www.mckinsey.com/business-functions/sustainability/our-insights/addressing-climate-change-in-a-post-pandemic-world> accessed 7 August 2020.

can be imagined)'.[33] The two together can cause, even in their milder incarnation, irrevocable harm to the world. To ensure this does not happen at least two moves have to be made. First, more attention has to be paid to 'the interactions between environmental change and infectious disease emergence' for there is 'growing evidence that causally links these two phenomena'.[34] Second, resources have to be found by governments to devote to climate action. But this is unlikely to happen in the face of ongoing recession in the global economy. Likewise, 'investors may delay their capital allocation to new lower-carbon solutions due to decreased wealth'.[35] In short both capitalist States and enterprises may avoid undertaking effective action to help fight climate change and pandemics. This brings the discussion back to deep structures of global order. Among other things, unless international law and institutions are able to promote appropriate reform of global capitalism that allows the global common good to be privileged over parochial interest environmental crises are likely to recur.

3.3   *Growing Crisis of Multilateralism, Law and Institutions*

But at the very moment that there is a need for active global cooperation to fight challenges posed by the pandemic and climate change, multilateralism is in retreat. The rise of populism and nationalism has made key States actively defer to narrow considerations at the expense of the global common good. It is the logic of anarchy that led the Trump administration to walk out of WHO diminishing its authority and depriving it of critical funding. While the Biden administration has returned to the organization it is far from clear what steps it will take to strengthen it.

The UN system which should have provided a lead in enhancing cooperation through generating ideas and resources is no longer in a position to do so. While the UNSG has taken the lead in diagnosing the state of the world, the initiative to respond to the looming global crises has moved to bodies like G-20 which has not responded with agility to either the pandemic or the global economic crises. The UN Security Council (UNSC), which could have issued binding guidelines to promote cooperation between nations to deal with the pandemic, is paralyzed by the differences between veto power States, especially US and China. While IMF has established a $1 trillion loan program to

---

33   ibid.
34   Moreno Di Marco and others, 'Sustainable development must account for pandemic risk' (2020) 117 Proceedings of the National Academy of Sciences of the United States of America 3888, 3889 <https://www.pnas.org/content/pnas/117/8/3888.full.pdf> accessed 8 August 2020.
35   Pinner, Rogers and Samandari (n 32) 5.

fight the pandemic and its consequences it continues to prescribe conditionalities to borrowing nations that have in the past encouraged the dismantling of the public health infrastructure. To put it differently, unless bodies like the UN Economic and Social Council (ECOSOC) are revived, and become the centres of global decision making in the world economy, there is not much hope for most of the Global South nations.

Meanwhile, the international trading system presided over by WTO has been undermined by trade unilateralism. It is not as yet clear if the Biden administration will seek to reinvigorate WTO. For nations of the Global South the crisis afflicting WTO means the worst of all worlds. These are likely to encounter protectionism without being able to recover legal and policy space ceded in the days of hyper globalization. What is more, the proposals for WTO reform emanating from US target among other things the special and differential treatment principle which accentuates the impact of the loss of policy space. While the Biden administration may back the liberal international order (LIO) it may not reject all the proposals advanced by the Trump administration. The Global South nations will also have to deal with vaccine nationalism, and the consequences of a hard patent regime, that may lead to pricing that will deny the poor access to vaccine. South Africa and India have already sought a waiver on the application of relevant parts of the TRIPS text to the production and distribution of the vaccine but the proposal is still being debated.[36] In sum, the undermining of LIO is troubling for nations of the Global South not simply because of its erosion but rather its partial and prejudicial rejection.

3.4   Crisis, Resistance and International Law

In response to any international crisis groups, peoples and nations that bear its consequences use appropriate means such as protests, social movements, and multilateral diplomacy to bring about necessary changes in the international legal order. The different types of crisis evoke distinct forms and scales of resistance. In the instance of episodic and regional crisis there is social and political mobilization on the part of global civil society, supported by concerned States, to deal with their consequences. A structural crisis spawns social movements with a greater geographical spread involving separate and intersectional class, gender or race based movements. An originary crisis can call forth global scale collective resistance of oppressed peoples and nations. An example is the challenge to colonial international law by postcolonial nations in the era

---

36   'Members to continue discussion on proposal for temporary IP waiver in response to COVID-19' (WTO, 10 December 2020) <https://www.wto.org/english/news_e/news20_e/ trip_10dec20_e.htm> accessed 24 December 2020.

of decolonization calling for its radical transformation. One manifestation of this effort at overhaul was the program and declaration of action on a New International Economic Order.

A central role of ongoing resistance movements lies in opposing and delegitimizing responses of international law and institutions that do not address the concerns of vulnerable and oppressed groups and weak nations. For instance, the Black Lives Matter (BLM) movement has successfully drawn attention to not only the racialization of internal and international relations but also to intersectional modes of oppression. Only collective resistance at the global level of the transnational poor and oppressed classes can hope to bring about meaningful change in the international legal order. But it would need to be backed by a coalition of nations of the Global South. Unfortunately, in the post-Cold War era the global coalitional strategy has been abandoned in favour of bilateral negotiations or issue based coalitions that bring together States with similar interests in particular domain areas. While this strategy may work in the instance of an episodic crisis it is unlikely to deliver where a regional or structural crisis of international law and institutions is concerned. From a disciplinary perspective, while critical approaches such as TWAIL make a strong argument in favour of the role of resistance in understanding a crisis and the reform of international law it has yet to find resonance in mainstream scholarship.

4   Conclusion

In moments of crisis new elements of disequilibrium are introduced in the international legal order threatening its effectiveness, stability, and legitimacy. But given its methodological weaknesses MILS is unable to assess the nature, extent and consequences of a crisis and recommend a suitable response to the international community. Its inability to explore the relationship of a crisis with deep structures of capitalism, imperialism, patriarchy, and racism means that the suggested responses can end up advancing the interests of the very social forces and States which are at the roots of a crises. In contrast critical approaches like TWAIL examine any crisis from an interdisciplinary and systemic standpoint and recommend changes that can help meet the concerns of the transnational poor, marginal and oppressed groups and realize the global common good. In the process TWAIL also exposes crises inside international law caused by static and incoherent doctrines that create hurdles in shaping just responses. In sum, TWAIL argues that MILS does not possess the epistemological resources to identify, differentiate, understand, and address different kinds of crises in the international legal order. Only critical approaches can offer the therapies and techniques that can help restore the health of modern international law.

CHAPTER 5

COVID and the Crisis Mode in International Legal Scholarship

Frédéric Mégret

Perhaps predictably, within weeks of the COVID outbreak, international law-yers were busy planning special issues, edited collections, and countless blog posts.[1] This is, after all, a crisis that affects us all in very individual and personal ways. It affects us as a discipline in at least the pedestrian sense that all of our conference planning and much that went with it has come crashing down. A profession that ordinarily feeds off its breezy cosmopolitanism suddenly found itself grounded, with no end in sight and some time to spare. It soon devoted its considerable potential for attention on the *sujet du jour*.

I myself gladly complied,[2] including to this very project, no doubt enjoying the sense of continued collegiality, albeit of the virtual kind. It is surely one of the more appealing facets of our profession that we can regularly count on each other to contribute to our many respective projects. Also, the neoliberal university encourages the production of "timely" policy inputs, even as we may be ambivalent about that push and what it may require us to do. At the same time, I could not help noticing how the emerging COVID-and-international-law agenda threatened to engulf every other topic that we had been attending to until then. As brilliant colleagues occasionally seemed to fall over each other to publish the first article or the first book treatment of the topic, I sometimes had the impression of a mad-train careening at full speed without a driver. Was it, maybe, already too late to jump?

---

1 Many of these are still in the making but even a quick look around reveals a range of initia-tives. See 'COVID-19' (*International Law Blog*) <https://internationallaw.blog/category/covid -19/> accessed 8 October 2020; 'COVID-19: Its Impact on International Law and You' (*American Bar Association*) <https://www.americanbar.org/groups/international_law/membership/ coronavirus-information-page/> accessed 8 October 2020.

2 Frédéric Mégret, 'Homeward Bound? Global Mobility and the Role of the State of Nationality During the Pandemic' (2020) 114 AJIL Unbound 322; Frédéric Mégret, 'COVID-19 Symposium: Returning "Home"–Nationalist International Law in the Time of the Coronavirus' (*Opinio Juris*, 30 March 2020) <http://opiniojuris.org/2020/03/30/covid-19-symposium -returning-home-nationalist-international-law-in-the-time-of-the-coronavirus/> accessed 7 October 2020.

In this short contribution, I want to reflect on how "crises" take hold of our imaginations and end up monopolizing our research attention. Drawing on Hillary Charlesworth's famous insights on international law "as a discipline of crisis",[3] I focus on a somewhat narrower issue, namely crisis as a mode of scholarship specifically and its relationship to crises – real or imagined. There is little doubt that there is a COVID crisis, but could it be that it is not a particularly meaningful crisis for international law? Even if it betrays a crisis for international lawyers, how is it distinctively an international law crisis rather than a crisis of globalization, modernity, or the State? What does it say about our discipline that we feel the need to immerse ourselves in crises and what are the limitations of doing so?

There are already several emerging genres in the international-law-and-COVID field. These include pieces addressing discreet problems both directly connected to the disease and to the broader pandemic; thinking about how international law can more broadly help alleviate some of its consequences; and work on how the pandemic might, more deeply, impact international law itself. Obviously, the jury is still out on how significant the impact of COVID will be for international law. I have read some good, insightful papers; and I have read others that felt more contrived, as if the author's heart ultimately wasn't in them. I suppose there are many ideas that we might otherwise have entertained, that can now be seen from a COVID perspective.

Yet it may also be that this rush to be present in the debate has more to do with international lawyers as a discipline than the significance of any contribution we might make to understanding the pandemic. The volume of what we produce speaks, maybe, to our obsession with relevance and also a certain plasticity of the discipline. There is no issue that cannot be treated as an international law issue, partly it should be said because international law has been led to mean almost anything. But the whole exercise sometimes reminds me of the tired "is there a doctor in the plane?" joke: "I am a doctor, I have a PhD in international law!" kept repeating the international lawyer, as everyone on board succumbed to a dangerous virus. Pushing ourselves on the front stage is part of an elaborate ritual of relevance that we often engage in, at our own risk.

The point is not that there are not issues that deserve attention but that the inflated sense of a "crisis" at a moment of intense mobilization creates its own distortions. What makes a crisis a "crisis", what is it a crisis of, who produces crisis discourse and to what ends? The intuitive, immediate framing of a major

---

3   Hilary Charlesworth, 'International Law: A Discipline of Crisis' (2002) 65 MLR 377. Also, Benjamin Authers and Hilary Charlesworth, 'The Crisis and the Quotidian in International Human Rights Law' (2014) 44 Netherlands Yearbook of International Law 19.

health crisis as an international law one raises more questions than it answers. This is not, for example, like Charlesworth's focus on the NATO intervention in Kosovo which at least raises some immediate and obvious questions for the jus ad bellum, a central stake of international law if ever there was one (although even there defining the exact parameters of that crisis was more challenging than it seemed). By comparison, the pandemic unfolds as a phenomenon that is more evidently removed from a central legal interrogation. That makes its characterization as an international legal crisis both potentially more interesting, but also more perplexing. The challenge, it turns, out is less "addressing" the crisis than the preliminary and contentious exercise of "defining" it as such.

One distinctively international legal issue to have garnered attention is the potential international responsibility of China. I was asked a couple of times as part of media requests. I initially turned them down as not worthy of a response, only to find that the idea was getting serious traction in the darker corners of the web and Florida courts. The issue has, in fact, since been entertained seriously in some blogs.[4] Personally, I cannot think of a framing that is more woefully inadequate and that more explicitly betrays international law's inadequacies. In the vast sea of responsibilities for COVID and the harm it has provoked, singling out one particular actor for what was at heart a systemic problem seemed little short of scapegoating. The question is not whether China could not have done things better, or the WHO for that matter. I'm sure they could. The question is what good does it do to even think in those terms? What kind of populist design are we lending our expertise to? One of the most distinctly legal issue to emerge from the pandemic, in other words, seemed to be esoteric and a distraction, and to expose our own professional irrelevance or meaninglessness. On the rare occasions that the media seemed to pay attention to international law, therefore, my role seemed to be that of dampening down enthusiasms with a mix of "it's complicated" and "it's not a good idea."

Beyond that, I could see a lot of discussions that led one to merely restate the doxa of international law: that we would need more international cooperation; more laws; more rights etc. This is the international lawyer in their admonishing, hand-wringing role: familiar, predictable, and not particularly useful. Maybe, then, this was just not our crisis or at least not in the way we understood it. I'm sure there will be a few institutional articles to write about the WHO's performance, but I doubt those would live up to the expectations of the moment. The one area where I would have hoped to have seen much more

---

4   Peter Tzeng, 'Taking China to the International Court of Justice over COVID-19' (*EJIL: Talk!*, 2 April 2020) <https://www.ejiltalk.org/taking-china-to-the-international-court-of-justice-over-covid-19/> accessed 7 October 2020.

is the COVAX Global Vaccines Facility, an ambitious program to share the costs and benefits of a vaccine. Here I thought is where the fundamental distributive questions lie. But however hard I searched, it seemed few international lawyers were speaking to the issue (I am optimistic it is only a question of time before some do but still it is intriguing that this has not captured the discipline's imagination more). I suspect that when it comes to the design of even mildly ambitious distributive schemes, the lawyers will not be in the front seat, and only be called in in an accessory capacity.

There are many ways in which even as we seek to academically capitalize on that crisis, it deeply eludes us as international lawyers. One is that it is a global and transnational phenomenon translating into renewed nationalism rather than a classic international crisis; this risks confirming the recurrent fear that our conceptual blueprint is increasingly unsuited for the world upon which we seek to intervene. Specifically, one concern is the world presiding over the pandemic has become so deeply privatized that the "public" in public international law seems increasingly irrelevant. As I turned to the debate on repatriation to the State of origin, for example, it struck me how the whole issue has been absorbed by purely private speculation on the obligations of airlines and insurance companies. To be sure, there were recriminations here and there that States could have provided more consular assistance, but these were clearly secondary. All of this also made me wonder about our role as gate keepers of what counts as good and bad international law topics and whether international law still has the capacity to fundamentally retool itself for the moment. One could also not help notice how the discipline went into overdrive after the crisis began to touch the inner sanctum of Western power. In short, I wondered if international lawyers would like what their discourse of crisis ended up revealing about themselves.

Aside from producing not very good research questions (a crisis, even properly conceived, is not a research question), I would suggest the crisis-mode in international legal scholarship suffers from a deeper and more pervasive flaw. It operates, essentially, as what is imagined as a "system absorbing exogenous shocks," where the crisis is imagined as a feature of the world outside the law and the law's task is if not to (help) solve it, at least to understand it from within its categories. What that view is at risk of getting most wrong is the idea that the challenge is coming from without. It risks reproducing an image of international law as perfectly self-constituted and dealing with outside "objects" that are not, in some crucial ways, objects of its own making. This may be an exaggeration in that no doubt many reflective international lawyers will point out ways in which COVID threatens to disrupt international law. But many do so in a way that has a kind of "I told you so" quality, where COVID is confirmation, for example, that we need more work to make international law real, true to itself or more effective. What this obviates is a sense that the crisis is at least partly of international law's making, so that it cannot entirely claim innocence from it. As Justina Uriburu and Francisco-José Quintana have brilliantly argued:

> dominant approaches to both international legal thought and practice have made valuable but dangerously depoliticizing contributions, which portray the pandemic as a largely external phenomenon, concealing the role of international law in the production of the conditions that led to the pandemic and the allocation of the suffering that this crisis has caused.[5]

What, then, if the crisis was less an external crisis than a crisis within, helpfully revealed by world events? And what if, instead of being an opportunity for more scholarship, it was used as an opportunity to rethink scholarship? In order to explore that question I want to provide a very brief and schematic presentation of how the crisis genre in international legal scholarship operates as one of three modes: digestion, hegemony, and retreat.[6]

Under the "digestion" model, much of international legal scholarship is conceived in the fashion of a regular updating of an ongoing project under the conditions of the present. The image that comes closest in my mind is of a constant process of *digestion* of the "real" into the categories of the "law." 9/11 is a good example of an event that international lawyers have been digesting for the better part of the last 20 years (and before that, the end of the Cold War). The question is how 9/11 has changed international law and, although the jury is still out, the general reassuring answer is ultimately not so much. In the process, the discipline grinds its wheels (and maybe imagines itself as flexing its intellectual muscles) and reassures itself that it is up to the task. It is predictable that some of this will happen to the "international law and COVID" debate and that, after having precipitously dramatized the stakes, not all of the resulting production will age well. The main idea, at any rate, is that the crisis provides an opportunity to reassert normalcy and therefore dominance, as part of a social competition over legitimate expertise.

---

5   Francisco-José Quintana and Justina Uriburu, 'Modest International Law: COVID-19, International Legal Responses, and Depoliticization' (2020) 114 AJIL 687, 687.

6   For a very helpful exploration of the current context of international legal scholarship, see Jan Klabbers, 'On Epistemic Universalism and the Melancholy of International Law' (2018) 29 EJIL 1057.

A second move is more specifically hegemonic. Where digestion denotes a relatively passive attitude, the hegemonic international lawyer is actively seeking out new terrains of the mind to conquer. International lawyers claim a certain problem which one would not normally have associated with them as their own. Because the number of good legal issues that we can put our minds to is finite (and there are only so many articles one can write about the same ICJ judgment or the Kosovo intervention for example), we often find ourselves scavenging for more. This is a constant process of appropriating parts of the non-legal world into the legal world, evidently helped by the fact that this is a largely illusory separation line in the first place. This is the vast realm of "international law and ...". We have all done it in some form or other. Sometimes, it involves looking around for the remains of other disciplines' feasts, but it also lends itself well to international law's inherent grandiosity as a normative discipline that tolerates no void and therefore thinks it must have (even through some Lotus style default rule) an answer to everything. There is no doubt some of this going on in relation to the COVID pandemic. Where Charlesworth faults international lawyers for too "thin" a rendering of what counts as a crisis in the case of Kosovo, understanding the pandemic as a crisis for international law involves a hyper-broad characterization that steps resolutely into the quotidian of pretty much all of humanity. The problem with this hegemony is that it stretches our expertise thin – and therefore the willingness of others to listen to us.

The third move is retreat and it is one that is more popular than it seems. It involves abandoning the "real" world to others and retiring to what we do best, which is engaging in discreet debates highly peculiar and internal to the discipline, for example writing articles about institutions that have "international law" in their *raison d'être*, such as international courts. Think of this as a form of familiar hibernation from the real. We might, for example, focus only on the handful of judicial cases that will no doubt emerge in due course in relation to COVID (vaccine litigation? Repatriation lawsuits?), and chose to see the whole crisis through their reassuring but probably powerfully distorting prism (why did these cases emerge where they did and when they did? How could they have been otherwise? What cases are not raised?). The point is not that there is no value to informed doctrinal discussion of latest judicial developments but that the ratio of the discipline is still too heavily tilted towards that kind of work that reeks of formalism and reductionism and that focuses on rarefied legal disputes at the expense of the vast realms of everyday law. The retreat, moreover, seems to concede too much to those who would like us in our modest place when, for once, we may have more to contribute (beyond delusions of *grandeur*). If the problem with hegemony was an expertise spread too thin, the problem with retreat is that it ultimately compromises our claim to relevance.

There is not much of a middle ground between these extremes. But all lead to a degree of opportunism and follow-ism, of simply tagging along the party lest we miss out on the action even as, diffusely, we understand the real party is happening elsewhere, in the halls of power, in the temples of justice even, where we have not been invited or are called in when the key decisions have already been made. I am concerned by how impoverishing of even our scholarship (let alone our real-world influence) this follow-ism is. In effect, it robs us of the initiative of what we write on, showing us as little more than a reactive discipline with little conceptual spine of its own. In the worst of cases, it makes us sound as if we are constantly second guessing tough real-world decisions from our armchairs; in the best case, it makes us appear like we are party-crashing (who invited the lawyer?).

For what are we in the end? One appealing view is that we are modest tradespersons who are the repositories of a long and fraught tradition and who may occasionally benefit from specific (if not unique) insights as a result of our peculiar position in the international system and the social world. There are the conversations we have between ourselves as highly specialized tradespersons, where we hammer out the details of how this or that mechanism works out. These are interesting to us, but they would elicit a polite yawn from almost everyone else. And then there are the conversations we have with others, in which we advance with a mixed of guarded protectiveness (as no doubt sometimes we should do) and inter-disciplinary hubris (wanting, in essence, to engage interdisciplinary conversations on our own terms).

Indeed, a more appealing view may be that, in the best of cases, we can be the sophisticated and even contrite articulators of our own crises and what they have done to the world rather than the other way round. The deep insight of Charlesworth was not that international law is about crises, or even that it is *in* crisis, but that it is a discipline *of* crisis. For many, the crisis is always outside the law; it is not specifically ours. In fact, it positively cannot be not ours since we are tasked with resolving it. Thus the outside crisis serves to mask our own, a crisis of our modes of understanding and, more often than not, the very real crises it repeatedly provokes in the world. The pandemic has, however, made painfully obvious, how international law is part of the very fabric of crises, neither sole enabler nor actively preventing them: the veneer of cosmopolitanism behind the brutal reassertion of nationalism; the stark limits of cooperation and international organization; the dominance of private agendas; the huge inequality.

Owning up to the sort of slow-motion crisis that is our discipline, then, might put us in an unenviable but intellectually more compelling spot: that of having gotten to the bottom of the pit and come back with the bad news that, alongside whatever few nuggets of wisdom we may have produced over the centuries but also the immense human toll and cost exacted, there really never was that much to be found: it was only a gold rush, and we all fell for it. Now we need to clean up, or at least own up to our own problematic legacy.

Finally, in an attempt to ground international law in everyday life, it may also be worth looking at what makes the production of scholarship possible. One thing that the pandemic has unmistakably done "for" scholarship is that it has changed some of its material conditions of production under a mix of neoliberal and political emergency conditions. In particular, it has introduced a series of significant temporal distortions. On the one hand, time seems to have ground to a halt as multiple commitments were cancelled, seemingly freeing up some space for imagination and contemplation. We live in an era, moreover, in which we have fully refined the art of conducting research projects in a networked, decentralized and delocalized fashion, meaning that the pandemic has hardly prevented the discipline from moving ahead, albeit in an increasingly disembodied and desocialized way. On the other hand, family obligations and (often heavily gendered) care work as well as the transition to online teaching have quickly redensified the little time that had been freed up. Rather than rebalancing international legal scholarship, the pandemic might end up reinforcing the same old voices, namely those who have the resources to thrive in a crisis. We should be wary.

In that vein, I think the question is how we could write differently? What would it mean to *not* write about COVID at all as international lawyers, or at least not directly? To be silent, for once? It is not as if the world cannot wait for our considered reflections on the virus. We are not in the race to produce a vaccine. Being silent could allow us to be mindful of the many issues that we are not focusing on as we chase the latest event. But being silent is hard when everyone and everything else has turned the volume up. How will that silence not be interpreted as dropping out, not caring or not living with the times? How might we reinvent an international legal scholarship of "looking elsewhere" or perhaps "looking beyond" when the challenges of the moment seem to call for all hands on deck?

Ultimately the discipline is defined by what we decide to write on and not write on. This non-contribution to the COVID and international law debate is written in this spirit: not wanting to entirely pass on the opportunity of a good crisis, yet feeling alienated by the discipline's omnivorous appetite for crises, and mindful of our responsibility to not surrender to the dominant crisis mode.

CHAPTER 6

Narratives of Solidarity in Times of Crisis

Tales from Africa

Makane Moïse Mbengue

We did not have the same past ... but we will have the same future, strictly speaking ... the time of singular destinies is over ... no one can live on self-preservation alone.[1]

∴

In April 2020, in the early times when the COVID-19 pandemic reached its global scale, a head of state of a West African nation published a piece in which he described the pandemic as an unprecedented crisis which revealed that efforts made in the four corners of the world exposed the limits of all national systems, even the most sophisticated ones. According to that head of state, all members of the international community, taken by surprise and overwhelmed, found themselves in a kind of rescue situation, revealing each other's shortcomings on a daily basis. The said head of state is President Macky Sall from Senegal. In the words of the latter, "the first lesson to be learned from this major crisis – where the infinitely small shakes the whole world – is that in the face of cross-border threats, big or small, rich or poor, we are all vulnerable".[2] President Sall's depiction of the implications of COVID-19 for the community of nations offers a blueprint of how a crisis narrative can serve as a narrative of the *existing* or *ideal* international legal order.

Sall's perception of COVID-19, as a global crisis, can be summed up as follows: it is a crisis that reminds the world of its own contradictions and paradoxes. Indeed, he observes: "The earth is certainly round, but something, somewhere, is not right. Humankind is constantly making progress in all directions,

---

1   Cheikh Hamidou Kane, *L'aventure ambiguë* (Julliard 1961).
2   Macky Sall, 'Africa, the world and COVID-19' (*The Africa Report*, 9 April 2020)accessed 2 July 2021.

pushing back the limits of science and technology every day, including the conquest of space. Meanwhile, on earth, there is a shortage of masks, test kits, personal protective equipment, beds, ventilators; so many products, materials and equipment that are crucial for the treatment of patients and protection of health workers, true heroes engaged in a risky and potentially fatal struggle against an enemy invisible to the naked eye. It is therefore time to come back down to earth!".[3] In Sall's view, the COVID-19 pandemic, just like the global environment crisis and the scourge of terrorism, confirms the objective limits of the nation-state in responding to cross-border threats. In other words, national sovereignty appears ineffective and inefficient to address the challenge of navigating global crises such as the COVID-19 pandemic. It is against this background that Sall concludes that "any nation-state, whatever its power and means, can no longer be self-sufficient and that in the face of global challenges or crises, we all need one another, especially when our common vulnerabilities are added to our individual frailties".[4]

Sall's crisis narrative is not only a narrative *on* the crisis. It is ultimately a narrative *of* the crisis. Narratives *on* crises are consequential; they focus on the effects – may they be positive or negative – of crises. Narratives *of* crises are structural; they query the causes and *raison d'être* of crises. And this is where President Sall's crisis narrative distinguishes itself from the other crisis narratives from most world leaders at the beginning of the COVID-19 pandemic. Sall's narrative of the crisis is an opportunity to engage into a broader narrative and to highlight another crisis: the crisis of the international (legal) order. Indeed, he considers that the current global crisis deriving from COVID-19 is intrinsically and extrinsically linked to the foundations upon which international cooperation has been built since the end of the Cold War. Sall's narrative *of* the crisis allowed him to call for a new international order. The new international order or the new world order he is calling for "requires mutual trust and a sincere willingness to cooperate on issues of common interest and shared values, while respecting our differences and diversities". Interestingly enough, it is through that pledge for a new world order that President Sall concomitantly addresses his criticism of the old world – if one considers of course that the COVID-19 crisis will ultimately reshape our world and with it the international community as a whole. In his view, a new international order demands above all "a new mindset that recognises that all cultures, all civilisations, are

---

3   ibid.
4   Sall (n 2).

of equal dignity; and that there can be no superior civilisational centre that dictates to others how to behave and how to act".[5]

Solidarity within the community of nations is, thus, at the cornerstone of Sall's narrative. He indeed concludes that "What is important today is to learn the lessons from the crisis and to pool our resources and our intelligence in order to confront, *in the same spirit of human solidarity*, our common enemy: a silent killer which scoffs at borders, ideologies and differences between developed and developing countries. The time has come to work together so as to bring about a world order that puts human beings and humanity at the centre of international relations".[6] In the context of what Josep Borrell, High Representative of the European Union for Foreign Affairs and Security Policy, labelled as the "global battle of narratives",[7] a narrative of solidarity is without doubt *the* narrative that is the most expected at least by developing countries. However, beyond developing countries, solidarity can also offer opportunities for a renewed partnership between developed and developing countries as well as international institutions. The joint statement in February 2021 by Emmanuel Macron, president of France, Angela Merkel, chancellor of Germany, Macky Sall, António Guterres, secretary general of the United Nations, Charles Michel, president of the European Council and Ursula von der Leyen, president of the European Commission is reflective of the strong potential of such a partnership.[8] In their joint statement, the six leaders underlined that "the most serious crises call for the most ambitious decisions to shape the future (...) this one can be an opportunity to rebuild consensus for an international order based on multilateralism and the rule of law through efficient cooperation, solidarity and coordination".[9]

Crises allow, therefore, to revisit solidarity at the international level. They show that the contours of solidarity are not static at the international level. The COVID-19 crisis, in particular, has prompted the emergence of a new kind of solidarity, i.e. solidarity in legal resilience. Legal resilience refers to the ability of states to shape together legal initiatives and instruments that would

5   Sall (n 2).

6   Sall (n 2).

7   Josep Borrell, 'The Coronavirus pandemic and the new world it is creating' (*European Union External Action Service*, 23 March 2020) <eeas.europa.eu/headquarters/headquarters-homepage/76379/coronavirus-pandemic-and-new-world-it-creating_en> accessed 2 July 2021.

8   Emmanuel Macron et al, 'Multilateral Cooperation for Global Recovery' (*Project Syndicate*, 3 February 2021) <www.project-syndicate.org/commentary/multilateralism-for-the-masses-by-emmanuel-macron-et-al-2020-02> accessed 2 July 2021.

9   ibid.

allow them to better recover after a crisis of a magnitude such as the COVID-19 pandemic. Here again, Africa has been a laboratory to develop strategies of solidarity for legal resilience during the pandemic. The solidarity towards the risk of investor-state dispute settlement in the context of the COVID-19 pandemic constitutes a good illustration.

On 24 November 2020, the African Union (AU) Ministers for Trade adopted a "Declaration on the Risk of Investor-State Dispute Settlement with Respect to COVID-19 Pandemic Related Measures" (the AU Declaration). The AU Declaration was later endorsed by the African Heads of States at the 13th Extraordinary Session of the African Union Heads of State and Government on the African Continental Free Trade Area (AfCFTA), held in December 2020.[10] With this Declaration, the AU was the first body at the international level – and till now the only one – to collectively respond to concerns that had been steadily growing since the beginning of the COVID-19 crisis – that investors could use investor-state dispute settlement (ISDS) found in almost all investment treaties to challenge states' measures imposed to deal with the crisis.

Concerns first started being voiced regarding the issue of ISDS challenges to states' COVID-19 related measures in or around April 2020. That month, the International Institute for Sustainable Development (IISD) published a paper calling for states to act to protect themselves against COVID-19 related ISDS claims.[11] The IISD paper raised the spectre of an unprecedented risk of foreign investors suing governments under the global web of international investment treaties. It called upon governments to cooperate to craft solutions to address this risk, emphasising in particular the option of a bilateral, regional, or multilateral agreement to suspend treaty-based investor–state arbitration for all COVID-19 related measures. IISD later published indicative language for a suspension agreement, developed in consultation with states, academics, and international investment law experts.[12] The publication of the IISD paper

---

10   'Thirteen Extra Ordinary Session on the African Continental Free Trade Area (AfCFTA): The Assembly of the Union adopts decision on the start of trading' (*Africa News*, 6 December 2020) <https://www.africanews.com/2020/12/06/thirteen-extra-ordinaty-session-on-the -african-continental-free-trade-area-afcfta-the-assembly-of-the-union-adopts-decision -on-the-start-of-trading/> accessed 14 May 2021.

11   Nathalie Bernasconi-Osterwalder, Sarah Brewin and Nyaguthii Maina, 'Protecting Against Investor-State Claims Amidst COVIS-19: A call to action for governments' (*International Institute for Sustainable Development*, 14 April 2020) <www.iisd.org/articles/protecting -against-investor-state-claims-amidst-covid-19-call-action-governments> accessed 14 May 2021.

12   International Institute for Sustainable Development, 'Draft Agreement for the coordinated Suspension of Investor-State Dispute Settlement With Respect to COVID-19- Related Measures and Disputes' (*International Institute for Sustainable Development*, 18

was followed by a call for a moratorium on ISDS during the pandemic from a number of civil society organizations in May,[13] and in June an open letter to governments was signed by 600 national and international NGOs in more than 90 countries.[14]

By mid-2020, scores of private international law firms had published client bulletins explaining how such claims could be crafted under the terms of most investment treaties.[15] Towards the end of 2020 and into early 2021, reports of threatened ISDS claims or notices of disputes (under both treaty and contract) started to emerge,[16] while commercial arbitration centres started to report that 2020 had been a record year for new case filings,[17] despite much of the global economy grinding to a halt.

June 2020) <www.iisd.org/publications/suspension-investor-state-dispute-settlement-covid-19> accessed 14 May 2021.

13   Columbia Center on Sustainable Investment, 'Call for ISDS Moratorium During COVID-19 Crisis and Response' (*Columbia Center on Sustainable Investment*, 6 May 2020) <ccsi.columbia.edu/content/call-isds-moratorium-during-covid-19-crisis-and-response> accessed 14 May 2021.

14   'Open Letter to Governments on ISDS and COVID-19' (*Seattle to Brussels Network*, June 2020) <s2bnetwork.org/wp-content/uploads/2020/06/OpenLetterOnISDSAndCOVID_June2020.pdf> accessed 14 May 2021.

15   See the many examples in this paper: Corporate Europe Observatory, 'Cashing in on the pandemic: how lawyers are preparing to sue states over COVID-19 response measures' (*Corporate Europe Observatory*, 18 May 2020) <corporateeurope.org/en/2020/05/cashing-pandemic-how-lawyers-are-preparing-sue-states-over-covid-19-response-measures> accessed 14 May 2021.

16   Lisa Bohmer, 'Chile is put on notice of treaty-based airport concession dispute' (*Investment Arbitration Reporter*, 20 January 2021) <www.iareporter.com/articles/chile-is-put-on-notice-of-treaty-based-airport-concession-dispute/> accessed 14 May 2021; Lisa Bohmer, 'Highway concessionaire initiates contract-based ICSID arbitration against Peru' (*Investment Arbitration Reporter*, 11 June 2020) <www.iareporter.com/articles/highway-concessionaire-initiates-contract-based-icsid-arbitration-against-peru/> accessed 14 May 2021; Lisa Bohmer, 'Zimbabwe's State-owned pharmaceutical company is threatened with contract-based arbitration over cancellation of COVID-19 kit contract' (*Investment Arbitration Reporter*, 14 July 2020) <www.iareporter.com/articles/zimbabwes-state-owned-pharmaceutical-company-is-threatened-with-contract-based-arbitration-over-cancellation-of-covid-19-kit-contract/> accessed 14 May 2021; Lisa Bohmer, 'Changes to Mexico's electricity regulation in light of pandemic prompt threats of investment arbitration claims' (*Investment Arbitration Reporter*, 18 May 2020) <www.iareporter.com/articles/changes-to-mexicos-electricity-regulation-in-light-of-pandemic-prompt-threats-of-investment-arbitration-claims/> accessed 14 May 2021; Lisa Bohmer, 'Chile Round-up: three threats, and one arbitration drawing to an end' (*Investment Arbitration Reporter*, 20 November 2020) <www.iareporter.com/articles/chile-round-up-three-threats-and-one-arbitration-drawing-to-an-end/> accessed 14 May 2021.

17   KC Vijayan, 'Singapore arbitration centre opens office in NY' (*The Straits Times*, 12 December 2020) <www.straitstimes.com/singapore/singapore-arbitration-centre-opens-office-in-ny>

The AU Declaration represented the consensus view of the 55 AU Member States that the risk of ISDS posed a tangible threat to the ability of African governments to deal with the public health and economic fallout from COVID-19. Going one step further than simply acknowledging the risks, the AU Declaration provided clear guidance to help Member States respond to those risks. The AU Declaration is yet another example of the investment law and policy innovations originating in the continent, following in the footsteps of such progressive and ground-breaking instruments as the Pan-African Investment Code (PAIC),[18] the Southern African Development Community (SADC) Model BIT,[19] the Common Market for Eastern and Southern Africa (COMESA) Common Investment Area Agreement,[20] and the Nigeria-Morocco Bilateral Investment Treaty (BIT).[21]

But it is first and foremost, an important momentum of solidarity among African nations on how to build legal resilience in times of crises. Although concise, the Declaration's recommendations address short term and immediate steps that AU Member States can take in response to the COVID-19 crisis while providing a clear framework for longer term, broader reforms to the investment protection regime to enable states to act in future crises. The Declaration offers another tale from Africa which reveals that crises can serve as critical junctures for the shaping of new visions within the international legal order.

It also signals that narratives in times of crises should not be about hegemony. Precedent crises have often led to hegemony at the international level – i.e. one state or one limited group of states deciding on the new world order. The COVID-19 crisis allows the creation of new paradigm shifts in terms of narratives and the shaping of a world order "based on cooperation, the rule of

accessed 14 May 2021; 'ICSID Releases 2020 Caseload Statistics' (*ICSID*, 28 January 2021) <icsid.worldbank.org/news-and-events/news-releases/icsid-releases-2020-caseload -statistics> accessed 14 May 2021.

18 African Union, 'Pan-African Investment Code' (*African Union*, 31 December 2016) <au.int/ en/documents/20161231/pan-african-investment-code-paic> accessed 14 May 2021.

19 Southern African Development Community Model BIT Template with Commentary, July 2012 <www.iisd.org/itn/wp-content/uploads/2012/10/SADC-Model-BIT-Template -Final.pdf> accessed 14 May 2021.

20 Investment Agreement for the Common Market for Eastern and Southern Africa Common Investment Area, May 2007 <investmentpolicy.unctad.org/international-investment -agreements/treaties/treaties-with-investment-provisions/3225/comesa-investment -agreement> accessed 14 May 2021.

21 Nigeria-Morocco Bilateral Investment Treaty, December 2016 <investmentpolicy.unctad .org/international-investment-agreements/treaties/tips/3711/morocco---nigeria-bit-2016-> accessed 14 May 2021, (hereinafter Nigeria-Morocco BIT).

law, collective action, and shared principles"[22] and which "rather than pitting civilizations and values against one another (…) must build a more inclusive multilateralism, respecting our differences as much as our common values".[23]

President Sall's piece might have been overlooked by many international lawyers and international policy-makers. Yet, his crisis narrative offers a window to rethink what a narrative of international law should be not only during a crisis but also in a post-crisis context. Referring to an old African saying according to which "The rainbow owes its beauty to the varied shades of its colours", Sall took the opportunity of his narrative *of* the crisis to emphasize that the new world order, in particular with respect to global health issues, "will have to exclude all forms of discrimination, stigmatisation and prejudice, especially towards our continent. Africa, as the cradle of humanity and a land of old civilisation, is not a no-man's land. Nor can it offer itself as a land of guinea pigs. Gone are also the doom scenarios that try to draw an apocalyptic future for the continent. This continent has undergone far more perilous and crueller trials. It has remained resilient and is standing stronger than ever!" It is, thus, to be hoped that the COVID-19 crisis will truly lead to a sustainable narrative of international law for all and from all.

22   Emmanuel Macron et al (n 8).
23   Macky Sall (n 2).

CHAPTER 7

International Law as a Crisis Discourse

The Peril of Wordlessness

Jean d'Aspremont

On ne fait pas n'importe quoi avec la langue.[1]

∴

International law lives off crises, lives its crises, and lives in crisis. International law is a discourse for crisis, about crisis, and in crisis. In short, international law is a crisis discourse. In that sense, engaging with international law from the vantage point of crisis hardly adds anything, let alone proves novel. International lawyers are the masters of a discourse that is all about containing, making, and surviving crises in an interventionist,[2] and managerial spirit.[3] Against this backdrop, the very extensive literature that burgeoned following the outbreak of the COVID-19 pandemic is nothing but business as usual for a crisis discourse like international law.[4] And yet, as I will try to demonstrate

---

1 Jacques Derrida, *Apprendre à vivre enfin* (Galilée 2005) 38.

2 I have looked at the interventionist dimension of international legal discourses elsewhere. See Jean d'Aspremont, 'Cyber Operations and International Law: An Interventionist Legal Thought' (2016) 21 Journal of Conflict & Security Law 575.

3 I have looked at the managerial dimension of international legal discourses elsewhere. See Jean d'Aspremont, 'Jenks' Ethic of Responsibility for the Disillusioned International Lawyer' (2020) 31 EJIL (forthcoming).

4 International lawyers have been extensively discussing whether the pandemic constitutes a situation covered by existing obligations and their exceptions under international trade law or international investment law, whether the situation created by the pandemic constitutes a circumstance precluding wrongfulness under the law of State responsibility, whether obligations in terms of human rights law and refugee law are suspended by virtue of the pandemic, whether the pandemic gives rise to new primary obligations in terms of international human rights law or international humanitarian law, whether the pandemic gives rise to an obligation of due diligence or an obligation to cooperate, whether the pandemic gives rise to a threat to international peace and security under the international law of collective security, whether cyber operations by States that have consequences for the research, trial, manufacture and distribution of a vaccine are prohibited, whether domestic

in this short chapter, international law's revelling in crises may prove to be, within a few decades, the very cause of international law's self-debilitation, self-exhaustion, and self-depletion.

What international law does to the world, it does it with words. In fact, international law's interventions in crises and management thereof hinge on there being words to capture what international law purports to do and what international law is meant to apply to. Short of any adequate terminological apparatus, international law loses most of its interventionist and managerial edge. As this chapter seeks to demonstrate, it is because of this dependence on words that the omnipresence of crisis narratives in international legal thought and practice may prove most alarming. Indeed, if any phenomenon deemed to be out of normality comes to be elevated to, reduced to, or, simply made, a crisis, one may wonder what words international law can and should brandish in facing the seemingly most pressing and greatest cataclysm of recent human history, namely the looming climate catastrophe.[5] It is argued here that, should international law let the looming climate catastrophe – as well as the calamitous consequences of the measures necessary to avert it – be absorbed in its crisis narratives and in what is called here its 'normally abnormal normality', international law would be condemned to wordlessness. This would be so despite having had the luxury of being able to foresee it.

This short chapter starts by sketching out the way in which international law comes to function as a crisis discourse, that is, a discourse for crisis, about crisis, and in crisis (1). It then elaborates on why crisis narratives are omnipresent in international legal thought and practice, showing that crises amount to a discursive necessity for international law (2). This chapter then develops its main argument according to which crisis-centred international law,

---

measures to contain the pandemic breach international human rights law, whether the pandemic and the behaviour of States in relation thereto can fall within the jurisdiction of international courts – to name only a few of the legal issues that drew attention in the recent literature. This literature on COVID-19 and international law is, less than a year since the outbreak of the pandemic, already too abounding to be referenced comprehensively. See, however, the numerous blog entries on <www.ejiltalk.org>. See also the legal scholarship referenced in the *Oxford University Press COVID-19 content hub* <https://academic.oup.com/journals/pages/coronavirus>. See also the overview provided by Armin von Bogdandy and Pedro Villareal, 'International Law on Pandemic Response: A First Stocktaking in light of the Coronavirus Crisis' (2020) MPIL Research Paper 2020-07 <https://papers.ssrn.com/sol3/papers.cfm?abstract_id=3561650> accessed 19 April 2021; See also the special symposium dedicated to 'The International Legal Order and the Global Pandemic' in (2020) 114(4) AJIL.

5   Whilst this chapter focuses on the climate catastrophe, other catastrophes are surely on the horizon and could also be mentioned like the collapse of biodiversity, a global nuclear fallout, the Kessler syndrome, etc.

confronted with the upcoming greatest catastrophe of recent human history, is at risk of being wordless and of losing its world-making role in a matter of a few decades (3).

Two important caveats are warranted at this preliminary stage. First, the point developed in this chapter cannot be reduced to an arcane and detached literary exercise, let alone a nihilistic one. If anything, caring for the words of international law means caring for what international law can potentially be doing. Indeed, words matter because they constitute the first step of any intervention on the part of international law on the "outside".[6] It is through words that international law does what it does, and thus destroys, silences, and discriminates but also shapes, guides, and prompts action. In that sense, as far as international law is concerned, there is nothing more concrete than words. For that reason, wordlessness is no minor threat for international law. Second, it must be acknowledged that the argument made in this chapter may itself be articulated around a certain idea of crisis. After all, the idea of the peril of wordlessness could be construed as just another variant of the crisis narratives that populate international legal thought and practice. In that sense, the discussion provided in this chapter could be critically scrutinised in the very same way as it itself evaluates the way in which international law functions as a crisis discourse, let alone be charged for indulging in a performative contradiction.[7] Yet, it is argued here that that the resort to the idea of the peril of wordlessness in this chapter – and thus to a possible crisis narrative – is no conceptual, methodological and theoretical obstacle to this chapter's inquiry in the functioning of international law as a crisis discourse.[8]

1   A Discourse for Crisis, about Crisis, and in Crisis

International law, as a crisis discourse, is a discourse based around crisis, for crisis, and in crisis. That is, it is a discourse that lives off crises, lives its crises,

---

6   See generally, Jean d'Aspremont, 'Wording in International Law' (2012) 25 LJIL 575.

7   This objection is an objection commonly made by Jürgen Habermas, *The Philosophical Discourse of Modernity: Twelve Lectures* (Frederik Lawrence tr, Polity Press 1987) 185–186, 279. See also Alasdair MacIntyre, *Three Rival Versions of Moral Inquiry: Encyclopaedia, Genealogy, and Tradition* (University of Notre Dame Press 1990) 55–56.

8   In the same vein, see Jean-François Lyotard, *La Condition Postmoderne* (Editions de Minuit 1979) 51; Theodor Adorno and Max Horkheimer, *Dialectic of Enlightenment* (Verso 1997) 7–9. See also the remarks of Susan Marks, 'False Contingency' (2009) 62 CLP 1, 1–21.

and lives in crisis. This section sketches out three of the main features of what it means for international law to be a crisis discourse.

First, international law is a discourse *for crises* that lives off crises. It is the tool which is summoned whenever a phenomenon deemed to be outside normality is experienced. When international lawyers face a type of cruelty, indecency, poverty, complacency, or bankruptcy which they judge to be outside normality, they brandish an international legal rule or the formal powers of an international legal institution.[9] Interestingly, international lawyers are not alone in invoking international law whenever a phenomenon is deemed to be outside normality. They are often assisted by policymakers, journalists, activists, one-line self-taught lawyers, etc. who commonly feel at ease raising international legal claims and who speak on behalf of international law to address the crises which they witness and experience. As a discourse for crisis, international law can be seen as a discursive tool that is on standby, charging in the garage, until it is fired up by international lawyers (and their associates) to tackle any new crisis appearing on their horizon.[10] From this perspective, international law is a discursive tool that supposedly accumulates knowledge through its repeated deployment and application to crises, and is a tool that is being constantly upgraded and enhanced.[11] As a discourse for crises that lives off crises, international law is permanently profiled and vindicated as a tool that is fully adaptable according to an evolving and ever changing world.[12]

Second, international law is a discourse *about crisis* that lives its crises. It portrays the world as rhythmed by crises and revels therein. Crises are part of the world-making performances of international law.[13] When it is mobilized,

---

9   This has occasionally given rise to specific branches of international law entirely dedicated to crisis. On the idea of a disaster law, see Kristian Cedervall Lauta, *Disaster Law* (Routledge 2015); Rosemary Lyster, *Climate Justice and Disaster Law* (CUP 2015). On the idea of an international disaster response law see Andrea De Guttry, Marco Gestri, and Gabriella Venturini, *International Disaster Response Law* (TMC Asser Press 2012). On the idea of an international disaster relief law, see Stephen Green, *International Disaster Relief: Toward a Responsive System* (McGraw-Hill 1977).

10   On the idea of crisis as impetus for action, Joseph Powderly, 'International criminal justice in an age of perpetual crisis' (2019) 32 LJIL 1, 3–6.

11   On the idea of crisis as a tool for the development of international law and for an opportunity to fill the gaps, Hilary Charlesworth, 'International Law: A Discipline of Crisis' (2002) 65 MLR 377, 380.

12   This is part of what I have called elsewhere the self-confirming modes of thinking on which international law is organized. See Jean d'Aspremont, 'A Worldly Law in a Legal World' in Andrea Bianchi and Moshe Hirsch (eds), *International Law's Invisible Frames* (OUP 2021).

13   See generally, Monica Hakimi, 'The Work of International Law' (2017) 58 Harv Int'l LJ 1. See Charlesworth (n 11) 382–383.

international law contributes to the making of the crisis onto which it is projected as much as the crisis triggers the application of international law.[14] A very elementary illustration thereof is non-compliance with an international legal obligation.[15] Non-compliance is commonly understood as a crisis that triggers a need for international law's response and yet it is a crisis that is constituted by international law itself. That international law is a discourse about crisis is no minor thing. It should be recalled that like any idea projected onto the world, crises function as horses' blinders. For example, it is because migration is deemed a crisis rather than a normal expression of life or of human movement on earth, that it comes to call for an extraordinary response, limitations, containment, repression, etc. In that sense, international law's deployment of crisis narratives and thus the portrayal of a phenomenon as constituting a crisis is never neutral. Not only does international law elect certain crises and ignore others,[16] but, more fundamentally, it reduces very complex phenomena to a limited set of extraordinary and pathological facts, thereby dramatically restricting how such phenomena are experienced, perceived, and approached.[17] In short, as a discourse about crisis that lives its crises, international law defines normality and abnormality in the world, thereby carrying out some of its most dramatic world-making performances.[18]

Third, international law is a discourse *in crisis*. It constantly lives in crisis as it presents itself as being riven by interpretations or institutional practices that potentially undermine it, or as being inadequately equipped, or in need of reform.[19] In doing so, international law constantly fuels a demand for reform and reformers,[20] the latter being a role which international lawyers are commonly prompt to volunteer for.[21] At the same time, being in a state of crisis

---

14   On self-confirming thinking in international law see d'Aspremont (n 12).

15   For a discussion of the common elevation of violations of international law into crises, see Charlesworth (n 11) 380.

16   ibid 384.

17   See generally, Henri Bergson, *La pensée et le mouvant* (Flammarion 2014) 181.

18   See generally, Georges Canguilhem, *Le normal et le pathologique* (Presses Universitaires de France 2013). See also Michel Foucault, *Histoire de la folie à l'âge classique* (Gallimard 1976).

19   See Anne Orford, 'The Destiny of International Law' (2004) 17 LJIL 441; Charlesworth (n 11). On the extensive debates about the state of crisis of international criminal law, see Frédéric Mégret, 'The Anxieties of International Criminal Justice' (2016) 29 LJIL 197; Elies van Sliedregt, 'International Criminal Law: Over-Studied and Underachieving?' (2016) 29 LJIL 1; Powderly (n 10).

20   On the idea that crisis allows rewriting, see Alasdair McIntyre, *Whose Justice? Which Rationality?* (Duckworth 1988) 363.

21   On the idea that crisis promotes a certain type of heroism within the discipline, see Charlesworth (n 11) 387.

serves a self-reproducing function for international law.[22] Indeed, this self-declared state of crisis allows international law to constantly recognize its imperfection, while conveying a constant acknowledgement that it must be adjusted to the world and adapt its interventionist and managerial ambitions to what that world requires. In that sense, being a discourse in crisis, international law comes to look defective. And yet, such projection of its own limitations constitutes a cynical move on the part of international law, for this is what allows international law to affirm its full flexibility and thus its permanent state of renewal.[23] As a discourse in crisis that lives in and with its own crisis, international law cynically makes itself vulnerable for the sake of affirming its invincible flexibility.[24]

2   Crises as Discursive Necessities

It is submitted in this section that living off crises, living one's crises, and being in crisis is not the result of a convention, a convulsion or an obsession but corresponds, more fundamentally, to three distinct discursive necessities of international law.[25] This means that for any proposition under international law to be considered international law proper it must be seen as responding to the three crisis-related discursive necessities mentioned in this section. Short of responding to such crisis-related discursive necessities, any saying under international law would fall into discursive irrelevance and be demoted to a saying located outside international law.[26] As the following paragraphs will

22   On the idea that modern discourses are always at the mercy of crisis and that this is something they do to themselves, see Peter Sloterdijk, *Critique of Cynical Reason* (University of Minnesota Press 1987) 7, 76.

23   For a scholarly example of the elevation of crisis as a moment of self-reflection and self-examination, see Francisco-José Quintana and Justina Uriburu, 'Modest International Law: COVID-19, International Legal Responses, and Depoliticization' (2020) 114 AJIL 687.

24   On this aspect of international law, see Jean d'Aspremont, 'International Legal Methods: Working for a Tragic and Cynical Routine' in Rossana Deplano and Nicholas Tsagourias (eds), *Handbook on Research Methods in International Law* (Elgar 2020). See more generally David Kennedy, 'When Renewal Repeats: Thinking Against the Box' (1999–2000) 32 NYU J Int'l L & Pol 335.

25   On the idea that a field's anxieties are part of the fields' condition (with an emphasis on international criminal law), see Mégret (n 19).

26   It is important to highlight that the three crisis-related discursive necessities discussed in this section are not exclusive of other discursive necessities. For instance, international law is also informed by a constant sense (and staging) of imminent change. This is something which John Haskell and I have explored elsewhere. See John D. Haskell and

show, each of the three crisis-related discursive necessities to which any saying under international law must respond takes the form of distinct ruptures by virtue of which international law justifies, affirms, and grounds itself. Living off crises, living one's crises, and being in crisis enable international law to articulate itself around specific ruptures which are necessary for international law to do what it does.

First, international law is nurtured by crises, for crises perpetuate the idea of there being *ruptures from normality* without which international law's interventions cannot be justified. As long as there are crises, there are projections of ruptures in the normality of the world, thereby creating the experience of a need for the restoration of normality. In that sense, crises secure the permanence of rupture from normality and thus of the need for normality-restoring interventions by international law.[27] Said differently, crises enable a rupture from a state of normality where international law would have been neither justified nor relevant.[28]

Second, international law is informed by crisis narratives as international law is in a constant search for a *rupture from the past*, which allows it to affirm its uniqueness and relevance in the present.[29] Indeed, each crisis which international law is called to tackle re-affirms, re-locates, and re-designates international law in the present. This means that each crisis is a new, and permanent, beginning for international law.[30] In other words, crises enable a rupture from a past where international law would have been both static and anachronistic.[31]

Third, international law is riven by its own crisis which allows for a *rupture from ontology, metaphysics, and contemplation*.[32] To be sure, the crisis which international law is permanently undergoing works as a reminder that international law was never a given inherited from metaphysics but is merely a

---

Jean d'Aspremont (eds), *Tipping Points in International Law: Critique and Commitment* (CUP 2021).

27 On the idea that crises legitimize action and create a sense of urgency, see Benjamin Authers and Hilary Charlesworth, 'The Crisis and the Quotidian in International Human Rights Law' (2014) 44 NYIL 19, 21, 25.

28 Terry Eagleton, *The Function of Criticism* (Verso 2005) 105: 'The fact that we are always in crisis secures deconstruction a safe, indeed, interminable future'.

29 Paul Ricoeur, *La mémoire, l'histoire, l'oubli* (Seuil 2000) 386–387.

30 According to Jürgen Habermas this is a central feature of modern discourses, also something which can be ascribed to Hegel. See Jürgen Habermas, *The Philosophical Discourse of Modernity: Twelve Lectures* (Frederik Lawrence tr, Polity Press 1987) 5–7.

31 On the extent to which crises and progress are intertwined, see Walter Benjamin, *Sur le concept d'histoire* (Olivier Mannoni tr, Payot 2013) ch 4, 65–66.

32 On the idea that modern discourses put an end to contemplative thinking, see Hannah Arendt, *The Human Condition* (2nd edn, University of Chicago Press 1998) 14–21.

human creation, and one that has no other foundations than those that the discourse gives to itself.[33] As a discourse in crisis, international law reminds its users that its conventional foundations are permanently re-discussed, re-determined, and re-affirmed, thereby making foundational contestation permanent.[34] Crisis and foundational conventionality are two sides of the same coin. From this perspective, crises transcend international law from the onto-logical, essentialist and metaphysical validation[35] of which international law would have not been able to find viable foundations.[36]

It must be acknowledged that the abovementioned distinct ruptures which are enabled by crisis narratives – and the discursive necessities to which they correspond – work in parallel but not together. In fact, the above sketch of the extent to which crises manifest three key discursive necessities should suffice to shed light on the possible contradictions between them and show that international law, as a crisis discourse, is certainly not a consistent discursive construction.[37] For instance, it may be that the necessity of a rupture from the past contradicts the necessity of a rupture from ontology, metaphysics, and contemplation as the making of international law as a human creation necessarily historizes it and thus calls for its anchoring in the past. Likewise, the necessity of a rupture from normality may contradict the necessity of a rupture from ontology, contemplation, and metaphysics, for the conventionality to which the latter confines international law simultaneously condemns it to an indeterminate normality.

Actually, such contradictions between the three abovementioned crisis-related discursive necessities do not matter as long as they are not disabling

---

33   Jacques Derrida, 'Force de Loi: Le 'Fondement Mystique de l'Autorité'' (1990) 11 Cardozo L Rev 920, 942, 944; Michel Foucault, *L'achéologie du savoir* (Gallimard 1969) 87; Michel de Certeau, *L'écriture de l'histoire* (Gallimard 1975) 74; Habermas (n 30) 7.

34   According to Anne Orford, responses to crises include conventional attempts to find a new sovereign ground for the law, whether that be in the form of international organizations or of powerful national sovereigns who stand outside the law and guarantee its operation: Orford (n 19).

35   This is not exclusive of international law functioning in an ontological way. See Jean d'Aspremont, *International Law as a Belief System* (CUP 2017).

36   This does not mean that international law has ever succeeded in providing itself viable foundations. See Jean d'Aspremont, 'Three international lawyers in a hall of mirrors' (2019) 32 LJIL 367.

37   On the contradictions of modern discourses in general, see Paul Ricoeur, *La mémoire, l'histoire, l'oubli* (Seuil 2000) 399; Peter Sloterdijk, *Critique of Cynical Reason* (University of Minnesota 1987) 8, 11–12, 88–90. On the idea that scrutinizing these contradictions is one of the goals of critique, see Roberto Mangabeira Unger, *The Critical Legal Studies Movement. Another Time: A Greater Task* (Verso 2015) 15.

to the discourse – and I believe they are not as far as international law is concerned. More interesting, in my view, is the fact that crises are not only a state of the discourse – as discussed in section 1 – but also a necessary condition for it. Indeed, as has been indicated in this section, crises respond to a series of discursive necessities without which no proposition could be properly made under international law. This means that crises are an indispensable part of the normal state of international legal discourse.[38] Crises are accordingly also a source of that discourse. And yet, at the same time, crises are defined by a presupposed normality set by international law (e.g. a stable climate, an absence of war, unimpeded trade, etc.). In that sense, crises are always both the source and the product of international legal discourse.[39] Being generated by and generating the international legal discourse, crises materialize what is called here the *normally abnormal normality* of international law. As a crisis discourse, international law absorbs all the phenomena to which its application is envisaged into its own normally abnormal normality.

3 The Peril of Wordlessness in the Face of the Climate Catastrophe

As was indicated in the previous sections, international law is a crisis discourse whereby all the phenomena to which the application of international law is envisaged are absorbed into the latter's normally abnormal normality. This section reflects on the possible implications of international law's tackling the looming climate catastrophe as it tackles the pandemic crisis, the world institutions' crisis, the migration crisis, the cyber-security crisis, the financial markets' crisis, the sovereign debts' crisis, the terrorism crisis, etc. In particular, this section raises the question of what international law has to say about the looming climate catastrophe that threatens to ravage the world if it is apprehended through its own mundane crisis vocabulary? It is argued in this final section that, as long as international lawyers let the looming climate catastrophe be absorbed in the normally abnormal normality of international law and

---

38 On the idea that crisis becomes part of the order which international lawyers are responsible for, See Fleur Johns, Richard Joyce, and Sundhya Pahuja, 'Introduction' in Fleur Johns, Richard Joyce, and Sundhya Pahuja (eds), *Events: The Force of International Law* (Routledge 2011) 1–17.

39 Compare with the argument of Benjamin Authers and Hilary Charlesworth according to which international human rights law is produced by crisis and dependent upon crisis. See Authers and Charlesworth (n 27).

let it be captured as just a crisis, they expose international law to the peril of wordlessness as well as to the impossibility to perform any world-making role in relation to the climate catastrophe.

A very important caveat is warranted before this argument is developed further. The point here does not seek to imply that the pandemic crisis, the world institutions' crisis, the migration crisis, the cyber-security crisis, the financial markets' crisis, the sovereign debts' crisis, or the terrorism crisis are phenomena of second importance compared to the climate catastrophe. These "crises" of course matter as they relate to situations of very widespread and intolerable distress and suffering. One could claim that by absorbing these phenomena in the normally abnormal normality of international law, international lawyers already belittle the distress and the suffering caused by these crises. If this is the case, what is there to say about the consequences of absorbing the looming climate catastrophe in the normally abnormal normality of international law?

The claim made here, that the treatment of the looming climate catastrophe as a crisis and its absorption into international law's normally abnormal normality can lead to international law's wordlessness and its loss of any world-making role, will be substantiated in this section by responding to four counterarguments that can be anticipated in response thereto. The first counterargument pertains to the urgent nature of the abnormality and the impossibility of international law adjusting to it. In fact, in defence of international law (and of international lawyers), it could be contended that, as far as the pandemic crisis, the world institutions' crisis, the migration crisis, the cyber-security crisis, the financial markets' crisis, the sovereign debts' crisis, the terrorism crisis, etc. are concerned, international law could only be mobilized "instantly", "without preparation" or "on the spot", leaving no other option than absorbing these phenomena in international law's existing normally abnormal normality. In other words, it could be said that the aforementioned crises erupted in a way that provided no time for equipping international law properly. This is the common *we-have-no-time-for-a-rethink-but-must-act* narrative. Whatever the weight of this argument, this is not a claim that can actually be entertained in relation to the looming climate catastrophe. Never has a catastrophe been anticipated and foreseen so long in advance as the looming climate catastrophe. Few would dispute the fact that this catastrophe is a long looming one, and one that leaves ample time for international law to reinvent its vocabularies as well as its narratives and to do away with its normally abnormal normality. This is not to say that there has been no effort to systematize international law's response to climate change, as is illustrated by the attempt to design an 'international law on climate change'[40] or a 'climate disaster law'.[41] Yet, these scholarly endeavours, however remarkable and lofty they may be, have remained short of a new vocabulary that raises to the level of what the looming climate catastrophe demands. Whatever the merits of the abovementioned scholarly enterprises, urgency can be no excuse for international law's complacency and by-default reliance on its usual crisis narratives.

The second counterargument that ought to be mentioned is that of the actual word-makers in international law. It could be argued that this whole debate about the wordlessness of international law *vis-à-vis* the looming climate catastrophe is not a scholarly matter for it lies in the hands of the actual international law-makers who define the main legal categories through which international law intervenes in response to the problems of the world. This is the mundane *States-make-international-law* narrative often heard in – orthodox – scholarly circles. It is submitted here that scholars can hardly exculpate themselves by ascribing the possible wordlessness of international law *vis-à-vis* the looming climate catastrophe to the passivity of policy-makers, diplomats, legal advisers and all those who allegedly pull the strings behind the veil of the State. In other words, international legal scholars cannot seriously claim that they are themselves not the ones carving the words of international law and thus the terms of international law's action on climate change. Whilst the formal repositories of the discourse, i.e. the treaties, may well be made by States and all the policy-makers, diplomats, and legal advisers that come with them, the vocabulary of international law, and thus the words through which international law acts upon the "outside", are used, uttered, invoked, filled, interpreted, and substantiated by a wide range of actors, including scholars, who have the ability to (re)invent, (re)interpret, (re)calibrate, (re)organize, and (re)appropriate the words of international law.[42]

The third counterargument that can possibly be raised – and proved equally unconvincing – is that international law, as a crisis discourse, has inevitably learnt from the multiple situations of crises to which it has been applied over the last century. This counterargument bespeaks the old modern ideal[43] of

---

40   See e.g. Benoit Mayer, *The International Law on Climate Change* (CUP 2018). See also the references mentioned by Rosa Giles Carnero, 'Climate Change and International Law' in Tony Carty (ed), *Oxford Bibliographies in International Law* (OUP 2017).

41   Rosemary Lyster and Robert Verchick (eds), *Research Handbook on Climate Disaster Law: Barriers and Opportunities* (Edward Elgar Publishing 2018).

42   I have explored this elsewhere. See d'Aspremont, 'Wording in International Law' (n 6). See also Jean d'Aspremont, *Epistemic Forces in International Law* (Edward Elgar 2016).

43   See generally, Bruno Latour, *La fabrique du droit. Une ethnographie du Conseil d'Etat* (La Découverte 2004) 235; Jean-François Lyotard, *La Condition Postmoderne* (Editions de Minuit 1979) 52. On the idea that each crisis looks alike and that what is accumulated is

accumulated knowledge which is so commonly espoused by international lawyers[44] and corresponds to the *international-law-improves-through-practice* narrative which is so cherished in practice-centric circles.[45] It is submitted here that this counterargument is not more persuasive than the *we-have-no-time-for-a-rethink* and the *States-make-international-law* narratives. Given that each intervention of international law in the continuously renewed crises of the world are only the materialization of a normally abnormal normality, there is nothing to be learnt from the common functioning of international law. Crises, understood as a materialization of international law's normally abnormal normality, only confirm and perpetuate what international law has always been doing. In other words, crises, being defined by international law according to its setting of normality and being indispensable to international law's functioning as discourse, exclude the possibility that anything can be learnt from themselves. Crises cannot simultaneously constitute international law, be constituted by international law, and be the source of accumulated knowledge about what international law does with crises.

Last, but not least, it could also be counterargued that the climate catastrophe can yet be averted and that there is no need for a rethink of international law's vocabulary and narratives as long as the catastrophe can be warded off. This echoes the *don't-verse-in-cheap-catastrophism* narrative. It must be acknowledged here that the looming climate catastrophe remains looming and that hope for preventive action remains – which is why the latter must definitely and unambiguously be pursued. Yet, it is argued here that averting

---

an accumulation of resemblance, see Michel Foucault, *Les mots et les choses* (Gallimard 1966) 45.

44   See e.g. Jean d'Aspremont, 'The League of Nations and the Power of "Experiment Narratives" in International Institutional Law' (2020) 22 International Community Law Review 275.

45   On the concept of practice in international law and practice-centricism of international legal literature, see Andrea Bianchi, *International Law Theories: An Inquiry into Different Ways of Thinking* (OUP 2016) 7. See also Jean d'Aspremont, 'Theory and History: Ordering Through Distinctions' in Jean d'Aspremont (ed), *The History and Theory of International Law*, volume I and volume II (Edward Elgar 2020). See also Isaiah Berlin, 'The Pursuit of the Ideal' in Henry Hardy (ed), *The Crooked Timber of Humanity: Chapters in the History of Ideas* (2nd edn, Princeton University Press 2013) 1–20, esp. 5: 'With the new methods discovered by natural science, order could be introduced in the social sphere as well – uniformities could be observed, hypotheses formulated and tested by experiment; laws could be based on them, and then laws in specific regions of experience could be seen to be entailed by wider laws; and these in turn to be entailed by still wider laws, and so on upwards, until a great harmonious system connected by unbreakable logic links and capable of being formulated in precise – that is, mathematical – terms, could be established'.

the climate catastrophe will itself bring its own calamity, for the shift from a carbon-dependent to a carbon-free economy, albeit the better alternative, will itself bear disastrous consequences.[46] This means that the disastrous consequences of the measures necessary to prevent or mitigate it should themselves not be absorbed in the normally abnormal normality of international law either. The looming climate catastrophe, as much as the calamitous measures necessary to avert it, demands that international law rise to the level of action demanded by the climate catastrophe and not limit itself to the comfort zone of its mundane crisis narratives.

Whilst seeking to debunk some of the most anticipated counterarguments about the need for a reinvention of the vocabularies of international law to prevent international law's wordlessness and its loss of any world-making role in front of the looming climate catastrophe (and of the disastrous consequences of the measures necessary to prevent or mitigate it), the previous paragraphs have so far fallen short of elucidating what precisely the contours of such new vocabulary – and the range of narratives that enabled thereby – can possibly be. Yet, at the risk of disappointing the possible readership of this chapter, it is important to stress that defining the vocabulary and the narratives that would allow international lawyers to evade the crisis narratives, and the normally abnormal normality of international law, ought not to be the aim of the discussion conducted here. First, the main goal of the foregoing has primarily been to make international lawyers more familiar with the techniques, conditions, and limitations of their action on the world.[47] Second, and more fundamentally, spelling out a possible new vocabulary and set of narratives that could possibly allow the looming climate change crisis to be approached outside international law's current normally abnormal normality can simply not be the answer to the problem of international law's wordlessness and loss of world-making power. Indeed, the point made here is not that the current *crisis* narratives of international law should be mechanically replaced by – say – a new set of *catastrophe* narratives. Such mechanical terminological substitution or an increased dramatization and differentiation in international law's narratives would not bring about the much-desired departure from international law's normally abnormal normality.[48] This would simply be a type of

---

46 See Editorial, 'Is it the end of the oil age? Power in the 21st century' *The Economist* (London, 19–25 September 2020) 18–21.

47 For a few remarks on the benefits of such exercise, see Henri Bergson, *Le possible et le réél* (Quadrige 2011) 5.

48 On differentiation being a central aspect of the working of modern discourses, see Michel de Certeau, *L'écriture de l'histoire* (Gallimard 1975) 59.

normally abnormal normality replacing another. Nor is it the claim made here that inventing a vocabulary or a set of narratives that provides a truer or more "scientific" representation of the reality of the looming climate catastrophe is required. In fact, international lawyers have now been sufficiently exposed to critical theory to appreciate that the "state of things" and "the natural order" are always the result of a performance[49] and that "reality" and "nature" constitutes terribly powerful regimes of truth.[50] For that reason, the question of vocabulary that is raised here should not be construed as a quest for better empirics.[51]

If the point made here is not about mechanically replacing crisis narratives by catastrophe narratives or about inventing a better representation of reality, what is it then that this chapter calls for? It is argued at this ultimate stage of the discussion that rising to the level that the climate catastrophe demands requires not only that the climate catastrophe be acknowledged as *the* catastrophe of all (present) times but, above all, that it be subject to a perpetual re-determination, re-appropriation, and re-narrativization that upholds the gravity of the catastrophe concerned and preserves international law's capacity to respond to it.[52] This means more concretely that, instead of immobilizing the climate catastrophe – and the disastrous consequences of the measures necessary to prevent or mitigate it – in a fixed vocabulary and uniform narratives,[53] international lawyers' engagements with the climate catastrophe should materialize in a vocabulary that can be constantly *re-determined* and *re-appropriated*[54] and in new sets of narratives that enable a permanent *re-eventalization*[55] of the looming climate catastrophe. The alternative to the immobilization of crises narratives with respect to the looming

---

49   Judith Butler, *Gender Trouble: Feminism and the Subversion of Identity* (2nd edn, Routledge 1990) 45; Michel Foucault, *Les mots et les choses* (n 43) 11; Steven Winter, *A Clearing in the Forest. Law, Life and Mind* (University of Chicago Press 2001) 105, 114.

50   On the notion of truth regime, see Michel Foucault, *Naissance de la biopolitique. Cours au Collège de France (1978–1979)* (Gallimard Seuil 2004) 22.

51   Compare with Bruno Latour, 'Why has Critique Run out of Steam? From Matters of Fact to Matters of Concern' (2004) 30 Critical Inquiry 225, 231: 'The question was never to get away from facts but closer to them, not fighting empiricism but, on the contrary, renewing empiricism'.

52   Comp. with George Steiner, *Errata. An Examined Life* (Weidenfeld and Nicholson 1997) 5.

53   On this being a common trait of modern thinking, see Henri Bergson, *La pensée et le mouvant* (Flammarion 2014) 192–194.

54   In the context of gender, compare with Butler (n 49) 42.

55   On this notion, see Michael Foucault, 'Question of method' in Graham Burchell, Colin Gordon and Peter Miller (eds), *The Foucault Effect: Studies in Governmentality* (University of Chicago Press 1991) 73, 76.

climate catastrophe and to the disastrous consequences of the measures necessary to prevent or mitigate it thus lies in the possibility of a permanent
re-determination, re-appropriation, and re-eventalization of the looming
climate catastrophe outside current crisis narratives.[56] Only a permanent re-
determination, re-appropriation, and re-eventalization of the looming climate
catastrophe outside current crisis narratives can prevent international lawyers
from letting the looming climate catastrophe be reduced to *an* event – as it currently is under international law's crisis narrative – that can be either denied
or banalized. It is also the only thing that can prevent international law from
being reduced to a single set of formalistic responses that can be anticipated
and easily rebutted by climate change deniers, the post-truth delinquents, the
institutional vandals, the self-declared and self-taught twitter experts, and all
the cynical climate change profiteers.[57]

The time has come to conclude this short essay. It has been stressed a few
times in this chapter that the question of the wordlessness of international
law in front of the looming climate catastrophe cannot be demoted to a purely
literary exercise as it raises central questions about international law's ability
to perform a world-making role. It should be added that this whole debate is
not only about the world-making role of international law but simultaneously
touches on international law's destiny. Should international law fail to raise to
the level of response demanded by the looming climate catastrophe and instead
limit itself to absorbing the latter in its normally abnormal normality, the (his)
story[58] of international law may well end with a tragedy. Indeed, if tragedy is
understood as a story of an average person, institution, discourse incapable of
rising to the level of what the moment asks for, the (his)story of international
law and climate change may well be tragic. After finding itself wordless in front
of a ravaging of the earth, international law would simply turn, in the post-
climate-catastrophe world, into an obsolete irrelevant discourse recorded in an
Encyclopaedia of defunct discourses, next to Middle Age palliative medicine
and flat earth physics. And this is not where the tragedy would end. It may also
be that, in the post-climate-catastrophe world, international law comes to be

---

56   Henri Bergson, *La pensée et le mouvant* (Flammarion 2014) 241.

57   For a discussion of some of the limitations of the current formal constraints on international lawyers' capacity for action with respect to climate change, see Maiko Meguro,
'Litigating climate change through international law: Obligations strategy and rights strategy' (2020) 33 LJIL 933.

58   On the limits of the distinction between story and history, see Hayden White, *Tropics of
Discourse: Essays in Cultural Criticism* (John Hopkins University Press 1978) 121. See also
Paul Ricoeur, *Temps et récit, Volume 1, L'intrigue et le récit historique* (Seuil 1983) 17 and Paul
Ricoeur, *Temps et récit, Volume 2, La configuration dans le récit de fiction* (Seuil 1984) 292.

portrayed as the discourse that facilitated the ravaging of the world under the complacent sight of the climate change deniers, the post-truth delinquents, the institutional vandals, the self-declared and self-taught twitter experts, and all the cynical climate change profiteers.[59] As international law continues to live off crises, live its crises, and be in crisis, international lawyers should seriously rethink their vocabularies and narratives, not only to do something for the world with their words, but also to salvage the legacy of international law.

---

59 Compare with Pierre Schlag, *Laying Down the Law* (New York University Press 1996) 166: 'Maybe what comes next is that we stop treating "law" as something to celebrate, expand, and worship. Maybe we learn to lay down the law'.

CHAPTER 8

COVID-19 as a Catalyst for the (Re-) Constitutionalisation of International Law
One Health – One Welfare

Anne Peters

There is a single species that is responsible for the COVID-19 pandemic – us.[1]

∴

How many and who must die before international law responds? COVID-19 starkly illustrates how a virus affects all, but in an extremely uneven way. The disease hits with disproportionate negative effects the poorer countries, and in each and every country, the poorer populations.[2] COVID-19 is thus exacerbating the cleavage between rich and poor, the wealth disparities inside States and across States.[3] The indigent have got worse, the better off have thrived[4] (sec. 1).

COVID-19 is also a reminder that diseases have always been a companion, both driver and outcome of international relations, now globalisation. In fact, the foundations of international law have been laid by infecting *the others*. Diseases, notably zoonoses, have also stimulated institution-building on the international plane (sec. 2).

---

1 Josef Settele and others, 'COVID-19 Stimulus Measures Must Save Lives, Protect Livelihoods, and Safeguard Nature to Reduce the Risk of Future Pandemics' (*The Intergovernmental Science-Policy Platform on Biodiversity and Ecosystem Services*, 27 April 2020) <https://ipbes.net/covid19stimulus> accessed 18 March 2021.

2 WHO, WHA, 'COVID-19 response', Second plenary meeting, A73/VR/2 (Doc. 73.1. of 19 May 2020), Preamble, 'Recognizing that the COVID-19 pandemic has a disproportionately heavy impact on the poor and the most vulnerable, …'.

3 CESCR, 'Statement on the coronavirus disease (COVID-19) pandemic and economic, social and cultural rights' (UN Doc. E/C.12/2020/1 of 17 April 2020) paras 6–7.

4 World Bank Group, *Poverty and Shared Prosperity 2020: Reversal of Fortune* (World Bank 2020); PricewaterhouseCoopers and UBS (Switzerland), *Riding the Storm: Market Turbulence Accelerates Diverging Fortunes* (Billionaires Insights, PwC and UBS 2020).

Acknowledging that international law has contributed to harming people, animals, and the planet, this essay presupposes that it can be a force for good. Based on this premise, I argue in favour of an activation of international law's positive potentials. The crisis should be used as an opportunity for the modification and operationalisation of the so-far underdeveloped One Health approach, informed by the international constitutional principle of solidarity (sec. 3).

1 Jurisfiction: Three Lives and Deaths under COVID-19

This is how three females experienced the first wave of COVID-19 in the spring of 2020.

For an academic in a rich and well-managed State, call her Marie, the border closure between Germany and Switzerland on Monday morning, 16 March 2020 at 8.00 was an extraordinary event. Marie had just spent one week of holidays in the Swiss mountains with the family. When she returned the key of the rented chalet in the *agence immobilières*, telephones were constantly ringing there. Tourists were inquiring about the situation, because on that day, Saturday, all skiing facilities in Switzerland had closed, and the winter season was terminated prematurely.

Home in the city of B on Sunday, Marie received a WhatsApp message from her neighbour in her house in the German city of H, telling her that the border would be closed next morning. Because Marie did not have her German identity card with her, she decided immediately to go back to H. This was a tough decision because she had an appointment with the veterinarian for her moribund cat on Monday early morning, and Marie had planned to return to her office in H only after that. Nevertheless, she packed her small bag and boarded the train on Sunday afternoon. Crossing the border was a bit spooky. Around midnight, her husband called her on the phone and told her that the cat had died (at the age of almost 18). For Marie, COVID will always be connected with her failure to accompany that death.

The next weeks of strict lockdown were paradisiacal. Everything was totally calm, all trips and meetings cancelled. Following something like a recommendation of the German minister of health, Marie stayed in self-confinement for 14 days. Zoom was not yet known in her quarters then. The weather was unusually cold and sunny. Instead of submitting her book manuscript in a rush she sat two weeks just polishing it, going out for a solitary walk in the evenings.

She wished she had known more about her great-grandfather who had died from the so-called Spanish flu in 1917 at the age of forty-something. He had left two young daughters, one of whom was Marie's grandmother, who both studied medicine (among the very first female students) in Berlin at the Humboldt university. Due to their father's premature death they had to finance their studies themselves by working in factories. Marie had never worked in factory nor financed her studies by herself. She had no reason to fear a flu anymore. Nevertheless, she decided to get a flu shot offered for free by her employer. At no point Marie felt that her life was in danger, not even her lifestyle.

Merait, a 55 year old textile worker in Bangladesh, experienced the pandemic differently. She lives in the slum-like suburbs of the city of D. When she arrived at the factory on 23 March, she was informed by the local manager that the plant would be temporarily shut down, and that all workers should just go home until they would be called back, and that they would be paid. She received her salary for the rest of the month and has been waiting since for the call, without getting any money.

Together with a group of colleagues, she turned to the local union which had already helped her sister, likewise a textile worker, seven years ago, after the big fire in the firm.[5] But this time, no compensation or reparation was in sight. The lay-offs were perfectly lawful, based on the economic emergency. Orders for clothes worth millions of Euro had been cancelled by the European and US-American client firms.[6]

Merait missed her mother. Mother had celebrated her 80th birthday on 25 March. But the week after she had developed a nasty cold, which forced her to stay in bed, and probably became a pneumonia. They did not even go to the hospital which was overrun with COVID patients. Maybe Merait's mom also had COVID but actually they never knew. She had breathing problems and one morning did not wake up anymore.

Luckily, the children were already grown-up. Merait's son normally sold plastic toys at the cross-roads in the nearby metropole. When the national lockdown was proclaimed he walked the 100 kilometres back to the town of D on foot to join the family. It took him three days to reach home. Since then, he

5 Cf. the *Sustainability Compact for Continuous Improvements in Labour Rights and Factory Safety in the Ready-Made Garment and Knitwear Industry in Bangladesh* (a joint declaration of the government of Bangladesh, the EU and ILO of 8 July 2013) and the *Ready-Made Garment Sustainability Council,* established on 14 January 2020.

6 Some of the firms later committed to pay in full for orders completed and in production. See 'COVID-19 Tracker: Which Brands Are Acting Responsibly towards Suppliers and Workers?' (*Workers Rights Consortium,* 17 December 2020) <https://www.workersrights.org/issues/covid-19/tracker/> accessed 18 March 2021.

has been spending his days queuing up in front of the local job centre, so far without success.

Merait's daughter was married off last year. But in the lockdown, her husband's temper soured. When his wife complained about money he replied that the dinner was not good and even threw a plate at her.

Posters had been hung up in the neighbourhood, showing pictures about handwashing, masks and social distancing. The community service distributed soap and masks. However, the soap bar lasted only two weeks. The water stations in the neighbourhood were always crowded. Merait's husband decided to discontinue the TV in order to save money. Merait had no smartphone of her own and was therefore cut off from the news. She could not sleep and wondered how long the lockdown would go on.

The third story is about Minkie, a small animal with beautiful, black, soft, and glossy fur. Minkie did not feel the lockdown. She was confined all her life (which lasted five months) in a cramped cage anyway. She is or rather was one of 4.5 million minks kept in 128 mink farms in the Netherlands. Minkie got COVID but she did not develop symptoms. She may have felt a bit weak, but because she did not have any space to move nobody noticed. It is unclear who was sick first: the worker who handled the machines that spit out the food, the worker who cleaned the waste, or Minkie. In any case, one worker infected a mink, the mink infected others, and the disease spread over the factory which held 35,000 minks. COVID circulated not only across one but across 27 farms. What is clear is that a mink–human transmission took place in whatever direction.[7]

The local veterinary agencies decided quickly: Minkie was gassed, together with 1.1 million companions. It was not done the usual way, by electrocution through the anus, but by carbon monoxide. This activity is not called murder, although it is a premeditated taking of life for profit. It is not even called killing but just 'culling'. The episode sped up the phasing-out of the mink farms in the Netherlands.[8] Parliament adopted a law prohibiting the ugly business, coupled

---

7   WHO, 'COVID-19 Virtual Press Conference' (22 June 2020) <https://www.who.int/docs/default-source/coronaviruse/transcripts/virtual-press-conference---22-june---covid-19.pdf?sfvrsn=6da8bbf7_2> accessed 27 August 2021. See also Statement of the Dutch government of 19 May 2020 <https://www.government.nl/latest/news/2020/05/19/new-results-from-research-into-covid-19-on-mink-farms> accessed 18 March 2021.

8   The closure of the Dutch mink farms will most likely boost the farms in Denmark, Poland, and China (the three biggest mink fur producing countries), until a global prohibition is imposed, or import bans on mink products are issued by countries with market-power, or consumers altogether stop buying mink fur products.

with financial compensation of the fur-farmers.[9] Of course, not 1.1 million deaths mattered, but the profit lost over 1.1 million corpses, and the infections of humans.

What Minkie never knew, of course, was that in Denmark, which produced 17 million mink pelts per year, a novel variant of COVID-19 broke out, infecting at least 214 humans and uncounted minks. This led to the immediate culling of *all* animals.[10] The news wrote about a 'death knell'[11] – but not of more than 17 million minks but of 'the industry.'

These three life-and-death-stories are fictitious, their bits and pieces were taken from the news. The only thing they have in common is the virus. It is not the first time in history that an animal-borne virus disrupts the lives of entire populations.

2   Diagnosis: Once Again a Disease Drives the Development of International Law

COVID-19 is a zoonosis, i.e. an infectious disease caused by a pathogen that has jumped from a non-human animal to a human animal and from there spreads to other humans.[12] Well known recent outbreaks of zoonoses in human society were HIV in the 1980s (transmitted from monkeys), the highly pathogenic avian influenza (HPAI, the so-called bird flu) that was transmitted to humans

---

9   Tweede Kamer der Staten-Generaal, *28 286, No. 1112, Dierenwelzijn Motie van de leden Geurts en Bromet over een fatsoenlijke stopregeling voor de nertsenhouderij*, proposed 10 June 2020, adopted 23 June 2020. See the judgment by Hoge Raad, Uitspraak, 16 December 2016, Eerste Kamer 16/00921, LZ/EE. See also Katharina Braun, 'COVID-19, people, and other animals', (*Völkerrechtsblog*, 12 November 2020) <https://voelkerrechtsblog.org/covid-19-people-and-other-animals/> accessed 17 April 2021.

10   Press conference on the statement of the Danish Prime Minister of 4 November 2020 <https://www.regeringen.dk/nyheder/2020/danmarks-minkbestand-aflives-grundet-mutation-af-coronavirus/> accessed 16 April 2021. See also WHO, 'SARS-CoV-2 mink-associated variant strain – Denmark' <https://www.who.int/emergencies/disease-outbreak-news/item/2020-DON301> accessed 27 August 2021.

11   Nikolaj Skydsgaar, 'Denmark tightens lockdown in north, mink cull devastates industry' *Reuters* (London, 5 November 2020) <https://www.reuters.com/article/health-coronavirus-denmark-mink/denmark-to-lock-down-regions-after-mutated-coronavirus-traced-to-minks-idUSKBN27L1I1> accessed 18 March 2021.

12   We do not yet know whether the novel virus originated from the wild animal market in Wuhan or from the bat laboratory next to the market. But what is obvious is that COVID-19 has come upon us as a result of human use and abuse of animals. See seminally on the governance aspects of zoonoses: William Karesh and others, 'Ecology of zoonoses: natural and unnatural histories' (2012) 380(9857) The Lancet 1936.

from ducks and geese in 1996, and SARS (probably from bats and civet cats) in 2003.[13]

But zoonoses go back in history, to the rise of agriculture thousands of years ago. At that time, the diseases of cows, pigs, geese, ducks, and many other species of animals that were domesticated in Europe befell humans and became what we now call measles, tuberculosis, smallpox, flu, and so on.[14]

Conquest and colonisation, constitutive for international law as we know it today, began with zoonoses. Following Columbus' arrival in the 'new World', about 90 to 95 percent of the indigenous populations in the Americas were killed by measles, smallpox, and influenza carried by the Europeans.[15] The European weapons, important as they were for the destruction of the American political units and for the establishment of colonial empire, 'paled' against 'the real killer that made European victory possible' – the European germs that were initially spread unwittingly but later employed deliberately for extermination purposes.[16] The overpowering and supplanting of local populations by European immigrants who were initially very few in numbers 'might not have happened without Europe's sinister gift to other continents – the germs evolving from Eurasia's long intimacy with domestic animals.'[17]

Besides this germ warfare, animals and a food-ideology were an integral part of the colonial and neo-colonial projects. The Europeans spread stories of the Indigenous' cannibalism which justified not only the forced education of the 'barbarous' but also the importation of cattle as a source of animal food.[18] Through this 'animal colonialism', the colonisers destroyed not only the local populations, but also the local fauna, flora, and the traditional livelihood.[19]

---

13   According to Wiebers and Feigin, three out of four emerging diseases are zoonoses: David Wiebers and Valery Feigin, 'What the COVID-19 crisis is telling humanity' (2020) 5(30) Animal Sentience 1 <https://www.wellbeingintlstudiesrepository.org/cgi/viewcontent.cgi?article=1626&context=animsent> accessed 18 March 2021.

14   Jared Diamond, *Guns, Germs, and Steel: The Fates of Human Societies* (W.W. Norton 1997) 195–214.

15   Noble David Cook, *Born to Die: Disease and New World Conquest, 1492–1650* (CUP 1998) 206; Diamond (n 14) 210–213. In contrast, the 'new world' had no lethal crowd diseases at all. Jared Diamond explains the absence of infectious diseases in Indian populations which would have been able to infect Spaniards with less contacts between livestock and humans in the Americas (in comparison to intense co-habitation of livestock and humans in Europe and Asia): ibid 213.

16   Cook (n 15) 205, 213.

17   Diamond (n 14) 214.

18   Anthony Pagden, 'The Forbidden Food: Francisco de Vitoria and José de Acosta on Cannibalism' (1981) 13 Terrae Incognitae 17.

19   Mathilde Cohen, 'Animal Colonialism: The Case of Milk' in Anne Peters (ed), *Studies in Global Animal Law* (Springer 2020) 35–44.

Zoonoses have continued to drive the development of international law. The presence of lethal tropical diseases in Africa, Asia, and Indonesia offers one explanation why the European conquest and colonial portioning of those areas was accomplished only 400 years later than the European apportionment of the Americas.[20]

The recurring Cholera pandemics in the 19th century gave rise to one of the first proto-international organisations, the *Conseil Supérieur de Santé*, established in Constantinople in 1838.[21] That Council was founded by a decree of the Ottoman Sultan, but the majority of the 18 to 20 members were delegates of the foreign powers with embassies in the city. In 1870, the Council had around 800 staff. The task of this hybrid, internationalised body was to coordinate several hospitals, oversee sanitary offices and secondary observatories.[22]

Another early international organisation is the Office International des Epizooties/World Organisation for Animal Health (OIE), founded in 1924 by 28 States.[23] Its narrow original objective was to promote international cooperation in controlling the spread of zoonoses notably in the context of transboundary live animal trade.[24] It has since then evolved significantly and has in 2002 extended its mandate from animal health to include animal welfare.[25]

---

20   Diamond (n 14) 214.

21   After the foundation in 1838, a 'Règlement organique du Conseil de santé à Constaninople pour les provenances de mer' was signed on 10 June 1839. This *règlement* was filed in the international Treaty Series: F. Murhard (ed) Martens Nouveau Receuil (Dieterich Goettingen 1842) vol. 16, 2nd part, 920–26. According to its additional Article, the *règlement* was the fundamental and organisational act of the Council ('fera foi comme acte organique et fondamental').

22   Jean-David Mizrahi, 'Politique sanitaire et impérialisme à l'heure de la révolution pastorienne: Le Conseil sanitaire de Constantinople 1838–1923', in Walid Arbid et al. (eds), *Méditerranée, Moyen-Orient: Deux siècles de relations internationales. Recherche en hommage à Jacques Thobie* (L'Harmattan 2003) 221–242 (esp. 222–223). See for the complicated mixed status: Benno Toll, *Der oberste Gesundheitsrat von Konstantinopel in seiner völkerrechtlichen Bedeutung* (Piloty 1922) who characterises the Council as an Ottoman agency which involved foreign delegates because otherwise the capitulations exempted foreigners from the Ottoman jurisdiction. Toll qualifies the connected 'quarantine association' as an international body without international legal personality (ibid 63–67).

23   International Agreement for the Creation of an Office International des Epizooties in Paris, with Appendix: the Organic Statutes of the Office International des Epizooties, of 25 January 1924 (57 LNTS 135).

24   Organic Statutes (n 23) Art 4.

25   International Committee of the OIE, 'Animal Welfare Mandate of the OIE', Resolution No. XIV of May 2002 (in OIE Doc. 70 GS/FR – PARIS, May 2002, 31 *et seq.*), based on: OIE, Third Strategic Plan 2001–2005 (Paris, OIE 2002), 23, point 6.

These historical fragments show how diseases, notably zoonoses, impacted on international transactions and how they boosted the building of international governance structures. This trajectory can easily go on. Theoretically, COVID-19 could trigger, for example, a global vaccine development and distribution programme which could in turn be a model for the creation of other so-called global public goods.[26] I submit that the momentum should be seized.

3   Remedy: One Health as an International Constitutional Principle

COVID-19 compels us to recognise the idea of One Health as a full-fledged principle of international law, to adapt it to the current needs, and to operationalise and implement it fully.

3.1   *One Health in Response to Zoonoses*

In its May 2020 meeting on the 'COVID-19 response', the World Health Assembly requested the WHO General Director to apply the 'One-Health Approach' and to continue to work closely with the OIE and the FAO in order 'to identify the zoonotic source of the virus' which would allow 'targeted interventions and a research agenda to reduce the risk of similar events occurring.'[27]

The One Health approach is defined in a recent UNEP publication as 'the collaborative effort across multiple disciplines to attain optimal health for people, animals and the environment. This approach has emerged as a key tool for preventing and managing diseases occurring at the interface of human, animal and environment health.'[28] The One Health paradigm came up in the aftermath of the 2003 outbreak of SARS, a zoonotic disease transmitted probably from bats, too. The veterinarian and activist Dr William B. Karesh seminally wrote that '[g]lobal health will not be achieved without a shift from the expert-controlled, top-down paradigm that still dominates both science and

---

26   The German Chancellor Merkel spoke of the vaccine as a 'globales öffentliches Gut': Press Conference of 24 April 2020 <https://www.bundeskanzlerin.de/bkin-de/ aktuelles/pressestatement-von-bundeskanzlerin-merkel-im-rahmen-der-who-spenden -videokonferenz-1746960> accessed 22 April 2021.

27   WHO, WHA, 'COVID-19 response' (n 2) para 9(6).

28   United Nations Environment Programme (UNEP) and International Livestock Research Institute (lead author Delia Grace Randolph), *Preventing the Next Pandemic: Zoonotic diseases and how to break the chain of transmission* (Kenya 2020) 37.

medicine. A broader, more democratic approach is needed, one based on the understanding that there is only one world – and only one health.'[29]

Today, One Health is no longer just a buzzword but informs legal decision-making. For example, the Islamabad High Court mandated the release of zoo elephants with the argument that 'the current pandemic crisis (...) has highlighted the interdependence of living beings on each other, (...) and (...) it has conspicuously brought the essence, meaning and significance of 'life' into the spotlight.'[30] This can be read as an implicit application of the One Health principle. Another example is the Convention on Biodiversity (CBD) COP decision of 2018 'Health and Biodiversity'[31] which was imbued by the One Health approach albeit without mentioning the word.

A One Health approach is inevitable facing the ongoing human-induced explosion of zoonoses. According to the Intergovernmental Platform on Biodiversity and Ecosystem Services (IPBES), '[a]n estimated 1.7 million currently undiscovered viruses are thought to exist in mammal and avian hosts. Of these, 540,000 – 850,000 could have the ability to infect humans.'[32] As the Lancet pointed out: 'New zoonotic diseases are emerging and re-emerging at an exponentially increasing rate. (...) Not all zoonotic diseases become pandemics, but most pandemics are caused by zoonoses and they have become characteristic of the Anthropocene era.'[33] The reasons for the growing risk of zoonotic pandemics are the exponentially increasing anthropogenic changes of the earth system. These include land use and extraction, the clearing of land for farming and grazing, the intensive, industrialised livestock farming, and increased human encroachment into wildlife habitats.[34] Also deforestation frees microbes many of which have not yet been encountered by people. A key factor for the great acceleration of the spread of zoonoses is the exponential intensification of international travel and trade, key components of globalisation. UNEP sums this up as follows: 'The frequency of pathogenic microorganisms jumping from other animals to people is increasing due to unsustainable

29   William B. Karesh and Robert A. Cook, 'The Human-Animal Link' (2005) 84 Foreign Affairs 38.

30   Islamabad High Court, Islamabad (Judicial department) W.P. No. 1155/2019 Islamabad Wildlife Management Board through its Chairman v. Metropolitan Corporation Islamabad through its Mayor & 4 others, judgment of 21 May 2020.

31   CBD/COP/DEC/14/4 (2018).

32   IPBES, *Workshop on Biodiversity and Pandemics, Workshop Report* of 29 October 2020 (unredacted and not peer reviewed version) 5.

33   Editorial, 'Zoonoses: beyond the human-animal-environment interface' (2020) 396(10243) The Lancet 1.

34   IPBES (n 32) 6.

human activities. Pandemics such as the COVID-19 outbreak are a predictable and predicted outcome of how people source and grow food, trade and consume animals, and alter environments.'[35]

3.2   *Expansion of the One Health Approach in Three Dimensions*

Understanding the reasons for the proliferation of zoonoses is the key to combating them. The UN Framework for the Immediate Socio-economic Response to COVID-19, published in April 2020, *inter alia* asks for 'efforts to arrest ecosystem encroachments and harmful practices, restore degraded ecosystems, close down illegal trade and illegal wet markets', and here refers to the three relevant conventions: The Convention on International Trade in Endangered Species of Wild Flora and Fauna, (CITES), the Convention on Migratory Species (CMS), and the Convention on Biological Diversity (CBD).[36] The UN Framework thus implies a One Health-based approach.

A robust response moreover demands the intensification and modification of the One Health approach in the following three dimensions. First, One Health must take livestock more decisively into its purview, beyond the already acknowledged issue of antimicrobial resistance. Inspiration can be found in a 'solutions scan', published by a Cambridge-led international team of wildlife and veterinary experts in June. It gives a list of options for reducing the risk of another pandemic.[37] The team mentions, inter alia, the following: 'Reduce animal density both within and between farms;' '[t]ake measures to reduce stress in farmed animals including maximum permissible stocking densities and other basic welfare standards;'[38] '[i]ntroduce licencing or certification system for the transport of live animals or animal parts, to ensure hygiene and welfare standards are adhered to.'[39] The group finally mentions the options to '[p]romote the development and commercialisation of synthetic alternatives (e.g. synthetic fur, leather or lab-created meat)' and to '[i]nfluence consumer attitudes to increase acceptability of lower-risk substitute products (e.g. plants or synthetic substitutes for food, clothing or medicine instead of

---

35   UNEP 2020 (n 28) 7.

36   *UN Framework for the Immediate Socio-economic Response to COVID-19* (United Nations: April 2020) 28, see also 35.

37   Silviu O Petrovan and others, 'Post COVID-19: a solution scan of options for preventing future zoonotic epidemics' (OSF 2020). The 'solutions scan' was initiated as a collaboration between BioRISC (the Biosecurity Research Initiative at St Catharine's College, Cambridge), Conservation Evidence based in the Department of Zoology, University of Cambridge, and numerous other researchers worldwide.

38   ibid 33.

39   Petrovan and others (n 37) 38.

animal products, particularly those from high-risk species).'[40] According to the IPBES, '[p]andemic risk could be significantly lowered by promoting responsible consumption and reducing unsustainable consumption of commodities from emerging disease hotspots, and of wildlife and wildlife-derived products, as well as by reducing excessive consumption of meat from livestock production.'[41] A well-known geophysicist points out: 'To prevent future pandemics (...) we must rethink our relationship with animals, and livestock in particular. The main upshot of this rethinking is the need to eat less animal-based food, including markedly reducing our consumption of beef'.[42]

Second, additional international institutions and international legal regimes must be drawn in. The One Health-oriented collaboration of the above-mentioned three international organisations (FAO, OIE, and WHO) began in 2010 with a tripartite concept note that lays the basis for their 'coordinating global activities to address health risks at the animal-human-ecosystems interfaces.'[43] Besides these three organisations, further institutions and regimes should be directly involved, notably the WTO (notably via the Codex Alimentarius Commission and the SPS-Agreement), the Convention on Biodiversity (CBD),[44] and the Convention on International Trade in Endangered Species of Wild Fauna and Flora (CITES).

In addition, CITES would need to be expanded in scope to domestic trade with international repercussions. The necessity is illustrated by COVID-19. The pangolins that were probably an intermediate host for the COVID-19 between the bats and humans are listed in Appendix I of CITES, which basically prohibits all international trade in the species.[45] However, CITES as it stands does

---

40   Petrovan and others (n 37) 42.

41   IPBES (n 32) 6.

42   Gidon Eshel, 'Pandemic leadership failures and public health, Commentary on Wiebers & Feigin on Covid Crisis' (2020) 5(30) Animal Sentience 365.

43   FAO, OIE, WHO, 'The FAO-OIE-WHO collaboration, Sharing responsibilities and coordinating global activities to address health risks at the animal-human-ecosystem interfaces' (April 2010) 3 <https://www.who.int/influenza/resources/documents/tripartite_concept_note_hanoi_042011_en.pdf?ua=1> accessed 27 April 2021: 'This tripartite relationship envisages complementary work to develop normative standards and field programs to achieve One Health goals'.

44   Convention on Biological Diversity (adopted 5 June 1992, entered into force 29 December 1993) 1760 UNTS 79.

45   CoP18 Doc. 75 (2019) – CITES, Species specific matters, Pangolins (Manis Spp.): 'At the 17th meeting of the Conference of the Parties (CoP17, Johannesburg, 2016), all eight species of pangolin were transferred from CITES Appendix II to Appendix I.'

not apply to the inner-Chinese trade with endangered species.[46] A dynamic interpretation of the treaty in the direction of covering all trade in endangered species that deploys substantive transboundary effects would theoretically be possible but likely to be perceived as illegitimate by State parties.[47] Therefore, the elaboration of an additional protocol in that sense would be advisable.

Third, the COVID crisis suggests that the One Health Approach which has so far addressed the human-animal-environmental-interface needs to be conceptually developed so as to encompass a North-South dimension. One Health should be understood as demanding a North-South solidarity in prevention and treatment of infectious diseases. One Health should thus comprise both a trans-species perspective and a trans-society perspective. This also implies that the One Health approach which currently unites medical, veterinary, and environmental expertise needs to be complemented by social science, economic, ethical, and legal expertise for addressing better the social, economic, and governance causes of the emergence and spread of zoonoses.

The legal argument providing the basis for this 'social' extension of the One Health approach is the principle of solidarity. In parallel to a whole range of nationalist reflexes and actions, pandemic-related legal pronouncements have invoked global solidarity. Both COVID-related UN-General Assembly Resolutions appeal to solidarity,[48] and the WHO Assembly does it, too.[49]

This new talk (some might say 'cheap talk') on global solidarity can build on a pre-existing textual basis which has however not given firm contours to the concept.[50] Despite this vagueness, solidarity has been identified as an

---

46   Convention on *International* Trade in Endangered Species of Wild Fauna and Flora
      (CITES) (adopted 3 March 1973, entered into force 1 July 1975) 993 UNTS 243 (emphasis
      added).

47   CITES Art. I lit. c) defines 'trade' as 'export, re-export, import and introduction from the
      sea'. Cf. also Willem Wijnstekers, *The Evolution of CITES* (11th edn, CIC – International
      Council for Game and Wildlife Conservation 2018) 60.

48   'Recognizing also that the COVID-19 global pandemic requires a global response based
      on unity, *solidarity* and multilateral cooperation, [...]' (UN GA res. 74/270 and res. 74/274;
      emphasis added).

49   WHA (n 2), 'Calls for, in the spirit of unity and solidarity, the intensification of cooperation
      and collaboration at all levels in order to contain and control the COVID-19 pandemic and
      mitigate its impact'.

50   'Solidarity' is mentioned in numerous hard and soft texts of international law. See for the
      latest document in the relevant process of the Human Rights Council: Draft declaration
      on the right to international solidarity and Report of the Independent Expert on human
      rights and international solidarity (UN Doc. A/HRC/35/35 of 25 April 2017).

'emerging structural principle of international law'.[51] Moreover, given the fundamental importance and the principle's firm constitutional entrenchment in many State constitutions of the world,[52] solidarity has not without merit been qualified as a 'constitutional' principle of the international legal order.[53]

The existence of a political, moral, and to a limited extent legally relevant discourse both on solidarity and on One Health suggests a mutually harmonious interpretation of both principles.[54] One Health can be interpreted in the light of solidarity, and solidarity in the light of One Health. One Health thus becomes a trans-social concept, and solidarity becomes a trans-species solidarity. But of course, both One Health and solidarity can be no more than a rough guideline pointing in the direction of a commitment to work collectively towards a shared goal (combatting the virus, stopping encroachment of wildlife habitat and high-density farming), and towards sharing benefits (e.g. the vaccine) fairly.[55] Along that line, One Health flows into a trans-species and trans-social 'One Health – One Welfare'-perspective, as espoused notably by the African Union.[56]

---

51 Rüdiger Wolfrum, 'Solidarity amongst states: an emerging structural principle of international law', in Pierre-Marie Dupuy and others (eds), *Common Values in International Law: Essays in Honour of Christian Tomuschat* (Engel 2006) 1087–1101.

52 See for the EU i.a. the European Charter of Fundamental Rights, Title IV 'Solidarity' (Articles 27–38). See for German constitutional law: Uwe Volkmann, *Solidarität: Programm und Prinzip der Verfassung* (Mohr Siebeck 1998).

53 Karel Wellens, 'Revisiting Solidarity as a (Re-)Emerging Constitutional Principle: Some Further Reflections' in Rüdiger Wolfrum and Chie Kojima (eds) *Solidarity: A Structural Principle of International Law* (Springer 2010) 3–54. See for the full argument Anne Peters, 'Global Constitutionalism: The Social Dimension', in Takao Suami and others (eds), *Global Constitutionalism from European and East Asian Perspectives* (CUP 2018) 277–350.

54 Such systemic integration of fundamental principles strengthens the coherence of the international legal order and can therefore be seen as aspects of its *procedural* constitutionalisation (Anne Peters, 'The Refinement of International Law: From Fragmentation to Regime Interaction and Politicization' (2017) 15 ICON 671).

55 Cf. Andrew Mason, 'Solidarity', *Routledge Encyclopedia of Philosophy* (Version 1.0, Taylor and Francis 1998) <https://www.rep.routledge.com/articles/thematic/solidarity/v-1> accessed 27 April 2021.

56 African Union – InterAfrican Bureau for Animal Resources, 'Animal Welfare Strategy for Africa' (2017) 11: 'principles of one health and one welfare'. See in scholarship R. García Pinillos, *One Welfare: A Framework to Improve Animal Welfare and Human Well-being* (CABI 2018). In scholarship, the idea has been further extended to a 'one rights'-approach. See Saskia Stucki and Tom Sparks, 'The Elephant in the (Court)Room: Interdependence of Human and Animal Rights in the Anthropocene' (*EJIL:Talk!*, 9 June 2020) <https://www.ejiltalk.org/the-elephant-in-the-courtroom-interdependence-of-human-and-animal-rights-in-the-anthropocene/> accessed 17 April 2021.

4   Conclusion

Simply invoking One Health can of course not stop the human encroachment on wildlife habitat. Quite to the contrary, the global public's focus of attention on COVID-19 has allowed environmental crimes to go unchecked. For example, the deforestation of the Brazilian rainforest has peaked again in the spring of 2020.[57] But, as always, offering a legal vocabulary to address injustice can form one (small) building block for a path towards change.

The COVID-19 crisis erupted in a political climate dominated by nationalism, populism, and international law-scepticism. It has accelerated these pre-existing factual and accompanying legal trends. COVID-19 so far neither produced one single mega-trend nor has it been a legal game changer. This can be viewed as a good thing or as a bad one, depending on whether one places hopes in the law, specifically international law, or not. Facing the virus, '[l]aw can serve as both an enabler and a barrier to global health, equity, and justice.'[58]

Marie, Merait, and Minkie have so far benefitted from international law in different ways. A BIT facilitated the establishment of the factory which employed Merait but did not oblige the firm to improve its social security scheme.[59] Had the WHO's explicit recommendation 'against the application of travel or trade restrictions'[60] been followed by Germany, Marie could have

---

57   Human Rights Watch, ' "The air is unbearable": Health Impact of Deforestation-Related Fires in the Brazilian Amazon' (26 August 2020) <https://www.hrw.org/report/2020/08/26/air-unbearable/health-impacts-deforestation-related-fires-brazilian-amazon> accessed 17 April 2021.

58   Alexandra L Phelan and others, 'Legal agreements: barriers and enablers to global equitable COVID-19 vaccine access' (2020) 396(10254) The Lancet 800, 800.

59   Peter Egger and Michael Pfaffermayer, 'The Impact of Bilateral Investment Treaties on Foreign Direct Investment' (2004) 32 Journal of Comparative Economics 788. Empirically speaking, the impact is controversial.

60   See, e.g., WHO, 'Statement on the second meeting of the IHR emergency committee regarding the outbreak of the 2019-nCoV' (30 January 2020) <https://www.who.int/news/item/30-01-2020-statement-on-the-second-meeting-of-the-international-health-regulations-(2005)-emergency-committee-regarding-the-outbreak-of-novel-coronavirus-(2019-ncov)> accessed 18 March 2021: 'The Committee does not recommend any travel or trade restriction based on the current information available'; WHO, 'Updated WHO recommendations for international traffic in relation to COVID-19 outbreak' (29 February 2020) <https://www.who.int/news-room/articles-detail/updated-who-recommendations-for-international-traffic-in-relation-to-covid-19-outbreak> accessed 18 March 2021: 'WHO continues to advise against the application of travel or trade restrictions to countries experiencing COVID-19 outbreaks'. The legal basis of these statements are the International Health Regulations which require that the WHO Director General's temporary recommendations 'avoid unnecessary interference with international traffic'

stayed with the dying cat. A stronger and more legally imbued sense of solidarity would lead Germany to put more money into the vaccination platform COVAX, and improve access to a vaccine for Merait and her family.[61] Minkie's kinfolk would need an outright international prohibition of fur farming, or at least a radical cap on stocking densities. The insight that human health, a public interest objective, will benefit from such measures, too, would help legalising closures of factories that interfere with property rights. It is the responsibility of Marie and her colleagues to make these arguments.

---

and that they 'are not more restrictive of international traffic and trade (...) than reasonably available alternatives that would achieve the appropriate level of health protection': International Health Regulations (adopted 23 May 2005, entered into force 15 June 2007) 2509 UNTS 79, Art 15(1) and Art 17(1) lit. d).

61   See 'COVAX: The Vaccines Pillar of the Access to COVID-19 Tools (ACT) Accelerator – Structure and Principles' (9 November 2020) and other documents: <https://www.gavi.org/covax-facility#documents> accessed 18 March 2021.

CHAPTER 9

The COVID-19 Pandemic Crisis and International Law

A Constitutional Moment, A Tipping Point or More of the Same?

Yuval Shany

I used to think of history as a sort of long scroll with thick black lines ruled across it at intervals. Each of these lines marked the end of what was called a 'period', and you were given to understand that what came afterwards was completely different from what had gone before ... And though, of course, those black lines across the page of history are an illusion, there are times when the transition is quite rapid ...[1]

∴

1 Introduction

Bruce Ackerman's famous 'constitutional moments' theory[2] posits that moments of crisis can facilitate significant changes in constitutional law and practice. Arguably such exceptional moments are impregnated with a sense of moral urgency, a feeling of grandeur and uncertainty about the long-term political fallout (a relative 'veil of ignorance'), that can facilitate constitutional reform. When applied to the history of international law, Ackerman's theory can perhaps link major historical events, such as the 30 Year Wars, the end of the Napoleonic Wars, the two World Wars, the end of the Cold War and 9/11, to major structural changes or power shifts (or 'epochs')[3] in international law. Alongside the narrative of abrupt change, one often finds in the literature on the history of international law a progressive narrative of incremental change brought about by gradual external developments in technology, economics,

---

1 George Orwell, 'The Rediscovery of Europe' *The Listener* (London, 19 March 1942).
2 Bruce Ackerman, *We the People: Foundations* (Harvard University Press 1991) 22.
3 See generally Wilhelm Grewe, *The Epochs of International Law* (De Gruyter 2000).

© YUVAL SHANY, 2022 | DOI:10.1163/9789004472365_011

social consciousness, politics etc., which are matched by organic growth of legal norms and institutions, reacting to and reflecting these changes.[4] The emergence of international organizations in the 19th century, the resurgence of human rights law in the 1970s and the expansion of international investment law in the late 20th, early 21st centuries may exemplify instances of such incremental change.[5]

Significantly, these two narratives of historical development of international law are not mutually exclusive. First, certain developments can be understood as clean breaks from the past, whereas others are the product of a long-term process. Second, identifying historical trajectories depends on the focal length of the historical lenses used: what is viewed as a major shift in direction at the time in which events take place, might be regarded decades or centuries later as a minor course correction, a short period of instability, or a mere point on a pattern showing the overall trajectory. And third, the two narratives may merge to generate processes of change, accelerating in particular moments in time due to 'tipping points' generated by certain dramatic events.[6] Indeed, it would appear that certain important developments in international law can be described as part of long-running trends punctured by sudden fluctuations correlating to dramatic events. For example, the evolution of norms of international humanitarian law, governing non-international armed conflicts, can be narrated as stemming from a gradual process of restraining violence in and around the battlefield that started picking up momentum in the mid-19th century, with certain regulatory peaks occurring after and in connection with major international crises such as World War Two, Vietnam and the Global War on Terror (e.g., Common article 3 in 1949, the 1977 Additional Protocols, and the development of laws governing transnational or asymmetric armed conflicts in the 2000s).

---

4 See e.g., Ignacio de la Rasilla, 'The Turn to the History of International Adjudication' in Ignacio de la Rasilla and Jorge Viñuales (eds), *Experiments in International Adjudication: Historical Accounts* (CUP 2019) 32, 45; Nico Krisch, 'International Law in Times of Hegemony: Unequal Power and the Shaping of the International Legal Order' (2005) 16(3) EJIL 369, 377. See also generally Thomas Skouteris, 'The Idea of Progress' in Anne Orford, Florian Hoffmann, and Martin Clark (eds), *The Oxford Handbook of the Theory of International Law* (OUP 2016) 939.

5 See generally J.H.H. Weiler, 'The Geology of International Law – Governance, Democracy, Legitimacy' (2004) 64 Zeitschrift für ausländisches öffentliches Recht und Völkerrecht 547, 553–561.

6 See eg, Martha Finnemore and Kathryn Sikkink, 'International Norm Dynamics and Political Change' (1998) 52(4) Int'l Org 887, 901.

2   The COVID-19 Pandemic as the Harbinger of a
       Constitutional Moment

The question before us is whether COVID-19 has the potential for generating
a constitutional moment or a tipping point for the development of international law separating between epochs or significantly accelerating already-
occurring trends. Discounting serendipitous changes in the course of history
(the 'unknown unknowns' of historical change), such a question invites an
assessment of whether a structural change in international law can be anticipated in the near future, and whether the current crisis might facilitate such a
change or accelerate existing trends going in this or the other direction. If the
answers to these questions are in the negative, then the reaction to the COVID
crisis is likely to showcase 'more of the same' for international law.

   One possible vision of a percolating crisis that might lead to a new epoch in
international law is found in the writing of my Hebrew University colleague,
the historian Yuval Noah Harari. Among the major challenges confronting
humanity in the 21st century, which he has identified, are nuclear war, ecological collapse, and technological disruption (e.g., dangerous applications of AI
and biotechnology).[7] What's common to these challenges is their potential for
catastrophic consequences, and the need for close global cooperation in order
to effectively address them. In addition, they all fit into a Frankensteinian crisis narrative: Scientific, technological, and economic progress getting out of
control and creating a threat to the survival of human civilization (at least in
its current form). Noah Harari advocates in response to the looming threats a
change of paradigm of international relations, a new epoch perhaps, which is
based not only on tight global cooperation,[8] but also on giving a prominent
role for scientific knowledge in policy debates.[9] Arguably, such a new international relations paradigm would also require a corresponding new international law paradigm.

   Would the crisis surrounding the COVID-19 pandemic facilitate such a paradigm shift? Unlike the Frankensteinian threats identified by Noah Harari,
COVID is not, as far as we know, a man-made catastrophe. Rather, it is more
akin to a biblical plague (and more recent episodes of contagious diseases, such
as the Black Plague, the Spanish Flu and SARS). Furthermore, its introduction
was not significantly impacted by a race among nations to obtain superior economic, technological, or scientific capacity; in the same vein, suppression of

---

7   Yuval Noah Harari, *21 Lessons for the 21st Century* (Spiegel & Grau, Jonathan Cape 2018) 125.
8   ibid 116.
9   Noah Harari (n 7) 251.

the pandemic will not necessarily impact the international balance of power or the global spread of wealth. Compared to the efforts required to generate global cooperation with respect to matters such as the proliferation of nuclear weapons, climate change, or misuse of digital technology, it may prove politically easier to introduce reforms aimed at dealing collectively with a crisis like COVID that – (1) potentially affects the population of all States; and (2) does not require certain States to surrender a scientific or technological advantage that they have obtained over the years, or to internalize a significant share of the costs of the technological solution.

At the same time, the COVID-19 crisis dictates a dynamic and logic of isolation: quarantine for those who have tested positive, blockade over the geographical areas in the country where infection rates are particularly high and a travel ban isolating the country from travellers from other countries. From that point of view, the response to the pandemic has been, by and large, the opposite of a joint globalized effort; rather, it has featured the reemergence of strong national regulators, reintroduced border controls, mobilization of national resources to address the crisis, an international race for ventilators and vaccines etc. The perceived impotency of global and regional regulating bodies, such as the WHO, UN Security Council and the EU, in responding to the crisis, further underscores the vital importance of the State as a first and principal responder to serious crises of an overwhelming nature. (Note that unlike historical episodes in earlier centuries where pandemics were viewed as natural disasters and the response largely exceeded human capacity, in the 21st century, States are expected to find scientific, technological, and regulatory solutions to such public health problems). If the perception among the general public is that globalization is a pre-existing condition that promoted the spread of the virus and proved to be a very small part of the solution to the crisis, then it is very doubtful whether COVID-19 in and of itself is likely to mark a constitutional moment or a tipping point facilitating a shift to a more globalized world.

3   International Law and Reliance on Scientific Knowledge

The COVID-19 crisis may however have a significant impact on development of international law, through operating in more subtle ways than merely demonstrating the importance of international cooperation. This requires probably some zooming out from the current state of affairs and a return to a previous major paradigm shift – following the end of the Cold War. The new international legal order heralded at that point in time, featured the main aspects recommended by Noah Harari for the 21st century – a rise in global cooperation in fields such as international trade and international peace and security, including the development of a common response to global challenges in fields such as the regulation of Chemical Weapons and Climate Change, and increased reliance on scientific knowledge to address such issues. The prominent role of technical experts in these regimes has been, in fact, a source of criticism directed at the democratic deficits of the new modalities of international governance developed in the 1990s, at both the regional and global level.[10]

It far exceeds the scope of this short note to seriously grapple with the reasons underlying the gradual erosion of the international norms and structures created in the 1990s. Clearly, there are geopolitical reasons, such as the reemergence of China, and relative decline of the US and the EU that can explain some of the trends (at least from a Westernized perspective).[11] There are also reasons related to the growing focus of domestic politics in several key countries on the negative implications of globalization for broad constituencies (e.g. immigration, shifts in production, increased regulation and cross-border terrorism), resulting in the rise in the political fortunes of extremist and/or anti-globalization movements.[12] It has also been observed that the passage of years has also rendered the deep causes for the post-World War Two shift from nationalism to international cooperation – armed conflicts, governmental oppression and economic recession – a distant memory for new generations of voters.[13]

---

10   See e.g., Steven Wheatley, *The Democratic Legitimacy of International Law* (Hart 2010) 72–79; Peter Lindseth, 'Democratic Legitimacy and the Administrative Character of Supranationalism: The Example of the European Community' (1999) 99 Colum L Rev 628, 646. Similar criticism had been directed at earlier attempts to introduce "rule by experts". See Madeleine Herren, 'International Organizations, 1865–1945' in Jacob Katz Cogan, Ian Hurd and Ian Johnstone (eds), *The Oxford Handbook of International Organizations* (OUP 2016) 91, 95.

11   See generally, for example, Joseph HH Weiler, 'Europe in Crisis – On "Political Messianism", "Legitimacy" and the "Rule of Law"' [2012] (Dec) Sing JLS 248; Robert Art, 'The United States and the Rise of China: Implications for the Long Haul' (2010) 125(3) Political Science Quarterly 359; Geir Lundestad, *The Rise and Decline of the American "Empire": Power and its Limits in Comparative Perspective* (OUP 2012).

12   See eg, Manuela Caiani, Donatella de la Porta and Claudius Wagemann, *Mobilizing on the Extreme Right: Germany, Italy and the United States* (OUP 2012) 168 *et seq.*

13   See eg, Ian Traynor, 'Peace in Europe may too often be taken for granted' *The Guardian* (London, 12 October 2012), <https://www.theguardian.com/world/2012/oct/12/peace-europe-taken-granted> accessed 19 March 2021.

Still, one possible reason for the increased disenchantment with international expert-based governance in the 21st century could be the rejection of science as a principal driver of policy, in national and international arenas. Again, the roots of this anti-science turn are deep and widespread. Another Hebrew University colleague of mine, the late Yaron Ezrahi, has linked this change to a fundamental epistemic shift in the political imagination of large population groups, moving from a dualistic cosmology, separating scientific facts and subjective beliefs (an epistemic stage he associates with the enlightenment movement),[14] to a new secular monistic cosmology representing a merger of science and culture.

The changing role of science in political life also relates to important political, sociological, and technological developments, which include the rise of identity politics, the broad acceptance of critical theory and increased access to information. Identity politics push politics away from being a competition of ideas about how to solve societal problems and develop new policies, to a form of expression of belonging. Scientific approaches to problem-solving and policy design have little currency in such a political environment. Critical theory approaches to knowledge as a form of power and to mainstream science as a form of power monopoly have generated scepticism towards scientific expertise and increased the association of knowledge-based policy proposals with political liberalism and elitism. And while new information technology has democratized access to knowledge in the technical sense, it has done so without addressing the challenges of scientific literacy that enables making informed choices between competing scientific claims and methods. The result of all of these developments has not only been the adoption of populist agendas and policies that are not evidence-based at the domestic level in several countries, but also their extrapolation to the international level.

Such a linkage is clear in some cases: climate change denial seems to underlie the withdrawal of the US from the Paris Agreement and misinformation and disinformation about international migration trends and the alleged violent propensities of migrants is likely to have led to the failure of the global pact on migration. In other cases, the paths connecting anti-science with anti-globalization are more obscure. Arguably, the move away from evidence-based evaluation of international governance projects – including, their effectiveness, efficiency, cost-effectiveness, impartiality and procedural propriety – to a sentiment-based evaluation renders such global projects that are almost inevitably distant, foreign and not embedded in any specific local culture and

---

14   Yaron Ezrahi, *Imagined Democracies: Necessary Political Fictions* (CUP 2012) 303.

tradition, more vulnerable to criticism and a sense of alienation. In the same vein, rather than comparing on a systematic basis competing alternatives – i.e. the pros and cons of international versus national governance, as would be required in a political environment relying on knowledge-based analysis – those who wish to retain power at the national level are often successful in manipulating the discussion by focusing only on one subset of the matrix: The disadvantages of international governance projects, ranging from the mythological Polish plumbers in the UK to the economic collapse of West Virginia coal country.

Can the COVID-19 crisis alter or exacerbate this dynamic? It has already been widely commented that one of the significant changes brought about by the pandemic has been a renewed interest in science as source of information, not only informing, but actually shaping the public debate, and providing real solutions (a panacea-like vaccine or treatment drugs).[15] Furthermore, there appears to be some degree of correlation between the anti-science stance of prominent politicians, the manner in which their countries handled the crisis and their political standing. At the time of writing, the 2020 US elections have not yet taken place, although it is notable that anti-science positions, which were expressed in a strong manner by the Trump Administration, have been toned down by the Trump campaign. In any event, regardless of the actual outcome of the US election, it is more than plausible than not that governments operating under the shadow of the COVID-19 crisis would find it more difficult than before to reject scientific knowledge and evidence-based policy (still, the risk of political appropriation of science remains).

If indeed science is going to re-emerge as a more prominent method and source for policy-making in the post-COVID-19 era, it would likely have significant implications on the level of international cooperation. This is because the logic of the scientific method of accumulating, processing, and disseminating knowledge is global in nature, regardless of whether the policy problem is itself local or not. The response to COVID-19 illustrates the point: Whereas the regulatory responses to the pandemic were mostly national (and local), the scientific efforts to find effective ways to prevent and treat the disease and to develop a vaccine, were very much global in scope and nature. Furthermore, even with regard to the domestic regulations adopted, a strong public expectation that they be evidence-based has emerged, and the experience of other countries has been often discussed in domestic decision-making processes.

---

15   See e.g. Mandë Holford and Ruth Morgan, '4 ways science should transform after COVID-19' (*World Economic Forum*, 17 June 2020) <https://www.weforum.org/agenda/2020/06/4-ways-science-needs-to-change-after-covid-19-coronavirus/> accessed 19 March 2021.

If, indeed, such a decision-making mode will become more prominent, the relevance of knowledge-based international mechanisms of cooperation, which collect, process, and share expertise is also likely to increase, inviting perhaps a return to the trajectory of the 1990s. The discourse about the need to reform the WHO and provide it with more legal powers and material capabilities is one immediate illustration of this new propensity. But, a shift to a knowledge-based decision-making is likely to strengthen other international mechanisms dealing with policy problems which have a strong scientific and planning dimension, such as the environment, economic development, and immigration.

4   Concluding Remarks

Two key questions raised by my two University colleagues remain however unanswered. First, would a renewed push towards evidence-based decision-making be sufficiently significant in order to overcome sharply divergent national interests that hinder close global cooperation? That is, would States agree to subject themselves to global regulatory power on rational evidence-based grounds, even if this would imply loss of relative powers vis-à-vis their political adversaries or competitors? We have seen that the evolution of international norms and institutions post-WW2 and post-Cold War was significant, but ultimately deferential to State sovereignty and relative power considerations. The retention of veto power by the P-5, the refusal of nuclear powers to disarm themselves and the preservation of WTO exceptions on subsidies illustrate such side-constraints. Still, the Frankesteinian mega-challenges identified by Noah Harari require taking global cooperation to another level of intensity. The inconsistent, at best, and hostile at worst attitude of the two last US administrations towards international frameworks such as the Paris Agreement, the WTO dispute settlement machinery and the ICC, shows that considerable obstacles would still have to be cleared in order to significantly advance international governance, even when the stakes are very high.

Second, it is doubtful whether the 'epistemic genie' – i.e. the critical attitude towards science as informed by cultural (or political) biases – can be fully returned to the bottle. In this respect, once the forbidden fruit – the fruit of knowledge about knowledge – has been tasted there might be no turning back. Furthermore, it is unlikely that the prominent role of science in democratic decision-making can be fully re-established, without dealing with problems of scientific literacy and elitism that have led to its marginalisation in recent years, and to reduced confidence in delegating power to scientists on a long-term basis. This is not impossible, but it would require a considerable effort at the national level that is likely to face considerable resistance from powerful ideological groups that are anti-science and anti-globalization. In a world where alternative facts and alternative science are culturally acceptable and represent a sound political investment, the prospects of a smooth slide to a new stage of knowledge-based international law appear slim.

The upshot of these speculations is that while the world needs a constitutional moment, current political obstacles suggest that the COVID-19 crisis has more potential to serve as a tipping point pushing international relations back towards a previous, more cooperative, stance. Still, even this is far from certain, and cultural and political forces may yet lead the post-COVID-19 world to conduct itself more or less the same way as the pre-COVID-19 world.

CHAPTER 10

Beyond War Narratives

Laying Bare the Structural Violence of the Pandemic

Eliana Cusato

Scrivere è sempre nascondere qualcosa in modo che venga poi scoperto.[1]

.·.

There has been much discussion about the importance of narratives for our understanding of the COVID-19 pandemic and its impact on the existing legal, political, and economic order.[2] The vast literature that emerged following the outbreak of the pandemic shows how members of international law interpretative community have leveraged different cognitive frames in support of particular normative and policy agendas. Thus, international lawyers have extensively debated the possibilities and perils that come with mobilising discrete legal regimes to respond to the pandemic, notably international human rights, public health, migration, and investment laws. This reaction can also be read as a (reassuring) indication of the capacity of the discipline to subsume the COVID-19 'crisis' into existing legal categories in order to make sense of it and manage its consequences.[3] In this chapter, I will consider some implications of the narrative framing the pandemic as an international peace and security issue, which can be seen as the epitome of crisis narratives. While I share the concerns expressed by other commentators

---

1 I. Calvino, *Se una notte d'inverno un viaggiatore* (Oscar Mondadori, 2016) at 193, tr. 'writing always means hiding something in such a way that it then is discovered'.
2 A. Roberts and N. Lamp, 'Is the Virus Killing Globalization? There's No One Answer', *Barron's*, 15 March 2020.
3 See J. D'Aspremont, 'International Law as a Crisis Discourse: The Peril of Wordlessness', in this collection.

about the 'securitisation' of the pandemic,[4] my aim is to contribute to this discussion from a different angle. Using the concept of structural violence, I intend to shed light on the socio-economic-ecologic violence that pre-exist and persist beyond the COVID-19 'crisis' and that the vocabulary of war/insecurity conceals. To put it differently, I am interested in exploring what is at stake in the acts of framing and, in Judith Butler's words, the 'orchestrating designs of the authority who sought to control the frame'.[5] If war talk, as other crisis discourses, allows for a simplified normative agenda, what gets elided in such accounts of the pandemic? What does this exclusion tell us about international law and lawyers?

I will start by outlining the role of legal practices in the securitisation/militarisation of the pandemic, which is in line with more general developments in international law, the most relevant example being the definition of climate change as a 'threat multiplier'.[6] The rhetoric of war/insecurity applied to complex social phenomena, such as global warming or pandemics, creates a shared sense of vulnerability vis-à-vis the enemy and obfuscates the differentiated effects suffered by the most marginalised. Following Johan Galtung and Paul Farmer, I will then re-define the pandemic, and its uneven impacts, as instance of violence that is 'built into the structure' and that cannot be accounted for by the dominant liability-based model of international law. Lastly, I will argue that the narrative framing the virus as the 'enemy', or an external threat to peace and security, obscures the complex interconnection between humanity, economy, and ecology. In reproducing this separation, international law shows (at least) a myopic attitude to the root causes of the pandemic, which are the same of the ecological breakdown: exploitation of fellow humans and nature.[7] I will conclude by reflecting on the responsibility that comes with 'naming' the violence of the pandemic and the prospects of changing master narratives in international law.

---

4 C. Connolly, 'War and the Coronavirus Pandemic', 15 TWAILR Reflections, 9 April 2020; C. Schwöbel-Patel 'We Don't Need a 'War' against Coronavirus. We Need Solidarity', Al Jazeera, 6 April 2020.

5 J. Butler, Frames of War: When is Life Grievable? (Verso 2009), at 12.

6 See Report of the Secretary-General on Climate Change and its Possible Security Implications, UN Doc. A/64/350, 11 September 2009.

7 On the relationship between exploitation and international law, see S. Marks, 'Exploitation as an International Legal Concept', in S. Marks (ed.) International Law on the Left (CUP 2008), 281.

1   **Smoke and Mirrors: COVID-19 and the War Rhetoric**

War metaphors are pervasive in public discussions of everything from political campaigns to battles with cancer to wars against organised crime, drugs, poverty.[8] Likewise, as put by Arundhati Roy, 'the mandarin who are managing this pandemic are fond of speaking of war. They don't even use war as a metaphor, they use it literally'.[9] Donald Trump declared himself a 'wartime president' and proclaimed in a Tweet 'We will win this war;[10] Boris Johnson announced that "We must act like any wartime government';[11] and Emmanuel Macron said 'We are in a war' in which 'nothing should divert us' from fighting an 'invisible enemy'.[12] The invocation of war in discussions on the pandemic is not limited to head of states. David Katz, founding director of the Yale-Griffin Prevention Research Center, observed that

> We routinely differentiate between two kinds of military action: the inevitable carnage and collateral damage of diffuse hostilities, and the precision of a "surgical strike," methodically targeted to the sources of our particular peril. The latter, when executed well, minimizes resources and unintended consequences alike. As we battle the coronavirus pandemic, and heads of state declare that we are "at war" with this contagion, the same dichotomy applies. This can be open war, with all the fallout that portends, or it could be something more surgical.[13]

The language of 'inevitable collateral damage' and 'precision warfare' are undoubtedly familiar to international lawyers. The regulation of hostilities is, after all, one of the most developed area of international law. While many international lawyers would agree that the war metaphor is entirely inaccurate for the situation we are facing, it is equally true that the professional discipline of international law has become an integral part of the securitisation and militarisation of international affairs.[14] If, as put by Judith Butler, 'the frames that, in effect, decide what lives will be recognizable as lives and which will not,

---

8   S.J. Flusberg 'War Metaphors in Public Discourse', 33(1) *Metaphor and Symbol* (2018) 1.

9   A. Roy, 'The Pandemic is a Portal', *Financial Times*, 3 April 2020.

10   https://twitter.com/realdonaldtrump/status/1244029041432244224.

11   https://www.bbc.com/news/av/uk-51936760.

12   https://www.bbc.com/news/av/51917380.

13   D.L. Katz, 'Is Our Fight Against Coronavirus Worse Than the Disease?', *New York Times*, 20 March 2020.

14   N. Tzouvala, 'COVID-19, International Law and the Battle for Framing the Crisis', *International Law Association Reporter*, 25 March 2020.

must circulate in order to establish their hegemony',[15] the role of international law – understood as a discipline, a normative project, and a practice – in the circulation of specific narratives deserves to be carefully considered.

Ongoing academic and policy debates on the whether the pandemic gives rise to a threat to international peace and security and fits within the mandate of the United Nations Security Council (UNSC) are an indication of the power and responsibility of the legal interpretive community.[16] In its remarks to the UNSC, in April 2020, the UN Secretary-General has called the coronavirus pandemic the 'fight of a generation' and a significant threat to the maintenance of international peace and security.[17] Antonio Guterres warned the UNSC that the pandemic had the potential to increase social unrest and violence, which would greatly undermine the world's ability to fight the disease. On 1 July 2020 the UNSC followed up and unanimously adopted Resolution 2532, recognising that the unprecedented extent of the novel coronavirus pandemic 'is likely to endanger the maintenance of international peace and security'.[18] The Resolution also "[d]emand[ed] a general and immediate cessation of hostilities in all situations on its agenda" (para. 1) and call[ed] upon all parties to armed conflicts to engage immediately in a durable humanitarian pause for at least 90 consecutive days (para. 2). However, interestingly, the general and immediate cessation of hostilities and humanitarian pause do not apply to military operations against the Islamic State in Iraq and the Levant (ISIL/Da'esh), Al-Qaida, and all other Council-designated terrorist groups (para. 3). The 'war on terror' seems, in other words, compatible with the 'war' against the COVID-19 pandemic.

For some commentators, framing COVID-19 as a peace and security issue is plausible and a natural outcome .[19] The precedent invoked is the UNSC's response to the Ebola crisis in West Africa, which Resolution 2177 (2014) characterised as a 'threat to international peace and security'.[20] As such, the conclusion is reached that there is an arguable case for the Security Council to act in response to COVID-19, although it remains unclear what kind of measures

15   Butler, supra note 5, at 12.
16   M. Windsor, 'Narrative Kill or Capture: Unreliable Narration in International Law', 28 *Leiden Journal of International Law* (2015) 743, at 765–768.
17   UN Secretary-General's Remarks to the Security Council on the COVID-19 Pandemic, 9 April 2020.
18   UNSC Resolution 2532, 1 July 2020, UN Doc. S/RES/2532 (2020).
19   M. Svicevic, 'COVID-19 as a Threat to International Peace and Security: What place for the UN Security Council?', *EJIL:Talk!*, 27 March 2020.
20   UNSC Resolution 2177, 18 September 2014, UN Doc. S/RES/2177 (2014).

the UNSC should take.[21] Security Council actions are, in other words, presented as a necessary and desirable means to manage and contain the 'crisis of disorder facing the world'.[22] Other international legal scholars, however, have warned that the militarised language may encourage counter-productive responses at the domestic and international level. Christine Schwöbel-Patel observes that '[a]lthough the enemy is invisible, war talk nevertheless creates the spectre of an enemy. And, because war is associated with the 'other', war talk has the tendency to create and build on ethno-nationalist sentiment'.[23] For Ntina Tzouvala the 'war' narrative has the potential of expanding executive power and increasing tensions between states.[24] Rather than encouraging international solidarity and compassion, the militarised language suggests the need for measures to defend ourselves against 'a shadowy enemy'.[25]

It is important to note that the securitisation of COVID-19 is not atypical, but in line with recent developments in international law. Over the last couple of decades the UNSC has been expanding its primary responsibility for the maintenance of international peace and security (under Article 24 of the UN Charter), by affirming its jurisdiction over a variety of issues, such as human rights violations, gendered violence, humanitarian disasters, illicit trade in natural resources, organised crime, and infectious diseases.[26] Recently, climate change has been approached through an international security lens and as a subject matter that could be addressed by the UNSC.[27] In 2007, 2011 and 2018 the UNSC hosted thematic debates on the implications of climate change for international security, thereby asserting a link between anthropogenic climate

---

21   E. Pobjie, 'Covid-19 as a Threat to International Peace and Security: The Role of the UN Security Council in Addressing the Pandemic, *EJIL:Talk!*, 27 July 2020.

22   A. Orford, 'The Politics of International Security', 17 *Michigan Journal of International Law* (1996) 373, at 400.

23   Schwöbel-Patel, supra note 4.

24   Tzouvala, supra note 14.

25   Connolly, supra note 4.

26   For a critique of the expansion of the authority of the UNSC over 'new' challenges to international peace and security, with specific regards to the Women, Peace and Security Agenda, see G. Heathcote, 'Women and Children and Elephants as Justification for Force', 4 *Journal on the Use of Force and International Law* (2017) 66.

27   See Report of the Secretary-General on Climate Change and its Possible Security Implications, UN Doc. A/64/350, 11 September 2009. In the literature, see e.g. S.V. Scott and C. Ku, *Climate Change and the UN Security Council* (Edward Elgar 2018); S.V. Scott, 'Climate Change and Peak Oil as Threats to International Peace and Security: Is It Time for the Security Council to Legislate', 9 *Melb J Int'l L* (2008) 495; K. Davies, T. Riddell, and J. Scheffran, 'Preventing a Warming War: Protection of the Environment and Reducing Climate Conflict Risk as a Challenge of International Law', 10 *Goettingen Journal of International Law* (2020) 307.

change and increased rate of violence.[28] However, in a field were sensitivities are rapidly shifting, the meaning of 'security' in relation to climate change is increasingly viewed as 'a site of contestation between alternative discourses' or world views.[29] This is illustrated by the statements made by developing and small-island states in the context of UNSC thematic debates mentioned above. Global South countries disproportionately impacted by climate change consider conventional notions of security, grounded on military intervention or stabilisation, as ineffective in coping with the complex reality of climate change.[30] Many countries also expressed skepticism as to whether the UNSC would be the appropriate institutional body to deal with climate change given the broader causes and consequences of climate breakdown.[31]

In a similar vein, the 'securitisation' of the pandemic raises the question of the nature of the 'threat' posed and to whom. As in the case of climate change, the uneven impacts of the pandemic upon the most marginalised individuals and communities are a matter of concern.[32] The rhetoric of war/insecurity creates a shared sense of vulnerability vis-à-vis the enemy, thus obfuscating the differentiated effects of the pandemic according to privilege or vulnerability. The depiction of COVID-19 as a peace and security issue diverts attention away from the heterogeneity of human societies and the 'geographies of injustice'.[33] As a result, it promotes an apolitical approach to deaths and suffering, and discourages the search for their underlying causes.[34] Hence, rather than looking at the violence allegedly 'caused' by the virus and falling in the trap

---

28   See UNSC, 5663rd Meeting, Security Council Open Debate: Energy, Security and Climate, UN Doc. s/PV.5663 and UN Doc. s/PV.5663 Resumption 1 (2007); UNSC, 6587th Meeting, Security Council Open Debate: Maintenance of International Peace and Security: The Impact of Climate Change, UN Doc. s/PV.6587 and UN Doc. s/PV.6587 Resumption 1 (2011); UNSC, 8307th meeting, Security Council Open Debate: Understanding and Addressing Climate-Related Security Risks, UN SCOR, UN Doc s/PV.8307 (2018), 11 July 2018.

29   M. McDonald, 'Climate Change and Security: Towards Ecological Security?', 10 *International Theory* (2018) 153, at 158.

30   See e.g. the interventions of the representatives of Nauru, Maldives and Trinidad and Tobago at the UNSC debate *Understanding and Addressing Climate-Related Security Risks*, UN SCOR, UN Doc s/PV.8307 (2018), 11 July 2018.

31   See e.g. the statement of the representative of the Democratic Republic of the Congo at the 2007 UNSC open debate, supra note 28, at 7.

32   K. Evelyn, "It's a racial justice issue": Black Americans are dying in greater numbers from Covid-19, *The Guardian*, 8 April 2020.

33   U. Baxi, 'Towards a Climate Change Justice Theory?', 7(1) *Journal of Human Rights and the Environment* (2016) 7, at 9.

34   L. Hartmann-Mahmud, 'War as Metaphor', 14 *Peace Review* (2002) 427, at 427–428.

of environmental/social determinism, in the next section I suggest that we should analyse the pandemic as an instance of structural violence.

2 Understanding the Pandemic via Structural Violence

Writing in 1969, Johan Galtung called attention to pervasive forms of violence that are 'built into the structure' and that manifest themselves as inequality of power, resources and life chances.[35] In a passage which seems to speak to the current situation, he claims that 'if a person died from tuberculosis in the eighteen century, it would be hard to conceive this as violence since it might have been quite unavoidable, but if he dies from it today, despite all the medical resources in the world, then violence is present according to our definition'. Anthropologist and medical doctoral Paul Farmer built upon Galtung's concept of structural violence to study the tuberculosis and HIV epidemics that killed millions of people in Haiti.[36] He found that historical political economic domination and inequalities created a society that is ravaged by these diseases, which could be avoided or at least made less severe. Both Galtung and Farmer warn that through focusing on forms of violence that are more immediately visible and directly carried out, we fail to appreciate the structures that systemically distribute life chances in an unequal way.

While the war metaphor and the language of 'crisis' distracts us from the 'politics of everyday life', to use Hilary Charlesworth's words,[37] by attending to the structural violence of the pandemic we are able to see forms of violence that pre-exist and persist far beyond the emergency. As Lutz Otte put it, COVID-19 has brought into sharp relief the 'systemic institutional shortcomings and the realities of precarious lives': weak public health systems, overcrowded prisons and immigration detention facilities are breeding grounds for infections.[38] The 'securitisation' of the pandemic disguises these structural issues that result in the pandemic being effectively out of control in many countries with the most vulnerable and disenfranchised being hit the worst. The coronavirus pandemic has revealed how a globalised economy based on profit accumulation and consumerism, sustained by international legal norms and institutions, has deepened existing inequalities between the Global North and Global South, as well

---

35 J. Galtung, 'Violence, Peace and Peace Research', 6(3) *Journal of Peace Research* (1969) 167.
36 P. Farmer, 'An Anthropology of Structural Violence', 45(3) *Current Anthropology* (2004) 305.
37 For a call to refocus international law on issues of structural justice, see H. Charlesworth,' International Law: A Discipline of Crisis', 65 *The Modern Law Review* (2002) 377.
38 L. Oette, 'How is Covid-19 impacting Human Rights?', SOAS Blog, 30 March 2020.

as within countries in the North.[39] In South East Asia, the virus has exposed the weak social protection for urban poor, especially migrant workers,[40] while for many African people working in the informal sector social distancing is a privilege they cannot afford.[41]

Do we have a legal vocabulary to account for this violence? One of the merits of Galtung's concept of structural violence is that it opens up the category beyond visible, direct and immediate infliction of harm to include social ills, such as poverty, subordination, and exclusion. According to Yves Winter, the traditional definitions restrict violence to the 'international, direct, immediate and visible infliction of physical harm, the assault or encroachment on the physical integrity of another human being or his or her property'.[42] Galtung argues that personal violence 'shows', whereas structural violence 'is silent, it does not show – it is essentially static, it is the tranquil waters. In a static society, personal violence will be registered, whereas structural violence may be seen as about as natural as the air around us'.[43] Of course, there is nothing 'natural' about millions of people dying for an infective disease, especially where evidence demonstrates the differentiated impacts across racial, gender, and class lines. Yes, the ceaseless repetition of this everyday violence makes it normal and thus invisible.

If we think about COVID-19 in these terms, one important insight for international lawyers is that this form of violence (contrary to 'personal' violence) does not presuppose an intentional agent as perpetrator and cannot be accounted for by liability-based models. It cannot be easily attributed to an 'enemy' (in our case, the virus) or to a state's conduct. This raises a number of challenges for a legal system built around the liberal notions of agency, attribution, control, and causation. It also suggests that we need a more resilient set of concepts that goes beyond the juridical grammar that requires every violence to be attached to a subject.[44] Further, as I will contend in the next section,

---

39   See e.g. J. Linarelli, M.E Salomon, and M. Sornarajah, *The Misery of International Law* (OUP 2018).

40   Chen Chen Lee, 'The Coronavirus Crisis Is Laying Bare Southeast Asia's Inequality Problem', *The Diplomat*, 8 April 2020.

41   K. Noko, 'In Africa Social Distancing is a Privilege Few Can Afford', *Al Jazeera*, 22 March 2020.

42   Y. Winter, 'Violence and Visibility', 34(2) *New Political Science* (2012) 195, at 196. The commentator outlines also the limits of Galtung's term, i.e. its vagueness and the neglect of 'the specific differences and historical variations of forms of injustice, their intersections, and the ways in which they are compounded'. Ibid. at 195.

43   Galtung, supra note 35, at 173.

44   Winter, supra note 42, at 197.

international law needs to overcome the artificial separation between humanity, ecology, and economy, which makes it unable to account for the root causes of the pandemic.

3 Root Causes: The Interconnection of Humanity, Ecology, and Economy

COVID-19 is an animal-borne disease which, according to the most diffused (yet controversial) reconstruction, was transmitted to a human by an animal kept in a wet market of Wuhan in China. The war narrative framing the virus as the 'enemy' or a threat to international peace and security is based upon an artificial separation between humans and nature. On the contrary, the rise in zoonotic diseases (like COVID-19) shows the profound interconnection between human wellbeing and the way we treat other living beings and entire ecosystems. The United Nations Environment Programme (UNEP) underlines that 60 per cent of all infectious diseases in humans are zoonotic, as are 75 per cent of all emerging infectious diseases.[45] In relation to previous outbreaks, UNEP notes that:

> The Ebola outbreak in West Africa [2014–2016] was the result of forest losses leading to closer contacts between wildlife and human settlements; the emergence of avian influenza [first detected in humans in 1997] was linked to intensive poultry farming; and the Nipah virus [1998–1999] was linked to the intensification of pig farming and fruit production in Malaysia.[46]

By defining the virus as something 'external' to our society, we turn a blind eye to the centrality of nature in the existing socio-economic order.[47] Industrial growth and production systems shape the ecological world and are in turn shaped by new and emerging ecological relations. As observed by Ntina Tzouvala, it is misleading to frame the virus as the product of Chinese underdevelopment; instead, we should see it as the result of the country's rapid

---

45   UNEP, *Six Nature Facts Related to Coronaviruses*, 8 April 2020, https://www.unep.org/news-and-stories.
46   Ibid.
47   T. Ferrando, 'Let's Not be Fooled: There's Nothing External and Symmetrical in the Global Economic Downturn', *Critical Legal Thinking*, 8 April 2020.

development and incorporation into a globalised economy.[48] The disruption
of forests and landscape fragmentation caused by rapid urbanisation and
intensive farming have created new opportunities for zoonotic diseases, by
helping to align the three core elements needed for disease transmission – a
pathogen, a host and a vector.

Rather than pointing the finger at wet markets, we should look at how unsustainable development practices, often facilitated by international legal norms
conceptualising nature as property or resource to be exploited,[49] resulted in
increased habitat and biodiversity loss. As ecologists tell us that shrinking natural
habitats and changing behaviour may create the conditions for new diseases like
COVID-19 to arise in future,[50] rethinking how we 'frame' the environment becomes
an urgent task.[51] The COVID-19 pandemic has given renewed weight to such concerns, but it is important to note that these arguments in themselves are not new.
Indeed, human–nature relations have occupied a significant place within feminist
and critical ecology literature.[52] Donna Haraway has pointed out that 'we must
find another relationship to nature besides reification and possession'.[53] Vandana
Shiva has emphasised the need to transcend the 'polarisation, divisions and exclu-
sions that place the economy against ecology, development against environment
and people against the planet and against one another in a new culture of hate'.[54]

The split between ecology and economy is something that critical legal scholars have also explored and challenged.[55] It has been observed that, although

---

48   N. Tzouvala, 'The Combined and Uneven Geography of COVID-19, or on Law, Capitalism
      and Disease', *Opinio Juris*, 2 April 2020.

49   U. Natarajan and K. Khoday, 'Locating Nature: Making and Unmaking International
      Law', 27 *Leiden Journal of International Law* (2014), 573; I. Porras, 'Appropriating
      Nature: Commerce, Property, and the Commodification of Nature in the Law of Nations',
      27 *Leiden Journal of International Law* (2014) 641; S. Pahuja, 'Conserving the World's
      Resources?', in J. Crawford and M. Koskenniemi (eds.) *The Cambridge Companion to
      International Law* (CUP 2012) 398.

50   J. Vidal, "Tip of the iceberg": Is Our Destruction of Nature Responsible for Covid-19?, *The
      Guardian*, 18 March 2020.

51   See e.g. G. Lakoff, 'Why It Matters How We Frame the Environment', 4 *Environmental
      Communication* (2010) 70.

52   See the seminal work of Donna Haraway, e.g. 'The Promises of Monsters: A Regenerative
      Politics for Inappropriate/d Others', in L. Grossberg, C. Nelson and P.A. Treichler (eds.)
      Cultural Studies (Routledge, 1992), 295. See also A. Biro (ed.) *Critical Ecologies: The Frankfurt
      School and Contemporary Environmental Crises* (University of Toronto Press, 2011).

53   Haraway, ibid. at 296.

54   V. Shiva, 'Earth Democracy: Creating Living Economies, Living Democracies, Living
      Cultures', 2 *South Asian Popular Culture* (2004), 5, at 11.

55   See e.g. A. Philippopoulous-Mihalopoulos (ed.) *Law and Ecology: New Environmental
      Foundations* (Routledge 2011); S. Humphrey and Y. Otomo, 'Theorizing International

conservation and destruction of nature are mutually constitutive processes, the discipline of international law separates conceptually the rules that apply to nature to those that regulate the economy.[56] International environmental law defines the 'environment' as an object of human protection, while international economic law constructs 'natural resources' as objects of appropriation and free commerce. Whereas the environment is regulated with the goal of stewardship, natural resources are governed with the aim of enabling their efficient exploitation. However, as agued by Julia Dehm and Usha Natarajan, 'when competing governance objectives are directed at an identical object, the result is regulatory dysfunction'.[57] If the ecological breakdown and the COVID-19 pandemic have the same root-causes, meaning overconsumption, extractivism, and the unrestrained pursuit of economic growth, by severing humanity, economy and ecology, international law condemns itself to have peripheral impact upon the most pressing challenge facing our interconnected world.

This brings to the fore another key limitation of the war/security narrative. War talk does not engage in a full exploration of root causes.[58] Lori Hartmann-Mahmud explains that the vocabulary of war 'does not have time for analysis, for understanding, for dialogue. That is at once its strength and its weakness; it cuts through the competing versions of why and how the enemy has emerged and sharply focuses on attacking and defeating the enemy'.[59] In doing so, it distracts attention from the very discussions that are indispensable for meaningfully addressing the problem.

4   Of Frames, Power, and Responsibility

Narratives in international law structure the terms of debate, as well as set limits on the kinds of policies and regulatory approaches regarded as suitable to address the issue at hand. Narratives, however, are not neutral, 'they investigate, but also suggest, create and legislate meanings'.[60] This short chapter sought to explore the normative implications of war metaphors and securitising

---

Environmental Law', in A. Orford and F. Hoffmann (eds.), *The Oxford Handbook of the Theory of International Law* (OUP 2016) 798.

56   Humphrey and Otomo, ibid. at 805.

57   U. Natarajan and J. Dehm 'Where is the Environment? Locating Nature in International Law', *TWAILR Reflections*, 30 August 2019.

58   For similar arguments in relation to the human rights discourse, see S. Marks, 'Human Rights and Root Causes', 74 *The Modern Law Review* (2011) 57.

59   Hartmann-Mahmud, supra note 34, at 431.

60   M. Aristodemu, *Law and Literature: Journeys from Her to Eternity* (OUP 2000), at 3.

narratives as applied to the COVID-19 pandemic. It showed that war narratives simplify complex social phenomena to the point of distortion. As war involves a fight between opposing forces with a clear distinction between us ('good') and the enemy ('evil'), we are compelled to think that we are all experiencing death and suffering in the same way. That is not true. The pandemic has shed light on the unequal distribution of rights (including health rights) and vulnerability within and across countries. Further, war narratives mislead, as they proceed from the assumption that the enemy is separated and distinct from our society. This approach distorts our vision of the pandemic, blocking any alternative view that may see it as a symptom of the socio-economic system in place, which treats nature as a 'resource' to be exploited in the pursuit of endless growth. The virus is not the enemy, it does not hate us, it does not even know that we exist. This is not a war because wars are fought with the aim of defending or preserving a certain lifestyle or order. If this pandemic, and its devastating consequences, are a manifestation of structural violence, as I claimed, this requires a radical transformation of our hierarchy of values and ways of thinking. As presciently argued by Anne Orford 'those international lawyers who represent the current period in world history as one of order threatened by chaos again represent only one perspective: that of those who had a stake in the old order'.[61] Luckily, the international legal community is not uniform, instead it is characterised by multi-perspectival narrations and cognitive frames,[62] as the discrete reactions to the COVID-19 'crisis' have highlighted. While some narratives are 'more equal than other', the possibility to contest dominant frames and create new ones should not be underestimated. Intellectual traditions that emphasise the interrelation of humanity and ecology, such as the ones recalled above, offer compelling visions to construct different frames. As put by Dianne Otto,

> We need an international legal framework that can build solidarity rather than foster division, promote redistributive values rather than private enrichment, challenge the entrenched inequalities of the quotidian rather than normalizing and exploiting them, advance positive peace rather than militarism, and ensure environmental sustainability rather than degradation.[63]

61　　Orford, supra note 22, at 400.

62　　Windsor, supra note16, at 765.

63　　D. Otto, 'Introduction' in D. Otto (ed.) *Queering International Law: Possibilities, Alliances, Complicities, Risks* (Routledge, 2018), at 2.

Breaking with a frame not only generates the possibility of new frames and new content, but significantly discloses a 'taken-for-granted' reality.[64] It is both illuminating and empowering. Ultimately, international lawyers should pay attention to the ends that are at stake in framing the pandemic (and other 'crises'), reject narratives that oversimplify the reality, and take responsibility for the knowledge we produce and the stories we decide to tell.[65]

Acknowledgments

An earlier version of this chapter was published in the blog of the European Journal of International Law (EJIL:Talk!) in May 2020. Many thanks to Marija Jovanovich for her thoughtful comments on an earlier version of this chapter, as well as to the editors for their feedback.

---

64   S. Dehm, 'Framing International Migration', 3 *London Review of International Law* (2015) 133, at 165, referring to Judith Butler's important work cited above.
65   Orford, supra note 22, at 408.

CHAPTER 11

Repetitive Renewal

COVID, Canons and Blinkers

Christian J. Tams

It's like déjà vu all over again.[1]

⠆

This short essay is written in the dying days of 2020. In the usual end-of-year mode, and buoyed by reports about vaccination approvals, newspapers wonder how, in the future, we will remember the COVID crisis. ('What will remain of the COVID experience?', asks one; 'How will COVID shape our lives?', another.) I take these questions as the starting point for a set of brief speculations. And as this is the season of gifts, I put my speculation in the form of two wishes: wishes that reflect my hopes for how, with the benefit of hindsight, international lawyers will look back to this curious year; what we will take away from it, and what we will make of the crisis discourse that took hold of much of the discipline in the course of 2020 (and that animates this book).

1 Expanding the Canon: A Greater Role for Global Health Law

My first wish imagines the COVID crisis as a catalyst for change. In this perspective – a dominant theme of much of the crisis discourse, in law and elsewhere[2] – COVID presents an opportunity to adjust. The adjustment that I am hoping for concerns the mainstream representation of international law: the

---

1 Yogi Berra.
2 See Reinhart Koselleck (Michaela W. Richter tr), 'Crisis' (2006) 67(2) Journal of the History of Ideas 357, 370: crisis as an "inescapable pressur[e] for action"; similarly Willem Genugten and Mielle Bulterman, 'Crises: Concern and Fuel for International Law and International Lawyers' (2013) 44 NYIL 3, 4 (referencing the "positive impact [of] a crisis ... on the development of international law").

way international law is taught, or more specifically, *what aspects of it* students are taught in standard courses. In other words, this first wish is about the canon (or curriculum) of international law.

My first wish is very modest: I hope that, following COVID, basic features of global health law will feature as part of this canon. That students who study international law in Chicago, Oran, Valparaiso, Islamabad, or Dundee will have, upon completion of their course, acquired a basic understanding of the International Health Regulations (perhaps then in their 2022, post-COVID, version?). That these same students, by the end of their course, will have begun to appreciate the complex interaction between the different layers of health governance, from the global to the local. And that they will, in their assessment of international law's performance, consider whether and to what extent it will have contributed to global health.

A modest wish, no doubt – but one that, unless I am mistaken, will require tangible change. For at present, global health law has remained the domain of specialists, curiously unconnected to the mainstream discourse about international law. My personal experience suggests that one could, at any point prior to early 2020, claim to be quite well-versed in international law (perhaps even claim to be a 'generalist'), but at the same time confess to knowing next to nothing about global health law. The basics of global health law did not matter in the way other particular fields of international law did, such as the law of the sea, the *ius ad bellum* or world trade law.

Textbooks offer some support for my anecdotal observation. Using them as proxies – as reflections and shapers of the canon – we appreciate quite how marginal global health law is.[3] The following is a list of textbooks I tend to rely on in class, identified by the author's name, followed by a digit indicating the number of passages that are devoted to global health as a matter for international law's concern. (Only one digit is needed.)[4]

---

3   Interestingly, Verdross/Simma's Universelles Völkerrecht, last published in 1984 but in many ways ahead of its time, devotes a section to the WHO: Alfred Verdross and Bruno Simma, *Universelles Völkerrecht* (Duncker & Humblot 1984) 191 et seq. ASIL's *International Law: 100 Ways It Shapes Our Lives* also marks an exception: it has an entire section focused on 'Public Health and the Environment' (American Society of International Law, *International Law: 100 Ways it Shapes our Lives* (2018) <https://www.asil.org/resources/100Ways> accessed 18 April 2021). Generally, *100 Ways* takes a refreshingly down-to-earth approach to international law, mentioning accomplishments such as standardised passports and treaties such as the 1965 Hague Convention on the Service Abroad of Judicial and Extrajudicial Documents in Civil or Commercial Matters. I have always found it useful to contrast its vision of international law to that of academic textbooks. But that is for a separate discussion.

4   Lest I be misunderstood, this listing certainly is not meant as criticism. I could hardly claim global health law has been part of my 'canon' so far: every now and then I have referred to

Klabbers – 0

Dixon/McCorquodale/Williams – 0 (though there is 1 reference to the
WHO advisory opinion and a reference to the WHO's responsibility for
particular human rights)

Shaw – 1 (plus a further reference to 'health regulations' as evidence of
international law's growing remit)

Dahm/Delbrück/Wolfrum – 2 (though more might have been added in
Part II, which the authors had initially envisaged)

Lowe – 0

Vitzthum/Proelß – 1

Crawford/Brownlie – 1

I presume – but of course I would be happy to be proved wrong – that the
result would not be much different for textbooks used by colleagues in courses
at Armenian, Brazilian, Chinese, Dutch, or Egyptian universities. Global health
law, at least pre-COVID, is not part of the canon, in the way other sectoral
regimes of international law are, among them those governing military force,
world trade, human rights, the environment.

Decisions about disciplinary canons are difficult to police; typically they are
not matters of right or wrong. The canon in any discipline reflects traditions,
the particular interests of the 'canonists' and their pedagogical judgment, the
complexity of issues, their historical relevance and present-day significance.
And in a field that is as breathtakingly broad as that of international law –
which is ubiquitous, covering everything from A(aland) to Z(ones of peace) –
only a few select matters can be taken up; most must be left to a side. But while
the need for selectivity will not change, priorities will. Canons, far from being
set in stone, evolve. As regards global health law, it seems to me they should.

Perhaps they should have long ago. As least as far as historical relevance and
present-day significance are concerned, the exclusion of global health law from
the canon should have seemed contentious well before COVID. Historically,
the fight against epidemics has been a driver for international cooperation,
prompting early forms of institutionalisation and standardisation through law,
i.e. common themes of interest.[5] For those viewing international law as an

---

the IHR when discussing sources, and used them to emphasise the importance of secondary
law-making; but that is about it. I am squarely inside the glass house.

5   In his entry for the Max Planck Encyclopedia of Public International Law, Makane Mbengue
traces the evolution back to the 'cornerstone year' of 1851, the year of the first International
Sanitary Conference in Paris (Makane Moïse Mbengue, 'Public Health, International
Cooperation', in Rüdiger Wolfrum (ed), *Max Planck Encyclopedia of Public International
Law (Online Edition)* (OUP 2011) para 1). See further Gianluca Burci, 'Health and Infectious

instrument designed to "ensure the survival of mankind",[6] global health ought to be the key challenge. To put it bluntly, if *survival* in the most immediate sense mattered (and numbers were our guide), international lawyers should long have stopped obsessing about inter-State wars; global health should long have become our benchmark: fatalities from inter-State wars have been declining so much, and are but a fraction of preventable deaths caused by poor health, absence of medication and malnutrition.[7]

But I have no real intention of playing off one challenge against another, and nor do I wish for international law textbooks to ignore the prohibition against inter-State military force.[8] My first wish is a modest one, after all. And so I will conclude it with an encouragement to textbook writers and teachers of international law, and on an optimistic note: In light of this year's experience, let us integrate questions of global health into the international law canon – depending on one's leanings, as a global challenge requiring a multilateral response, as a case-study praising or critically interrogating the role of international law and institutions in that response, as a driver for the development of international law, or as evidence of international law's failings. I am fairly confident that, however we rate the performance of international law in relation to global health, this year's experience with COVID will leave its mark on the canon. That the students of 2030, having worked with revised editions of Klabbers, Shaw, Lowe et al., will be *au fait* with say, States' basic obligations under the Pandemic Influenza Preparedness Framework (PIPF) and happy to recite by heart the conditions under which the WHO Director-General can declare a Public Health Emergency of International Concern (PHEIC). And

---

Diseases' in Thomas Weiss and Sam Daws (eds), *The Oxford Handbook of the United Nations* (2nd edn, OUP 2018) 679.

6 As the title of Christian Tomuschat's general course at the Hague Academy had it: see Christian Tomuschat, 'International Law: Ensuring the Survival of Mankind on the Eve of a New Century: General Course on Public International Law' (1999) 281 Recueil des Cours 1.

7 For an instructive visualisation see notably Max Roser, 'Battle Death Rate in State based Conflicts by Type (1946–2013)', *Our World in Data* <https://ourworldindata.org/uploads/2013/06/ourworldindata_wars-after-1946-state-based-battle-death-rate-by-type.png> accessed 18 April 2021. James Crawford made the point in his Hague Lectures of 2013, noting that "despite a slow start, the adoption of rules prohibiting armed force in international relations has coincided since 1945 with a sharp decline in deaths in inter-State conflicts"; warning against "a mono-causal relation" he went on to observe that "[d]eaths per 100,000 people in inter-State conflicts virtually disappeared these last 20 years": James Crawford, 'Chance, Order, Change: The Course of International Law, General Course on Public International Law' (2013) 365 Recueil des Cours 1, 45–47.

8 Though would it not be an interesting experiment? And it could well work: Brownlie's *Principles*, for the few decades, left the topic to the side.

that, a decade from now, it will be difficult to claim competence in international law without some basic understanding of its role in relation to global health. That at least is my first, modest wish, which looks at the COVID crisis as a catalyst for change.

2   Beware of Blinkers: International Law beyond COVID

My second wish is for something *not* to happen: I hope that, with the benefit of hindsight, we will *not* reduce the international law of 2020 to the COVID crisis and international law's role in (responding to) it. I hope that, in looking back, we will appreciate 2020 as a year of continuities *and* ruptures, of challenges to international law, but also its unremarkable, routine application. This second wish, like the first, is modest; but unlike with the first, the crisis narrative does not help. Because crises focus attention and – like blinkers – fix the gaze.

In moments of crises (real or perceived), commentators up the rhetorical ante and narrow the view. "Is public international law dead?", asked Jochen Frowein, not otherwise given to hyperbole, in an op-ed written shortly after the 2003 Iraq War.[9] The answer was 'no', in case readers wondered. But that the question was asked in those near-death terms is reflective of the force of crisis narratives: such is their power to monopolise attention that a debate about the proper interpretation of a handful of Charter provisions and Security Council resolutions in one particular instance was felt to be an existential threat to the entire discipline of international law.

The editors of this volume avoid the dramatic register, but - as is clear from their Introduction - their invitation, too, reflects the power of crises to monopolise attention. Contributors were encouraged to discuss the usefulness of crisis narratives, and these are linked to international law *tout court*, to the international legal profession *as such*, to *the* international legal literature and *the* international legal discipline. We were, in the editors' words, asked to reflect on the 'fundamental ambivalence' that confronts international lawyers, international law and the international legal discipline in the wake of the COVID-19 pandemic.

Why is this problematic? Because it reinforces a latent trend to extrapolate general claims from sectoral crises, and to assume that they are crises of

---

9   Jochen Frowein, 'Ist das Völkerrecht tot?' *Frankfurter Allgemeine Zeitung* (Frankfurt, 23 July 2003) 6.

the discipline in its entirety.[10] In our case, the invitation to view international law through the prism of COVID nudges contributors to ignore or marginalise developments that do not fit the crisis paradigm, among them 2020's rays of light, but more importantly the routine operation of international law in dozens of fields. This illustrates the general effects of focusing on crises, which (as was observed in a prominent piece) "skews the discipline of international law" and "restricts [its] substance".[11]

This is what blinkers do, of course; to focus means to narrow the vision. But it is problematic because crises render an existing problem more acute. At least in my perception, the discourse about international law, quite apart from COVID, generally is too focused. When discussing public international law with expert and general audiences, I often feel that, even outside crises of the COVID type, we are prone to "restrict the substance of international law",[12] and to judge international law on the basis of a very narrow set of issues – the *ius ad bellum* (a 'cornerstone' on which the entire edifice is said to rest), human rights (so that everything is subordinated to a 'humanised' vision of international law), or binding, peaceful dispute resolution (so that a backlash against courts is a backlash against international law).[13]

This is understandable, as the *ius ad bellum,* human rights, and binding dispute settlement matter (and as they are interesting). But we should be clear that our focus impoverishes the discourse, and it leads us to miss out on what, at least to me, seems its most obvious quality: international law's diversity; the absence of one overarching logic or rationale – the fact that international law is about cooperation *and* domination, about ending impunity for war crimes *and* about streamlining passport designs, about curbing State power *and* harnessing it for international causes. None of this is as such controversial; in fact, perhaps readers may think it rather banal. However, the banal observation explains why I feel ill at ease when asked to view an entire year of international law through the prism of one crisis – a crisis that has shaped many aspects of my life, no doubt, but not necessarily the life of international law. So, in the interest of bringing out international law's diversity, and its capacity

---

10   For (a little) more on the following, see Christian Tams, 'Decline and Crisis: A Plea for Better Metaphors and Criteria' (*EJIL Talk,* 7 March 2018) <https://www.ejiltalk.org/decline-and-crisis-a-plea-for-better-metaphors-and-criteria> accessed 18 April 2021.

11   Hilary Charlesworth, 'International Law: A Discipline of Crisis' (2002) 65 MLR 377, 390–391.

12   ibid 390.

13   As with my first wish, I am not meaning to point fingers; having spent a lot of time working on aspects of international law that – like court cases and the *ius ad bellum* – that probably receive too much attention. I am part of the problem.

to exist alongside crises, here are three alternative snapshots of international law in 2020:

2.1   *Regional Trade Facilitation*

While the European discourse has focused on the first-ever Trade Agreement that makes trade more difficult (the UK-EU TCA), elsewhere there have been significant movements towards facilitating cross-border trade. The Regional Comprehensive Economic Partnership (RCEP) and the Agreement establishing the African Continental Free Trade Area (AfCFTA) are relevant waypoints: the former "the world's largest trading bloc, covering nearly a third of the global economy",[14] the latter establishing "the largest free trade area in the world measured by the number of countries participating".[15] Are we paying enough attention?

2.2   *Slowly Embedding the Global Compact on Migration*

While RCEP and AfCFTA in any year outside COVID would be headline events, most initiatives agreed at the international level gradually trickle down, without making news or waves. The 2020 experience with the Global Compact on Migration is a case in point: agreed in 2018 as a soft law framework,[16] the Compact's fate depends on national implementation measures and a gradual change of perspectives. In a 2-year interim review, the UN Secretary-General offered a surprisingly upbeat assessment, highlighting "indications that the Global Compact has had a ripple effect in terms of formal and informal cooperation" and commending States for incorporating Global Compact priorities into their national strategies and action plans.[17]

Much of this may be polite UN speak; and reading the report, at least for me, made for a stark contrast to the feeling of shame and despair I felt when seeing (also in 2020) the Moria refugee camp in flames. But the Secretary-General's key message does stand out: "Global agreement on migration 'taking root' despite pandemic challenge".[18] Do our COVID blinkers allow us to recognise this?

---

14   Tim McDonald, 'RCEP: Asia-Pacific countries form world's largest trading bloc' (*BBC News*, 16 November 2020) <https://www.bbc.com/news/world-asia-54949260> accessed 18 April 2021.

15   Maryla Maliszewska and others, 'The African Continental Free Trade Area' (World Bank, 27 July 2020) <https://www.worldbank.org/en/topic/trade/publication/the-african-continental-free-trade-area> accessed 18 April 2021.

16   Global Compact for Safe, Orderly and Regular Migration, annexed to UNGA Res. 73/195 (19 December 2018) UN Doc A/RES/73/195.

17   Global Compact for Safe, Orderly and Regular Migration: Report of the Secretary-General (26 October 2020) UN Doc A/75/542, paras 30, 10–15.

18   UN News, 1 December 2020: Global agreement on migration 'taking root' despite pandemic challenge: Guterres <https://news.un.org/en/story/2020/12/1078942> accessed 18

2.3   *International Law's Majestic Mundanity*

As AfCFTA, RCEP and the Global Compact may still be too close to the news, my third snapshot leads us into the midst of international law's majestic mundanity. Judging from the UN Treaty Database, 2020 has been a year of significant activity and steady progress in international law's quest to ensure uniformity in road traffic. (One of its lesser quests, but still: this, *too,* is international law.) No less than 39 amendments to regulations adopted as annexes to the 1958 Geneva Convention on Uniform Conditions of Approval for Motor Vehicles Equipment and Parts[19] were registered with the UN Secretary-General: they dominate the UN Treaty Database, and not only because they all bear long titles.[20] If we sought to assess international law by treaty-making activity, the 1958 Geneva Convention would be right up there.

I am not suggesting that we should: I do not propose that our textbooks should try to explain international law via uniform road transport; in fact I am very happy for this *not* to be our focus. But I do believe that, in our assessment of international law, we need to be aware of its diverse quests and its "sedimentary" nature[21] – and that we would be well advised to take the mundane with the dramatic: so much in international law is about international commitments slowly 'taking root', so much is purposefully pedestrian.

This is not a plea to treat all things equal. But I believe that we ought to be more transparent in acknowledging that our discourse, even outside crises, draws on a very selective sets of issues; that we should offer justifications for being selective, accept that this selectiveness means we are missing out on a lot – and be at least open to entertain the possibility that our selective view leads to distortions. A focus on crises makes it more difficult to appreciate international law's diversity, its richness and banality. In a discourse centred

---

April 2021. Interestingly, the effects of COVID-19 are said to have been ambivalent: "The COVID-19 pandemic has disrupted efforts to implement the Global Compact in some areas while accelerating implementation in others"; "COVID-19 has been a disrupter, but also a leveller": see UN Doc A/75/542 (n 17) paras 86, 16.

19   For those who do want to check whether it exists: see Agreement concerning the Adoption of Harmonized Technical United Nations Regulations for Wheeled Vehicles, Equipment and Parts which can be Fitted and/or be Used on Wheeled Vehicles and the Conditions for Reciprocal Recognition of Approvals Granted on the Basis of these United Nations Regulations (adopted 20 March 1958, entered into force 20 June 1959) 335 UNTS 211.

20   See UNTC, Monthly Statements of Treaties Registered with the Secretariat (2020) <https://treaties.un.org/Pages/LatestTreaties.aspx?clang=_en> accessed 18 April 2021.

21   James Crawford, 'The Current Political Discourse Concerning International Law' (2018) 81(1) MLR 1, 2.

on COVID, even newsworthy developments such as the launch of a continental free trade area are marginalised, and international law's lesser quests will never feature. A focus on crises does, to reiterate Charlesworth's fundamental point, "skew the discipline". I hope that, as we look back on the international law of 2020, we will be able to resist the urge to reduce everything to COVID.

3   Déjà-vu All Over Again?

So, what is it that we can take away from the discourse about the sectoral crisis of COVID? How should international lawyers respond, ask the editors: does COVID call for a serious reinvention of international law, or have we been there before? It may be a little early to tell, as we are barely seeing light at the end of the COVID tunnel. But so far, I would lean towards the 'have been here before': many of the quick responses to COVID seem rather predictable – as if, faced with an unsettling crisis, we have all retreated to the certainty of the usual cures.

This is certainly true for my two wishes: pleas for 'containment' (keep crises in place) and 'adjustment' (learning from crises), as they might be summarized, are safely within the mainstream of crisis responses. Had I been asked a decade ago, about the international financial crisis, I might have responded along relatively similar lines. Twenty years ago, when the debates about military action in and around Kosovo, 9/11 and Iraq prompted much soul-searching, my plea for 'containment' would have been more emphatic, while I would have hoped for a different form of 'adjustment': the canon did not need to be expanded then; but perhaps the quick succession of debates illustrated that one of the canon's core features, the *ius ad bellum*, was *not* set in stone.

Usual cures come in different forms, and much depends on how we see our roles as international lawyers. But reading the various COVID *agorae* and 'rapid response' symposia, I certainly had a sense, in the immortal words of the great American baseball poet, Yogi Berra, of "déjà vu all over again": for so many of the responses follow standard patterns, reflecting, above all, different visions of what it means to do international legal research:

'Take China to court!' we are told – as for the litigators-at-heart, every crisis is a potential court case, and every major crisis a potentially huge case. 'We need stricter rules!', claim the believers, for whom 'more international law' is the obvious response to any crisis. 'Re-politicise international law now!', assert the stern critics – to whom every crisis is a problem of managerialism, and in whose view, we must now finally confront international law's dark spots and biases. 'Keep politics out', argue the purists – preferring to keep their international law technical and clean, focusing on the minutiae. Reflect and study before rushing to conclusions, note the hesitant – as every crisis can be situated, and there is danger in committing all too firmly. And so on and so forth: in a cycle of repetitive renewal, we retreat to our comfort zones and offer, à propos of COVID, the usual cures.

CHAPTER 12

International Law and Crisis Narratives after the COVID-19 Pandemic

Catherine Kessedjian

Increased cooperation is the way forward.[1]

∵

To start, I would like to challenge the topic that the editors of the volume have imagined. I would like to challenge the use of two concepts: "crisis" and "after".[2]

Let's start with "after". We would be better off if we recognized that the pandemic is still here, that we must learn to live with it and that, even if we overcome COVID-19, there will be other viruses or similar infectious diseases that we will need to overcome. Therefore, it does not help to think about international law through the concepts of "before" and "after". We are in the middle of it and it will stay with us in one form or another for many years to come. Indeed, we could also argue that the pandemic[3] started much before the end

---

1 This chapter was written in large parts in the summer of 2020. As I was putting a final note to this short contribution, the passing of Justice Ruth Bader Ginsburg struck a very sad note on the day. It is quite fitting to recall her words during a speech she gave to the International Academy of Comparative Law in 2010: 'I nonetheless believe the U.S. Supreme Court will continue to accord "a decent Respect to the Opinions of [Human]kind" as a matter of comity and in a spirit of humility. Comity, because projects vital to our well being ... require trust and cooperation of nations the world over. And humility because, in Justice O'Connor's words: "Other legal systems continue to innovate, to experiment, and to find ... solutions to the new legal problems that arise each day, [solutions] from which we can learn and benefit."' <https://aidc-iacl.org/ruth-bader-ginsburg-a-decent-respect-to-the-opinions-of-humankind-the-value-of-a-comparative-perspective-in-constitutional-adjudication/> accessed 18 September 2020.

2 Erri de Luca in his book *Impossible* (which I read in the translation in French) has a humoristic way to encourage us all to use precise language: 'La langue est un système d'échange comme la monnaie. La loi punit ceux qui impriment des faux billets, mais elle laisse courir ceux qui écoulent des mots erronés'. Erri de Luca, *Impossible* (Gallimard 2019) 113.

3 As I revise this text during the editorial process in March 2021, an author proposed the concept of "syndemic" instead of "pandemic" to show that many aspects of our lives were turned

---

of 2019, but we were simply blind to it. This has major consequences as to what kind of international legal regime we need.

The above bears an immediate consequence on the use of the concept of "crisis". I will not offer a pedantic analysis of the medical origins of the concept; neither will I dwell on the numerous other usages that have developed over time. However, one factor is essential: whether in economy, psychology or theatre, a crisis is a temporary phenomenon, not permanent, which is overcome after a short period of time and after proper measures are taken. What we are living through is here to stay, it is permanent. Hence it is not a "crisis". We are in a transformational period. We need to conduct a serious analysis of the permanency of the transformation before we can propose useful cures for the illnesses that the international system is suffering.

What are the consequences of these premises? First, the COVID-19 pandemic cannot be overcome only by temporary measures. Because it is here to stay, it changes the fundamental paradigm upon which we have regulated the world until now. Second, it creates a world of uncertainty.[4] How are we to define the rules of the game when everything is uncertain and can be turned upside down in a very short period of time? Third, it seems to upset all previous certainties. Can we build on previous certainties anymore? Can we build new certainties upon which international law may be grounded? A lot has been said about "the return of the State". But this "return" is a dramatic step in the dark past that, in my view, has shown its complete lack of cogency. Borders have been rejuvenated as if the only way to fight the pandemic was to isolate each territory and its population against its neighbours. What about world governance? The silence on this issue is deafening.

I will try to develop these ideas throughout the rest of this paper.

1   Surveillance of the Population

General lockdown or confinement of millions of people is an antiquated measure. It may have been necessary because of the total unpreparedness of most (if not all) of the authorities around the world. It is very important that we

---

upside down because of the virus. Richard Horton, "Offline: COVID-19 is not a pandemic", (2020) 396 Lancet 874.

4   See e.g. Jean-Luc Nancy, *La peau fragile du monde* (Galilée, 2020); Ilaria Gaspari, 'Vivre dans les limites de l'incertitude' *La conversation mondiale*, (France Culture, 28 August 2020) <https://www.franceculture.fr/societe/ilaria-gaspari-vivre-dans-les-limites-de-lincertitude> accessed 28 August 2020.

analyse properly the exact reasons that may have justified such a measure at the time, because we certainly want to avoid a renewal of such measures which have long-term effects on the wellbeing of the people at large, on the social fabric of our communities, on culture and on education of the youth.[5] There are, on the positive side, some advantages that have come from the lockdown: less environmental stress (but not enough to really stop destroying planet earth), some additional solidarity among neighbours (although not everywhere) and some realization that true values matter (although many would debate the meaning of "true values").

If we take for granted (for the sake of discussion) that we do not want to live through a new lockdown and do not accept massive additional deaths[6] until a vaccine is available, then what measures should be taken and how should they be implemented?

Unless I have missed something in the discourse in this area, the measures that need to be implemented to achieve the two goals mentioned above are (1) identify the people that are infected with the disease, and (2) require them to respect a quarantine (the exact number of days that an infected person must isolate is not 40 days, but may range from one week to 14 days, depending on who has the final decision on this matter). This identification renders compulsory a certain amount of surveillance of the population, with or without electronic means, as the recent discussions have shown in many countries, unless we might count on each citizen's sense of responsibility towards the community. The surveillance must be made all over the world. Hence increased cooperation is necessary. But that cooperation must be made via really independent people and bodies, and we cannot rely on the State only. Indeed, it would be all too easy for a State to use sanitary reasons to unduly limit people's freedom to an extent not absolutely necessary to monitor the sanitary situation. Can we rely on courts to provide a proper check and balance for States' actions? As much as I would like to answer positively, we have had too many examples of lack of independence of judges, that I would propose that judicial control won't be enough in many instances. We must also use mechanisms of civil society to monitor the strict

---

5   Education for young people is one of the dark corners of the pandemic. Numbers are frightening. According to some analyses, millions of children will not return to school soon, and many will never return. Most of these children live in poor areas. The pandemic is definitely aggravating the social, economic, and medical discrepancies between the poor and the well-to-do.

6   The balancing act on this matter is a very delicate one.

proportionality of the measures taken, alert the competent authorities when measures are going too far from the initial goal and monitor the changes that must be implemented.

Internationally, we need an independent institution, such as the WHO, but with mixed representations: State representatives, independent experts, civil society. International cooperation is crucial in order for the system to work, particularly when one thinks of mobility (see below). The new WHO should be much more visible and should be given additional powers, notably for coordination of research, cooperation in the implementation of necessary measures and the like. Common efforts should be put into the development of secured tests, that are easy to administer and whose results are fast to get. Travel may be made conditional on the showing of such tests being negative. We are used to all kinds of formalities when travelling. These formalities are limiting one's freedom for sure. But if the wellbeing of millions of people is at stake, it does not seem too much of a price to pay to add one more health formality. Cooperation across borders is crucial to achieve this goal. Tests must be "recognized" from one country to the other. That will be easier if coordination of research and production has been made *ex ante*. People returning positive tests will have to self-isolate for a certain period of time. If self-isolation entails adverse consequences on work-related activities, collective measures should be put into place to alleviate the consequences for the person at stake. Those of us who are old enough to hold in their wallet an "international vaccine passport" know that this may be revived with additional requirements. It is somewhat burdensome but, again, it is proportional if the measure has the power to save lives. What I just said for testing is true for all health-related issues. They must not be left to each State separately, but should be decided and implemented in coordination as a global necessity. If we achieve this for health issues, we will be able to use the template for other global issues such as climate change, water, agriculture, and each additional issue that impacts the wellbeing of humans and other living creatures.

2   Mobility – The Archetype of Globalization

Who would have predicted that, in the first quarter of the 21st century, international mobility would be entirely suppressed and that we would have to rely on electronic communications to keep in touch with people around the globe, whether for personal or professional reasons? Orwell did not think in those terms and Saramago was concerned about the moral values that are at stake when an entire population becomes blind, but one person.[7]

Globalization, as we have known it during the second half of the 20th century and the first quarter of the 21st, was built on mobility. Indeed, an organization such as the European Union has been entirely constructed around mobility. It is true that mobility was first and foremost mobility of goods[8] and, only gradually, of persons.[9] It is also true that capital mobility has not been stopped at all during the pandemic. Circulation of goods has continued and was lessened by two factors: the decrease in production because of the labour force being prevented, sometimes, from reaching industries' premises; the decrease in available transportation vehicles also for lack or decrease in the labour force. Some will rejoice about the "halt" to globalization that the lockdown has entailed. It is true that the lockdown has shown how necessary local production is. But we should not have needed a lockdown to administer that proof. Indeed, local production of essential goods should have always been at the forefront of public policies. Instead, local production was, very often, reserved to luxury goods resulting in one of the most extraordinary oxymorons.

Mobility of goods may still be necessary as some countries may have a "savoir-faire" not shared by others, or benefit from climate conditions that allow certain productions that are impossible under a different climate. So, globalization may still be useful but should be regulated in a global way, outside the model of competition, within a model of cooperation and reciprocal help. It is quite ironic that we need a virus to convince us that we all live on the same small planet and that we are all interdependent.

Consequently, physical mobility should be more reasoned and not be the alpha and omega of the dominant social and economic model. We all know that in order for forced migration to stop, we should trigger a safer environment in every and all countries and on all fronts. A child born in January 2020 will start her life in a small cocoon of parents, close neighbours, and a few friends. If she is lucky, she will see her extended family and more of her friends via the internet. Mobility may not be as crucial for that child as it was for the

---

7   José Saramago, *Ensaio sobre a Cegueira* (1995), (Geneviève Leibrich tr, *L'aveuglement,* Seuil, 1997). It is not fortuitous that the lead character in the book, not being contaminated by the disease, is a woman. See the discussions, during the confinement, when some have noted that countries that apparently dealt best with the pandemic have governments led by women.

8   Mobility of goods is many centuries old and not the prerogative of the 20th century. At best, there was a major acceleration of the phenomenon after the Second World War.

9   For persons, mobility is a very ambiguous phenomenon: the poor have no choice but to risk their lives by moving; the rich had all facilities to move around as they please; the middle class enjoyed mass tourism and easy mobility for pleasure or work.

generations following Second World War. And it should not be considered as a regression that we are prevented from travelling.

3   Global Governance and Law of Proximity

From the above, I conclude that we have, more than ever before, a need for global governance, but that what we call in private international law "the law of proximity" is still the level at which we should think of the law for human beings. This is not new, of course. I do not remember who invented the concept "glocal" i.e. "think global and act local". I argue that this is what we should have done a long time ago and it is about time to implement it.

Global governance should follow a cooperative/collaborative philosophy among States, other entities, and individuals alike. As I argued elsewhere, the competition paradigm, under which we have lived for most of the 20th and the beginning of the 21st centuries, has killed human values of solidarity and empathy[10] without which any society is unbearable. Every day we are given tragic examples of the lack of solidarity. How long are we going to continue along the same road? Well-conceived global governance will allow for the just and equitable allocation of raw materials, global resources (particularly water), energy and the like. Global governance will prevent conflicts, decide which communities need help and allocate funds towards general welfare. Global governance will mitigate the consequences of capitalism, if capitalism is maintained as the economic model.[11] Global governance will decide the amount that each human being has the right to receive, what some call a "universal minimum wage" (UMW), how it is to be calculated and paid, and what are the conditions (if any) under which the UMW will be distributed. Global

---

10   The difference between empathy and sympathy is quite important to remember: e.g. if you saw somebody who fell into a well, sympathy would make you jump; empathy would make you call the rescue ward or go and get a ladder.

11   Many, today, express doubts that capitalism, as we have known it in the past twenty years at least, could survive. There is also a trend among some multinational corporations according which shareholders' interests should not be the only focus for corporations. See for example the declaration of the Business Roundtable of 19 August 2019 that focuses on stakeholders rather than shareholders. But a contrary trend was the focus of headlines in France on 10 September 2020 announcing that some corporations had distributed ever-increased dividends during the height of the pandemic, above the level of their benefits. And the recent (February 2021) firing of Danone's CEO to please minority shareholders who complained, for not receiving enough dividends, is also a testimony of a battle that is still on going.

governance will also allow sharing scientific discoveries in a way that encourages innovation but does not make it dependent on the wellbeing of others. The current pandemic, with its fierce competition for the creation of a vaccine, is a pitiful example at play of the worst sides of human greed. In sum, global governance will define general principles of cooperation and complementarity. The rest will be decided at local level.

A general principle of law has been developed in private international law called "the principle of proximity", which requires that among all the laws potentially applicable to and all the courts potentially competent for a certain matter, it is always preferable to choose the law or the court that presents the closest connection with the matter and the persons at stake. The principle of proximity is in line with the principle of subsidiarity, according to which legislation and regulation must always be decided at the level that is closest to the citizen for more efficiency and acceptability.

The law of proximity has also the advantage that citizens may choose to be regulated by certain norms specifically crafted for them, by them, provided they comply with the overall goals and values of the community at large and do not overstep the legitimate interests of their neighbours. The balance is a delicate one to achieve, but this is the condition upon which we will continue to enjoy dignity and serenity in our lives.

In order to achieve these goals, we need urgent reform of the current governance of most (if not all) international institutions. Checks and balances must be put in place so that an inclusive governance, acceptable for all, sets the proper policies for global issues, without which we will continue to suffer through the chaotic rules that a COVID-19-like pandemic has triggered.

CHAPTER 13

Only Once ... Upon a Time?

Laurence Boisson de Chazournes

We have to learn to think in a new way.[1]

∴

An infinitesimally small virus has put the world into total disarray, leading to an "unthinkable" phenomenon that has affected and affects all human beings. It has turned out to be the source of dysfunction in many forms. The virus itself is not responsible for the many legal disruptions which have occurred, but it has highlighted the weaknesses in the rules, principles, and institutions of the international legal order in confronting such a phenomenon. This piece aims to identify those weaknesses and suggest responses to them. In doing so, an emphasis will be placed on the need for comprehensiveness and solidarity as the world emerges from this crisis.

1 The International Health Regulations: Is It Possible to Prevent Another "Unthinkable"?

Looking back at the negotiation of the International Health Regulations (IHR) adopted in 2005, it is fair to say that nobody imagined that this legal instrument could indeed be called upon to confront a pandemic of the magnitude of COVID-19, which has touched every part of the globe.[2] The primary focuses of the revised IHR were surveillance, containment and the strengthening of national capacities and responses. As the heirs of Descartes and affiliated schools of thought, we never thought that it might not be possible to take control of a health emergency. It was beyond the realms of imagination that a few

---

1   Russell-Einstein Manifesto (London, 9 July 1955).
2   The author participated in the negotiations of the 2005 International Health Regulations as a consultant to the Swiss Federal Office of Public Health, working closely with the WHO Secretariat.

months after the appearance of a virus, slightly fewer than 5 billion people would be in lockdown and that there would then be successive waves of lockdown, paralyzing in many ways non-domestic human activity. It was unthinkable that the prevailing economic system, which is obsessed with the avoidance of debt and balancing the books in a way that is intended to reassure the "market", would make an about-face to enable mass borrowing in order to compensate those who have been affected by the impact of an unthinkable crisis.

This account does not aim at diminishing the role that the IHR can play. On the contrary, their revision was aimed at tackling what was named a "public health emergency of international concern".[3] Their implementation in the crises that erupted in the subsequent years of their adoption – the Ebola viral disease, the H1N1 influenza and others – showed their utility but also their weaknesses. They highlighted the need for rethinking the levels of alert, the alert system as such, and the types of measures that should be recommended.[4] Communication, cooperation and sound management were identified as key pillars of this instrument to be reviewed. The COVID-19 pandemic has made even more pressing the need for their fundamental reform, especially in terms of preparation and anticipation.

The pandemic has also demonstrated the need for an international agency that gathers information and takes responsibility for alerting its members, exchanging information between them and framing the measures to be taken by them. That the agency, in the present case the World Health Organization, may not have acted with all the diligence that was required is a topic of debate and will hopefully be addressed shortly.[5] Besides, the pandemic has shown the need for an independent and fully reliable agent for the IHR to ensure that they are soundly and fully implemented. But States are currently the ultimate architects of global governance. The leeway and discretion they afforded to each other in terms of transmission of information and cooperation for

3   See International Health Regulations (adopted 23 May 2005, entered into force 15 June 2007) 2509 UNTS 79, Art 1. See Laurence Boisson de Chazournes, 'Le pouvoir réglementaire de l'Organisation Mondiale de la Santé à l'aune de la santé mondiale: Réflexions sur la portée et la nature du règlement sanitaire international de 2005' in Droit du Pouvoir, Pouvoir du Droit, Mélanges offerts à Jean Salmon (Bruylant 2007) 1157–1181.

4   See Gian Luca Burci, 'The Legal Response to Pandemics: The Strengths and Weaknesses of the International Health Regulations' (2020) 11 Journal of International Humanitarian Legal Studies 204.

5   On 8 July 2020, the Director General of the World Health Organization announced the establishment of the Independent Panel for Pandemic Preparedness and Response (IPPR), created pursuant to Resolution WHA73.1, 'COVID-19 response' (19 May 2020) <https://apps.who.int/gb/ebwha/pdf_files/WHA73/A73_R1-en.pdf> accessed 19 April 2021.

assessing the origin and extent of the pandemic in the context of the IHR[6] have appeared to be a critical cause of dysfunction in the context of the COVID-19 pandemic.[7] Will the architects agree to subordinate some of their sovereign prerogatives with regard to the scientific assessment of situations, their characterization and the triggering of investigations? If not, there is a risk that the international agent and its architecture would again not be able to deal in an effective manner with the "unthinkable" as the COVID-19 pandemic showed.

2 Comprehensiveness: How to Reach You?

When revising the IHR, it was felt that they could not play their role in isolation and that they would need to interact with a number of other rules, principles, and instruments. A pledge was made to ensure "full respect for the dignity, human rights and fundamental freedoms of persons".[8] The States also recognized "that the IHR and other relevant agreements should be interpreted so as to be compatible" but also that "the provisions of the IHR shall not affect the rights and obligations of any State party deriving from other international agreements".[9] No real political choice was made between these provisions. How should human dignity be asserted? By whom? What is compatibility when a choice has to be made between two sets of rules, as for example rules protecting people's health and rules promoting economic interests? Would compatibility through interpretation be sufficient? What is the meaning of "not affecting ... rights and obligations" as contained in other instruments?

It was thought in the early 2000s that the pieces of the international legal puzzle would gently find harmony with each other. These provisions were signs of a willingness to depart from compartmentalized approaches to international law or, to use the buzzword of that time, to confront fragmentation[10] and transcend it through a toolkit approach based on interpretative means and other treaty law devices. In retrospect, these provisions looked more like elements of a policy agenda with no real priority. *Qui trop embrasse mal étreint*

---

6   See International Health Regulations (2005) Art 43.

7   See Gian Luca Burci and Mark Eccleston-Turner, 'Preparing for the next pandemic: The International Health Regulations and the World Health Organization during COVID-19' (2021) 2(1) Yearbook of International Disaster Law 259.

8   International Health Regulations (2005) Art 3.

9   International Health Regulations (2005) Art 57.

10   See Report of the Study Group of the International Law Commission on Fragmentation of International Law: Difficulties Arising from the Diversification and Expansion of International Law, UN Doc. A/CN.4/L.682 (13 April 2006).

to use a French saying,[11] especially in times of COVID-19? It made it easy for fragmentation to come back on stage.[12]

The pandemic exemplified these problems with a whole host of issues, such as bans on exports of essential goods, border closures and travel restrictions without any coordination, health emergency measures raising fundamental rights issues, seafarers and other persons trapped on board ships, asylum seekers and migrants left in the void and the UN Security Council *aux abonnés absents* – or, more bluntly, not responding when it has a responsibility to do so – to name a few.

The resilience of the rule of law in its composite content is at stake. We need to develop a legal approach that prevents fragmentation trends and allows for a rule of law answer to the many problems that arise all at once. The COVID-19 pandemic is obviously not just a health law issue. It has had an impact on various legal regimes. Would it not be possible that a group of experts be established whose mandate would be to take stock of the various legal problems which arose and make recommendations on necessary adjustments to be made in the relationships between the various bodies of norms, in doing so highlighting the hierarchy to be established among certain principles and norms? Comprehensiveness is needed, and human dignity and fundamental rights must be front and centre of future endeavours.

3   In Whose Name?

The COVID-19 pandemic has shed light on social and economic disparities around the world and among populations within countries. The struggle against the pandemic has aggravated them and continues to do so. Many international organizations have warned against growing poverty and rising unemployment. Can the "unthinkable" lead to a reshaping of the international governance system in a way that would confront inequality and disenfranchisement?

Turning back to the time of the establishment of some of the most prominent universal organizations, what is striking is that the scourge of the devastating effects of the Second World War led to several governance initiatives which should have resonance in today's world. The constitutive acts of international organizations established in this period, be it those of the International

---

11   There is no accurate translation of this French saying. "Grasp all, lose all" could be one, with the caveat that you might not lose everything.

12   See Jaemin Lee 'IHR 2005 in the Coronavirus Pandemic: A Need for a New Instrument to Overcome Fragmentation?' (2020) 24(16) ASIL Insights.

Monetary Fund, the World Bank or the United Nations, those which were revised – the International Labour Organization constitution amended by the ILO Declaration of Philadelphia – or which did not come to fruition (the Havana Charter for an International Trade Organization), carried among their main objects and purposes "high levels of employment and real income", "raising (…) the standard of living and conditions of labour", "international cooperation in solving international problems of an economic, social, cultural, or humanitarian character, and in promoting and encouraging respect for human rights and fundamental freedoms for all without distinction as to race, sex, language, or religion", and "full and productive employment". This human-centred focus should be restored.

Seventy-five years have elapsed. The prevailing economic conditions are not the same anymore, scientific and technological knowledge has drastically evolved, political dynamics are much more plural, the protection of the environment has become a "common concern of humankind",[13] and international law has gone through the human rights revolution, with all people now under their protection. Words and actions need to be reconciled. Human rights and labour conditions should be reasserted as the primary purposes of the international governance system, together with environmental protection. Managerial approaches, programmes, reforms, or projects cannot constitute in themselves a "raison d'être" for institutions.

The 2030 Agenda for Development and its 17 Sustainable Development Goals is an important wake-up call. Besides the great risk that the 2030 Agenda lacks meaningful effectiveness, there is a need for more. Official restatements by each international organization – including more recently established organizations like the World Trade Organization – of the main purposes they should pursue, alone and in partnership, would help refocus on the tools and means to be resorted to and on the ends to be pursued. The pandemic crisis has already provoked upside-down trends in international economic relations. There is a need to take stock of these trends and think further if and how they should find their place in the relevant collective institutional and legal frameworks so as to ensure that a human-centred approach is promoted. The organizations should act as good shepherds, while at the same time being able to benefit from widespread political support in this endeavour.

The COVID-19 pandemic has given rise to an initiative that was considered "unthinkable" a few months before the world was upended by this crisis.

---

13 See, inter alia, Convention on Biological Diversity (adopted 5 June 1992, entered into force 29 December 1993) 1760 UNTS 79; and the United Nations Framework Convention on Climate Change (adopted 9 May 1992, entered into force 21 March 1994) 1771 UNTS 107.

With the aim of ensuring that the European Union member States are able to mitigate the social and economic impacts of the crisis, a truly innovative international tool has been agreed upon. It brings financial support which, while mainstreaming climate action and environmental sustainability,[14] will be distributed in an inverse ratio to the economic performance under COVID-19 of the different member States. This makes it a true solidarity instrument. Moreover, in the euro area, the funding is based on the European Union, acting as the borrower and reimbursing the creditors, without allocating the debts to the benefiting countries. Solidarity among the euro countries is the principle: borrowing by an international organization on behalf of all the euro countries for the benefit of some euro countries, i.e. those that have suffered the most from the consequences of the COVID-19 pandemic, and support by an international organization without asking the countries which have benefited – often in a substantial way – to repay what has been given. Couldn't this solidarity mechanism be replicated, entirely or partially, in other settings? The recent decision of the G20 ministers of finance dealing with the global debt initiative for the poorest countries[15] could hopefully go in that direction, if accompanied with special drawing rights emitted by the IMF to cover the debts of these countries. This would prevent cuts in public spending necessary to confront the multiple impacts of the pandemic. This institutional approach would be less innovative than it could appear at first glance, not least because it was resorted to in 2008 as a response to the financial crisis, which at that time severely affected certain Northern countries.[16]

4   A Humbling Task

Promoting respect for the rule of law is a humbling task. Humility should not be understood as an unwillingness to put oneself forward or as unworthiness.

---

14   "Proposal for a Regulation of the European Parliament and of the Council establishing a Recovery and Resilience Facility", Council of the European Union, 11538/20 (7 October 2020).

15   "Common Framework for Debt Treatments beyond the DSSI", Decision of 13 November 2020, Extraordinary G20 Finance Ministers and Central Bank Governors' Meeting, <https://g20.org/en/media/Documents/English_Extraordinary%20G20%20FMCBG%20 Statement_November%2013.pdf> accessed 20 November 2020.

16   Shimelse Ali, Uri Dadush, and Lauren Falcao, 'Financial Transmission of the Crisis: What's the Lesson?' (2009) *Carnegie Endowment for International Peace* <https://carnegieendowment.org/publications/index.cfm?fa=view&id=23284&prog=zgp&proj=zie> accessed 19 April 2021.

It is used to qualify an attitude that leaves space for doubt, and demonstrates an understanding of social, political, economic, or cultural problems at stake as well as a willingness to contribute to the furtherance of the rule of law. Rather than endless existential discussion that has a tendency to harm the discipline, there should be reflection on how to make international law more effective at confronting global problems, such as pandemics, climate change and poverty. The COVID-19 pandemic, with its grave and long-lasting impacts, calls upon all of us.

A French nursery rhyme keeps coming back to my mind. It starts with "Monday morning, the emperor, his wife and the little prince came to my house, to shake my hand. As I was gone, the little prince said: "Since that's how it is, we'll come back on Tuesday"." The same happens on Tuesday morning, Wednesday morning, Thursday morning, Friday morning, Saturday morning and Sunday morning. On that day, the little prince says: "Since that's how it is, we won't come back again".

CHAPTER 14

The Kaleidoscopic World Confronts a Pandemic

Edith Brown Weiss

We must, indeed, all hang together or, most assuredly, we shall all hang separately.[1]

.·.

More than 216.3 million people worldwide are infected with the coronavirus as of late August 2021 and more than 4.5 million have died.[2] And the numbers keep climbing. These data likely understate the extent of the crisis since testing is not widely available in many countries and deaths may go unreported.

The COVID-19 crisis affects people and countries unequally. It has the most severe effects on people with low incomes, indigenous peoples, minorities, people suffering discrimination, and people vulnerable through age or underlying health conditions. It severely harms countries that lack an adequate health care system, which unfortunately includes many countries, especially in Africa. In this crisis, each country has largely dealt with the problem on its own.

The COVID-19 crisis illustrates the workings of a kaleidoscopic world, in which patterns rapidly change, many actors beyond States are critical, flexible instruments are imperative, and scientific knowledge is evolving. The kaleidoscopic world stands in sharp contrast to the traditional view of an international system dominated by States in a rather static order, in which States enter binding agreements and are responsible for implementing them. The COVID-19 virus challenges this classical framework. It forces us to reconsider

---

1 Benjamin Franklin, on the occasion of the signing of the U.S. Declaration of Independence (1776): Walter Isaacson, 'Declaring Independence: How They Chose These Words' *Time Magazine* (7 July 2003) <http://content.time.com/time/magazine/article/0,9171,1005150 -3,00.html> accessed 27 April 27, 2021. The analysis for this essay was completed in November 2020.

2 WHO Coronavirus (Covid-19) Dashboard, https://covid19.who.int/ (visited 30 August 2021).

© EDITH BROWN WEISS, 2022 | DOI:10.1163/9789004472365_016

international law in order to broaden its scope, enlarge the range of actors, encompass different kinds of legal instruments, and recognize the imperative of norms.

1   Characteristics of the COVID-19 Pandemic

The coronavirus knows no geographical boundaries. It is readily transmissible and can easily hop a ride undetected to every corner of the Earth. Those people carrying and spreading the virus may be asymptomatic. International conferences, tourism venues such as ski resorts, and social, commercial, and religious places where people congregate en masse can become superspreader events, usually unknowingly. The international Biogen conference in Boston in late February 2020, for example, is estimated to have unknowingly caused the infection of 20,000 people in the Boston area alone.[3]

At the beginning of the pandemic, little was known scientifically about the virus, especially about whether it could be transmitted by those showing no symptoms. Scientific knowledge about COVID-19 has rapidly changed. We are still learning much about the virus: its transmission, susceptibility of children, mutations of the virus, immunity and re-infection, long-term effects from having the virus, effective ways to control it, and many other features. As knowledge develops, public health measures to control and manage it change, often quickly.

Controlling the virus is a public goods problem, in which rapid responses by governments and other actors are essential and in which collective actions are needed at the local, regional, and global levels. At the same time, it presents a private goods problem: development of a vaccine by private companies, although often with public support. COVID-19 presents us with the need for all actors, public and private, to collaborate and to respond quickly and flexibly.

The COVID-19 crisis is linked with other crises. The responses needed to confront COVID-19 dramatically affect daily life and lead to harsh economic effects. Thus, we are confronting two simultaneous crises: health and economic. While we treat these separately, they are intricately linked. Both are at the same time globalized and localized, even to the point of individual behaviour. They beg for global cooperation.

---

3 Jacob Lemieux and others, 'Phylogenetic analysis of SARS-CoV-2 in the Boston area highlights the role of recurrent importation and superspreading events' (*medRxiv*, 25 August 2020) <https://www.medrxiv.org/content/10.1101/2020.08.23.20178236v1.full.pdf> accessed 13 September 2020.

The health and economic crises co-exist with a third crisis: the climate crisis. The climate crisis is longer term, but the climate changes that are taking place already affect susceptibility to disease and efforts to control it. The climate crisis is advancing much faster than expected several decades ago and with greater severity. It will have significant implications for our capacity to address health and economic crises.

2   Limits of International Law for the COVID-19 Pandemic

The international legal system applicable to COVID-19 is centred on the World Health Organization (WHO). The WHO, with 194 member countries, has adopted binding international regulations and nonbinding legal instruments applicable to COVID-19.[4] The WHO International Health Regulations (2005), the relevant instrument, contains 66 articles and nine annexes and specifies requirements for preparedness for controlling global disease transmission, including surveillance, notification and sharing of information, infection prevention and control, border controls, and measures to maintain essential health services. If the Director-General (DG) declares a Public Health Emergency of International Concern (PHEIC), the DG can issue standing and temporary recommendations to States. There is agreement among experts that it is again time to update these regulations.

The WHO system is by its structure focused on member States. It acts through regional bodies of member States. The WHO depends upon States implementing its regulations and recommendations and having the capacity and resources to do so. In many countries, these resources are lacking, either because the health systems are under-developed and underfunded, or because they are not designed to handle epidemics. Implementation of measures at the national level is spotty at best. The force of the WHO regulations and recommendations also depends upon States' willingness to accept the authority of the WHO and upon the WHO's capacity to avoid being captured by geopolitical or commercial considerations.

COVID-19 sharply raises the question of whether international law as classically conceived can effectively deal with a global pandemic in the current rather anarchic world. The answer seems to be "No." It is certainly relevant and important, but not sufficient. In practice, we are seeing a widely diverse set of regulations and recommendations by many different entities, from States

---

4   See Lawrence Gostin, *Global Health Law* (Harvard University Press 2014).

operating alone at the national level, to subnational regulations, to very local measures, and to actions by actors other than States, including the private sector and industry, nongovernmental organizations, schools, and diverse networks.

The classical or legacy international legal system is based solely on States, which are sovereign, independent, territorially defined, and theoretically equal. It is horizontal in structure in that it governs relations between States. It focuses on a limited number of sources: binding international agreements, rules of customary international law, and general principles of law. It does not easily accommodate change. International law is also stove-piped in that separate areas of law have arisen for different subjects, as for example health, economic, security, environment, and human rights, sometimes without recognition of the common core elements. While the WHO has attempted to balance health concerns with trade and human rights concerns in its regulatory work, trade law generally has not reciprocated, except for the WTO Doha Declaration on the TRIPS Agreement and Public Health, which permits compulsory licensing of pharmaceuticals for "national emergencies" and "circumstances of extreme urgency," as determined by the WTO Member. The challenging economic crisis today, which is linked with the health crisis, involves a separate body of inter-national economic law.

In public international law, international and domestic law are fully dis-tinct, although in practice domestic laws may sometimes extend beyond the country, and international law may need national implementing legislation to become binding within a given country. Similarly, the lines between public and private international law are sharply drawn, though they have blurred in recent years.

This classical framework of international law, centred on the WHO in the context of the pandemic, is certainly relevant, but it does not encompass the many actors and legal instruments that are relevant to controlling COVID-19. The private sector and civil society are critical to addressing the pandemic, but they participate only on the fringes. Measures at the subnational and local levels are not included. Many different kinds of instruments are rele-vant, such as guidelines and best practices, which do not rise to the status of binding commitments. States' incentives (whether inducements or sanctions) to implement and comply with the international legal commitments that do exist are weak.

Many States seem to be seizing on the basic principle of national sovereignty to strengthen national barriers and focus only on conditions within their own country in the pandemic. Closing national borders to travel (or closing sub-national borders) to prevent importing the virus and quarantining those who enter respond to concerns about how easily the virus is transmitted. Most States seem to be acting on their own, with no consensus on criteria or without co-ordination. The European Union, in which States have generally not coordinated their actions, announced in October 2020, however, a new color-coded map indicating the travel risk for each of its 27 member countries, based on common criteria. It has further created an EU Digital COVID Certificate Regulation, which applies as of July 1, 2021.

Similarly, there is no consensus on the distribution of vaccines. A State that develops a vaccine can keep it for its own citizens as an exercise of national sovereignty. Other States, with WHO support, demand international access to a vaccine as an issue of equity. Moreover, national sovereignty can become a basis for controlling access to data and information needed to understand and respond to the pandemic. Accurate public information about the crisis is essential to enlisting public participation in addressing it. Controlling the virus is unnecessarily complicated when officials use the crisis to crack down on civil liberties or insist on libertarian ethics for personal or political gain.

3   Reconceptualizing Public International Law[5]

The COVID-19 pandemic is taking place in the context of a fundamental transformation of the international system. The emerging order is complex and often chaotic. It consists of 193 States that are members of the United Nations and two with observer status, about 69,000 international organizations (both governmental and nongovernmental), thousands of multinational corporations, multiple religious entities, many illicit actors and 7.8 billion people as of August 2021. Change is rapid as new issues and problems emerge, coalitions form instantly across national borders, and many different actors try to exercise authority. I have termed this landscape a kaleidoscopic world.

The kaleidoscopic world involves many actors beyond the WHO and States in the effort to control COVID-19. These include subnational governments, local communities, the private sector, nongovernmental organizations, scientific and medical networks, informal networks, and individuals. All are engaged in public activities in trying to control the virus and its effects, or in some cases, to undercut existing control efforts, or to promote alternative responses to

---

5   The material that follows is based on work developed for my General Course on Public International Law at The Hague Academy of International Law, Edith Brown Weiss, 'Establishing Norms in a Kaleidoscopic World, General Course on Public International Law' (2019) 396 Recueil des Cours 1.

measures recommended by public health experts for controlling transmission of the virus, as in the Great Barrington Declaration in October 2020.[6] These actors are part of the broader international legal system.

Information technology has enabled governments at many levels, the private sector, formal and informal groups and networks, and individuals to communicate instantaneously across the world. For example, Tumblr hosted 532 million blogs as of August 2021. Over 409 million people view more than 20 billion pages of WordPress each month; WordPress blogs are written in over 120 languages. Twitter launched a COVID-19 curated page, which over 160 million people have visited over 2 billion times as of July 2020.[7] Mobile phones have become ubiquitous with over 5.2 billion "unique mobile subscribers," as of August 2021.[8] Thus, many actors beyond States have become empowered to take actions dealing with problems that can have global effects. They reflect bottom-up empowerment and affect the development and implementation of international legal instruments. At the same time, information technology has enabled authoritarian top-down control to control the coronavirus and facilitated those political leaders who want to flout practices directed to controlling coronavirus transmission.

Effective collective action requires access to information, and importantly, transparency about the emergence of the virus, its tracks, its effects, and the efforts to control it. Addressing COVID-19 involves international and domestic law, public and private sectors, and civil society. It illustrates once again that the lines between international and domestic and between public and private are blurring and that the gaps between national and international and public and private actions need to be closed.

In a more broadly conceived public international law, legal instruments are more diverse than in the legacy framework. They include not only binding international agreements, customary international law, and general principles of law, but also a second tier of nonbinding legal instruments produced by consensus, and a third tier of individual voluntary commitments. The key characteristic of nonbinding legal instruments is that while States or other actors have agreed to a common text, they are not legally bound to comply with it,

---

6 Martin Kulldorf, Sunetra Gupta and Jay Bhattacharya 'Great Barrington Declaration' (4 October 2020) <https://gbdeclaration.org> accessed 13 October 2020.

7 Twitter has been deleting or placing warnings on tweets that violate its COVID-19 misleading information policy. As of 12 January 2021, Twitter had removed 8,493 tweets and challenged 11.5 million accounts.

8 'Data' (GSMA Intelligence) <https://www.gsmaintelligence.com/data> accessed 30 August 2021.

which means they cannot be brought into international or national courts for failure to comply. Practice indicates, though, that in some cases compliance may be as good as for binding international agreements. Voluntary individual commitments differ from the above in that they are not prescribed by a consensus but rather differ from each other. They may be undertaken pursuant to a common goal, as in the Paris Agreement on climate change. Corporations in particular have made such commitments for a range of environmental goals.

In controlling COVID-19, we need a mix of these forms of legal instruments and of other instruments affecting behaviour that do not rise to the level of a formal legal instrument. Controlling the COVID-19 pandemic means that formal and informal legal instruments, codes of conduct, and suites of best practices need to exist at many different levels, including the very local. They need to encompass many actors other than States and the WHO. To address COVID-19, all States, private actors, and civil society need to know about relevant laws, codes of conduct, best practices, and other instruments such as declarations for quarantines, wearing of masks, social distancing, etc. Sharing experience with implementing them and with their effects is important.

Nongovernmental institutions have a potentially important role to play. They can be a significant source of relevant laws and good practices and identify gaps and weaknesses in domestic policies and laws. The December 2019 International Conference of the Red Cross and Red Crescent, for example, adopted a new non-binding guidance document regarding legal frameworks for preparing for and responding to disasters.[9] The Conference and related resolutions drew attention to important equity issues such as the protection of vulnerable groups. Such documents help both the Red Cross and the Red Crescent, and other groups, to provide domestic assistance in disasters, including pandemics. They form part of the relevant frameworks.

The new COVID-19 Law Lab, formalized in July 2020, is an important step in bringing together the relevant laws, regulations, nonbinding legal instruments, good practices, policies and other relevant commitments by States and other actors. The Law Lab is a joint project of the United Nations Development Programme (UNDP), the World Health Organization, the Joint United Nations Programme on HIV/AIDS and the O'Neill Institute for National and Global

---

9   The Conference adopted Resolutions entitled "Disaster Laws and Policies that Leave No one Behind" and "Time to Act: Tackling Epidemics and Pandemics Together": see Rachel Macleod, 'Tackling Disasters and Pandemics Together with Laws and Policies that Leave No One Behind' (2020) 24(21) ASIL Insights <https://www.asil.org/insights/volume/24/issue/21/tackling-disasters-and-pandemics-together-laws-and-policies-leave-no-one> accessed 13 October 2020.

Health Law at Georgetown University. The database of legal instruments covers declarations of a state of emergency, quarantine measures, disease surveillance, mask-wearing, social distancing, and access to medication and vaccines.

The COVID-19 crisis illustrates the need for breaking down the walls between public national and international law and between public and private. It demonstrates that we need to aggregate and consider a variety of legal instruments and commitments. It supports reconceptualizing international law around the notion of "public" and integrating international and domestic, public and private law into a framework for considering, undertaking, and evaluating actions.

4   Recognizing and Maintaining Norms

In the kaleidoscopic world, States and other actors need to be guided by shared norms that reflect commonly held values embedded in diverse cultures. We assume an essentially social contract in which norms arise or are recognized from an interactive process. They serve as prescriptive obligations that actors generally accept. Such norms unify disparate elements and can provide stability in our emerging chaotic international system. In the context of the COVID-19 pandemic, shared norms foster collaboration for the public good, both globally and locally, to control the virus.

We can identify norms that are fundamental to a just, peaceful, and robust international system and central to generating and maintaining public goods: in this case, the control of the coronavirus. These include cooperation, avoiding harm, human dignity and equity, transparency, and accountability.[10]

Cooperation is a fundamental norm in international law. It is found in diverse cultures and has deep biological roots in the behaviour of animals. The norm of cooperation is embedded in international agreements and other legal instruments and in many private sector instruments. Cooperation enables people to achieve benefits that they could not achieve on their own or to prevent problems or situations from spiralling downward, often drastically so, and causing everyone to suffer. When we are locked into the same space for the foreseeable future, as we are with pandemics and other crises, the shadow of the future can lead to cooperation.

We can distinguish two different forms of cooperation: joint efforts, which we may refer to as collaboration, and coordination of a myriad of separate

---

10   Brown Weiss (n 5).

efforts. Scientists working on the coronavirus are often engaged in joint efforts. Coordination may be needed to ensure that international, national, and local measures to limit the virus are effective.

Many international agreements embody the norm of avoiding harm. It is linked to the norm of cooperation, because cooperation may be essential to avoiding harm. In the context of the COVID-19 pandemic, avoiding harm means controlling transmission, avoiding deaths, and providing a healthcare system that minimizes suffering. I would argue that it also implies respect for scientific evidence and an obligation not to make false statements and engage in behaviour that impedes measures needed to control the virus.

The norm of human dignity and equity is complicated in the context of a pandemic. The effects of COVID-19 fall disproportionately on low-income countries and on marginalized and vulnerable groups. Many States do not have adequate health care systems so that many people do not have access to routine health care or they do not have adequate resources to deal with a pandemic. This makes it much harder to identify, monitor, track contacts, and treat disease, which affects the human dignity to which all people are entitled.

The norm of transparency holds that information must be made available. In the context of COVID-19 and similar health crises, it means that a State must make information available as soon as the presence of the disease is known and continue to make information available about its transmission, effects, and treatment.

The norm of accountability calls for mutual accountability between all participants in the system. It provides the glue for the other norms. States are accountable to each other, but private companies, civil society organizations, communities, and even individuals must be accountable. In the kaleidoscopic world, accountability is especially difficult. In the context of the COVID-19 pandemic, leaders should be accountable when by their actions, thousands of people needlessly die, marginal and vulnerable groups suffer enormous hardship, and human rights are violated under cover of the pandemic.

In the context of the pandemic, we might also identify a norm related to scientific knowledge. Understanding the virus, its spread, its effect, and its treatment is critical. In the international legal order, we often view scientific knowledge as more or less static for a significant period of time in that our understandings exist for at least months, or even years. But the scientific knowledge about COVID-19 is dynamic and rapidly changes, which has implications for international law. Advances in scientific knowledge come from widespread participation in the scientific endeavours and from transparency in sharing the resulting knowledge. States need to facilitate this and not stand in the way of cooperation and transparency.

One can argue that we have a moral obligation to seek scientific knowledge so as to understand the virus, cure or prevent the disease, control its spread, and lessen its harmful, often devastating effects.[11] This carries both positive and negative obligations. On the positive side, it is an obligation to engage in scientific research and technological development, to monitor developments, and to disseminate data and information. On the negative side, it is an obligation not to impede research, monitoring, testing, and access to data. It is also an obligation not to falsify data or manipulate it for political purposes, and not to deliberately disseminate false information. While this moral obligation applies more broadly to other problems, it is particularly acute for pandemics and similar problems where scientific knowledge is especially dynamic. One could treat this as a norm regarding the dynamic process of generating and using scientific knowledge.

The norms outlined here are fundamental for a kaleidoscopic world in addressing pandemics. With the many different actors and varied legal and other instruments, they provide a means for bringing cohesion to producing and maintaining a public good, in this case controlling COVID-19.

5   Controlling COVID-19 as a Public Good in a Kaleidoscopic World

International law has addressed issues of providing a public good, as for example in controlling the depletion of the ozone layer. The COVID-19 pandemic poses the ultimate public goods problem in the context of a kaleidoscopic world. Control of the disease is at the same time an individual good, a community good, and a global public good. The virus knows no boundaries. In this sense it is similar to but more dangerous than other viruses that have threatened us in that it is more contagious than Ebola and more lethal than recent flu viruses.

A public good has two characteristics. It is non-exclusive in that others cannot be excluded from sharing in it, and it is non-rivalrous in that one person's consumption of the public good does not reduce the quantity available to others. Global public goods are those whose benefits are spread widely across space and time. Measures, including legal instruments, are needed to produce global public goods and to maintain them.

Global public goods are like other public goods, except that their effects are not confined within national borders but rather cross them. They may exist for

---

11   See Charles Weiss, *The Survival Nexus: Science, Technology and World Affairs* (OUP 2022).

a significant period of time. Global public goods are usually not pure public goods but rather have a significant private element. This configuration may change over time.

For the COVID-19 pandemic, the global public good is control of the disease. The measures for producing this global public good are critical and have major implications for our success in doing so and for international law. We can distinguish three different kinds of measures:[12] additive measures in which the public good is sum of contributions from different actors; best-shot measures in which the public good is determined by the technology producing the best outcome; and weakest-link measures in which the public good is only as effective as the weakest link in the chain. All three are relevant to the public good of controlling the pandemic.

At present, controlling the COVID-19 pandemic exemplifies the first category of measures in that it depends upon the sum of what States and many other actors are doing to control it and to prevent its spread. Here the record is spotty at best. The virus as of this writing is not under control. Some States have refused to develop a national strategy for dealing with the pandemic. Some States lack the capacity to do so. Only a very few, such as New Zealand, an island State, have been successful in controlling the virus within the State's borders.

States are individually exercising national sovereignty in an effort to stop virus transmission. They have closed their borders, and locked down cities, regions, or communities within their borders. They have imposed varying travel restrictions. Their efforts are *ad hoc*, reflecting in part changes in the status of the virus within their countries, and in part efforts to go it alone in addressing the pandemic. States are generally not coordinating with each other in their efforts.

Producing a public good generally requires cooperation and coordination of actions.[13] States and all the many other relevant actors are obligated to take certain measures or engage in certain behaviours and to refrain from certain behaviours or actions. In the context of the COVID-19 pandemic, this means that States, the private sector and civil society are obligated to take measures

---

12   William Nordhaus, 'Paul Samuelson and Global Public Goods' in Michael Szenberg, Lall Ramrattan, and Aron Gottesman (eds), *Samuelsonian Economics and the Twenty-First Century* (Oxford Scholarship Online 2009) <https://oxford.universitypressscholarship.com/view/ 10.1093/acprof:oso/9780199298839.001.0001/acprof-9780199298839-chapter-6> accessed 13 October 2020.

13   See Inge Kaul, Isabelle Grunberg, and Marc Stern, *Global Public Goods: International Cooperation in the 21ˢᵗ Century* (OUP 1999).

to conduct tests, monitor transmissions, provide access to data, and engage in certain practices to minimize transmission. While these measures need not be uniform, they do need to be taken pursuant to a common goal of pursuing the public good. Scientists need to participate in research and monitoring and the results need to be publicly shared.

Our treatment of drugs in international law provides a relevant example. To combat illegal drugs, States agreed to take certain actions within their countries and to co-ordinate with other States in doing so. The United Nations General Assembly report from its UNGA sponsored conference on drugs in 2016 articulated a doctrine of common and shared responsibility for this scenario. The doctrine is especially relevant for the COVID-19 pandemic, in which States and other actors need to co-ordinate their strategies and measures for effective collective action. Common and shared responsibility extends not only to States and international organizations but also to subnational institutions and to community level actions.

The public good of controlling the coronavirus also depends upon finding a safe and effective vaccine or vaccines and making these available worldwide. This is referred to as finding "the best shot technology." A handful of countries and many private companies are racing to do this. The problem is fraught with dangers. The medical scientific community has standards for determining when a vaccine is effective and safe to distribute broadly, but States may not necessarily accept these judgments and may try to suppress or alter these judgments for political reasons.

Widespread distribution of the vaccine or vaccines will be critical to controlling the coronavirus, but international consensus on how this will be done is still lacking. The World Health Organization established the COVID-19 Vaccine Global Access Facility for States to cooperate in developing a vaccine and to agree on its distribution. As of May 2021, the Russian Federation, the United States and certain other countries had not yet signed the commitment agreement.[14] The new COVAX Facility, co-led by WHO, is intended to assist low-income countries access the vaccines. Access to the vaccine raises profound ethical issues among countries and within them. Moreover, the anti-vaccine movement in the United States, which has been spreading through social media to other countries, could complicate efforts to achieve herd immunity when vaccines become available.

---

14 US President Biden has reversed the US position against working with the WHO and in February 2021 committed an initial $2 billion to the COVID-19 Vaccines Advance Market Commitment (COVAX AMC), and $2 billion more through 2021 and 2022.

The global public good of controlling the coronavirus especially depends upon the third category of measures: overcoming the weakest link in the chain. Otherwise the weakest link can defeat the effort. As long as there is no global community (herd) immunity and no effective vaccine globally available, we face the nasty possibility that the coronavirus can slip undetected into areas that have been free of it. While we have considerable experience in dealing with the weakest link problem in our efforts to control the depletion of the ozone layer, among other environmental problems, we face a greater challenge in doing so in a pandemic in which all of us are relevant actors. Our experience with limiting Ebola and SARS is relevant, but they were contained before they spread globally.

The COVID-19 crisis reveals the need to reconceptualize public international law to broaden its scope, to be more inclusive with regard to relevant actors beyond States, and to encompass other forms of legal instruments and commitments other than binding agreements. The refusal or hesitancy of certain States to collaborate only accelerates the need to recognize our shared values and to engage all actors in pursuing them to prevent and control the pandemic, a global and local public good, and to enlist private goods for the public interest.

Dealing with COVID-19 in a kaleidoscopic world is difficult. Just as governments and diverse groups can press for addressing social justice issues in the context of the pandemic, other groups can work transnationally to ignore these issues. In the kaleidoscopic world, it has become easier to undermine respect for the rule of law and to promote the flouting of it. Groups and even individuals can work transnationally to undermine trust in scientific opinion and effective responses in controlling the pandemic. To counter these dangers and avoid chaos, shared norms among governments and the multiple actors are essential. While legal instruments and actions will differ, the many actors must work toward the common public good. In the end, this is the potential force of international law.

CHAPTER 15

How Learned Are Our Lessons?

Mónica Pinto

... the Constitution is not a set of rules to maximize individual welfare on some global scale. Rather, it is a statement about how a society wishes to organize itself ...[1]

∴

On 19 March 2020, the World Health Organization (WHO) declared that the coronavirus disease 19 (COVID-19) had become a pandemic.

As in the movies, the cacophony started muting, the usual movements slowed down progressively and, finally, stopped. No human voices, no engine noises, silence. The world came to a lockdown that was strictly enforced for 60/ 75 days. Borders and skies were closed. For a short while, conflicts, especially armed conflicts, were put between brackets. Words like confinement, social distancing, essential and non-essential sectors, among others, invaded our everyday lives.

1 The World Is at War against the COVID-19

The situation was so unprecedented that world leaders lacked a specific language to deal with it. Some of them looked at what they considered to be the most difficult scenario. Suddenly, we were at war.

President Donald Trump of the United States identified himself as a wartime president. President Emmanuel Macron announced that France was at a sanitary war. Also, Prime Minister Boris Johnson of the United Kingdom invoked wartime language in the fight against coronavirus. In his first appearance

---

1 Owen Fiss, "The Immigrant as a Pariah" in *A Community of Equals* (New Democracy Forum, 1999) 17

during the pandemic, President Daniel Ortega of Nicaragua explained that he had been waging the battle against the COVID-19.

The (natural) reaction was to put in place wartime measures. Even curfew was declared in many countries or in given cities. Ban on travel to and from certain countries and then, shutdown on flights and road transportation followed.

No more personal decisions. Family and social meetings were forbidden because of the risk of infection. Same regarding your elders, your sons and daughters, grandchildren, best friends. No medical appointments except for COVID-19 reasons. Stay at your place, do not socialize.

2   Authoritarian Approaches to Deal with the Pandemic

The reactions to the pandemic have been more or less alike all over the world, with no great differences regarding the level of development or the democratic tradition of the community.

Fear permeated national societies and the field was open for governments to take measures to suspend basic rights, sometimes in the light of the requirements put forward in constitutions and human rights treaties, and others, avoiding them.

The general perception is that more rights than those strictly needed have been put between brackets in many societies, and lockdown measures have been extended not necessarily on the grounds of the pandemic.

In some countries, the confinement reached the state and it resulted in no legislative activity, no judicial work, only the executive branch continued operating and concentrating the highest level of power ever in democratic regimes. Believe it or not, judicial activity was not considered an essential sector by some governments.

The crisis became all powerful and omnipresent. It could provide support to any decision. Personal freedom and human rights looked like the obstacles that the liberal society advanced against the measures that the crisis imposed.

Authoritarian approaches have been prevalent. They conveyed the message that democracy, liberal democracy, deliberative democracy, cannot cope with the situation. Confinement, an interim measure which would help governments to refurnish their health facilities and to stop the circulation of the disease, was imposed as if it were a medical treatment.

Soon after the WHO proclamation, in some places, the pandemic and the confinement became two different, even unrelated, matters. The first burst one day and the world started a frenetic race to control it; the latter was imposed by local rulers initially on the grounds of the pandemic but then was extended on unclear grounds.

When human rights permeated the legal order and also medical sciences, some approaches changed. The pattern became the full capacity both in law and in health terms. Nowadays, the rule is that all human beings, with or without disabilities, should have full enjoyment of all human rights on an equal basis. Accordingly, for instance, measures of compulsory hospitalization in asylums are the exception to the rule, an exception that has to be supported on the grounds that there is no other less intrusive measure available for the case and able to produce analogous results.

The impact of human rights on medical treatments was measured in democratic terms. In that line, the rule of the full capacity of all human beings came hand in hand with the concept of informed consent, which imposes on medical professionals the duty to refrain from exercising paternalistic control and instead provides patients with the information necessary for them to decide which course of action to adopt.

All these achievements have been neutralized by the authoritarian decisions adopted during the pandemic. Initially, only epidemiological reasons supported decisions by public authorities. However, science driven decisions do not necessarily meet human rights criteria. Soon these decisions had to be nuanced in light of other considerations, including those emerging from the field of mental health.

Discrimination, anti-Semitism, racism, which had been decently managed, if not completely superseded long ago, found room in everyday life. As an example, a relatively good quality of life had turned racism invisible in the American landscape but it flourished with the murder of George Floyds. Fortunately, the situation also made room to the Black Live Matter movement.

Different kinds of violence – social violence, gender violence, violence against children, LGBTIQ+, indigenous peoples – increased all over the world. Victims of violence have been confined together with their aggressors. Home had become a cage. Conventional wisdom as well as empirical evidence revealed that the great majority of domestic violence victims are aggressed by their relatives or persons of their inner circle. However, that was ignored when deciding the scope and the extent of confinement measures in a great number of places.

The pandemic highlighted, once again, the role of women as unpaid care workers. Gender approaches have been generally absent in the pandemic, producing lots of sensitive situations that could have been avoided had women participated in the decision-making process. We are not part of the problem but part of the solution.

These emergency situations scarcely met the requirements set forth in international human rights treaties and only a bunch of States fulfilled the information duty provided for in such treaties.

3   Equality as the First Victim of the Pandemic

The uniqueness of the situation is unprecedented. Never before had the world been in pause as it was during the COVID-19 pandemic.

Even when some may still think that there is no such a thing as globalization, narratives challenging globalization were faced with the resounding evidence of its existence because of COVID-19.

This is the first time ever that a phenomenon has taken place all over the world, almost at the same time, in every single country. COVID-19 reached poor and rich countries, little and big States, powerful and powerless communities. It also reached the superpower and the head of its government and also those coming next in line.

Chilean President Ricardo Lagos used to say that globalization means a qualitative change regarding the way in which our countries establish their ties with the international life.[2] The debate is not whether there is globalization but instead how globalization may help to reduce poverty and asymmetries.

Equality, which is always struggling to have its existence acknowledged, was the first victim of this pandemic. This global situation stresses the inequalities among countries and among people. COVID-19 affects the rich and the poor, but the rich can survive better than the poor.

The legal and political order in force after the Second World War made a pledge regarding *the equal rights of men and women and of nations large and small* and the United Nations supported *the principle of the sovereign equality of all its members.*

Equality is, perhaps, the most revolutionary feature of the notion of human rights, one of the most important inventions of our civilization.[3] Even when nothing is more diverse than two human beings, we are all equal as rights-holders, because of a legal decision. That being said, it is not that (liberal notion of) equality that I am targeting here but a structural equality, one that incorporates historical and social data, which acknowledges the subjugation and systematic exclusion that affects wide sectors of society, including women.

---

2   Ricardo Lagos Escobar, 'Ética y Globalización' (1999–2000) Revista Jurídica de Buenos Aires 183, 184.
3   Carlos Santiago Nino, *Ética y Derechos Humanos* (2 edn, Astrea 1989) 1.

Structural equality has been a pending issue in many parts of the world, including the Latin American and Caribbean region. The pandemic is having tremendous impact on equality. The countries showing high levels of structural inequality should seriously consider dealing with it before it becomes irretrievable.

It is not an arithmetic rule but, generally, structural inequality coexists with structural poverty. A poverty that is much more than an insufficient quantity of resources to get a basic basket of goods and services to be able to live with dignity. It is not a purely economic question. Structural poverty prevents from reaching human development and it entails vulnerability and social exclusion. Poverty requires a human rights approach, an approach acknowledging that the poor are human beings, rights-holders on an equal footing with the rest of the society.

People in vulnerable situations, usually living under the threshold of poverty, now have less hope than before the crisis. The informal economy where they find a way of earning a life is more fragile. Those living on the edge between poverty and marginality have become extremely poor and have to make their lives as they can when they can. The tragedy of these people is that they are caught between a rock and a hard place because if they are confined, they do not get money and they die of hunger but if they are not, they die from COVID-19.

Migrants and refugees have been abandoned to their fate in highly developed countries of the world. Those traditionally in vulnerable situation, like indigenous peoples and/or LGBTIQ+, have a harder life now.

Only recently the WHO acknowledged how confinement impacts on poverty. States should stop turning a blind eye to poverty. Redress is needed before the next pandemic.

4 A Global Health Problem Looking for a Universal Approach

The United Nations General Assembly Resolution 74/270 of 3 April 2020 considered that the COVID-19 pandemic poses a threat to human health, safety, and well-being. Maybe this statement is too narrow given the wide array of issues that the pandemic affects.

In any case, situations like the present one challenge a government's ability to fulfil its obligations of protection in the field of public health while ensuring respect for human rights under its jurisdiction.

The pandemic revealed the weakness of health plans and medical facilities all over the world. Europe, which used to have a more than reasonable public health policy, could not afford the number of patients and their treatments. The US President Trump decided to rebrand the Affordable Care Act, also known as Obamacare, and issued an Executive Order on An America-First Healthcare Plan without getting into details and having as backdrop the incredibly high number of casualties of the COVID-19 in that country. Latin America had to put in place a decent scheme to face the crisis, and the same problems arise in Africa, perhaps with more difficulties, and Asia.

The focal point is the World Health Organization, a United Nations specialized agency, a technocratic organization with the capacity to produce and enforce international health regulations. It manages the right to health but also has to develop the capacity of predicting gaps in the rules and to ensure that they are duly filled. At the same time, it is not expected to be reckless in its statements. It is said that the WHO was disclosing the public health emergency in a timely manner and then, the pandemic. It acted on the grounds of serious scientific knowledge. As Jan Klabbers put it in a recent article, "the WHO is engaged in a host of non-binding highly authoritative forms of exercising public authority".[4]

The reactions to the WHO's statements are not attributable to the organization but to the States, among which those that still today challenge the idea of health care as a public policy.

5   Is the Pandemic a Turning Point for International Law?

The COVID-19 crisis is more global than the Second World War but it has not reached the same global consequences. It does not look as though it is a turning point in the framework of international relations.

International law will stay there, States will remain as the main actors in this field and Article 38 of the Statute of the International Court of Justice will not be rewritten because of this crisis.

As evidence that there have been no major changes, President Nicolás Maduro of Venezuela reacted to the declaration of the pandemic saying that COVID-19 is a disease of wealthy people created by the US; in turn, in the US, it was said that it was created in a Chinese laboratory, and vice-versa. No changes.

That being said, it does not mean that everything will be as it used to be. The world will have to deal with the 60 million people pushed to poverty because

---

4   Jan Klabbers, 'The Second Most Difficult Job in the World. Reflections on COVID-19' (2020) 11(2) Journal of International Humanitarian Legal Studies 270.

of the pandemic and the shutdown of advanced economies, as warned by the World Bank.[5]

This pandemic showed its global nature and that we need a global exit. We cannot get out of this individually. Perhaps some States will, but surely not the great majority. Multilateralism and international co-operation are two of the traditional avenues that are available to enhance the quality of global solutions. A more robust World Health Organization is needed. Its prevention programs and thresholds should be strengthened.

Relying on the scientific information managed by WHO, we should be prepared to face public health emergencies of international concern more frequently in the future. The pandemic revealed itself as a negative global common. As it happens with other global commons, we need international co-operation to deal with them. All have to be onboard. A universal health coverage is needed.

To be both effective and sustainable, the policy responses adopted need to include public agencies and the private sector as main actors of the prevention. A prevention that means universal access to vaccines and medical treatment but also to tap water and sewerage.

In the 1970s, the instruments of the New International Economic Order called upon developed States to act in solidarity with those in development of the Third World. The approach was not successful. However, at the end of the 1990s, when the hole in the ozone layer was an irreversible fact, developed and developing States found the way to establish a partnership which made room for shared but differentiated responsibilities. All had to be onboard. Same here.

As lessons learned from this ongoing crisis, both the rule of law and a human rights approach should lead to the wisest decisions. As in other matters, like artificial intelligence,[6] here too States have the duty to respect our human rights and to avoid arbitrary interference in their exercise. Human rights perform as hermeneutic tools that help in decision-making process. The *pro persona principle* should prevail when determining the proper restriction to our rights that is necessary in a democratic society.

As stated earlier in this paper, science driven decisions do not necessarily meet human rights criteria. Keeping people in confinement may be a tool to prevent diseases but at the same time it has serious implications in the

---

5 Jonathan Wheatley, 'Virus will push up to 60m into extreme poverty, World Bank warns' (*Financial Times*, 19 May 2020) <https://www.ft.com/content/85882871-1b61-49e2-b170 -cc3f159b8f88> accessed 20 April 2021.

6 Daragh Murray, 'Using Human Rights Law to Inform States' Decisions to Deploy AI' (2020) 114 AJIL Unbound 158.

development of other human capacities and skills as well as in other fields of activities.

I am aware that the argument cuts both ways. Let's consider climate change. We should pay attention to what science and scientists have to tell us so as to prevent more degradation. But in order to do so, we have to engage in a serious conversation on the search for appropriate balances. A democratic debate on the goals that are pursued, the scope of the eventual intervention and the means used to that end is necessary.

The international law agenda has to include these conversations. We are, indeed, facing complex and busy times.

CHAPTER 16

Hobbes and the Plague Doctors

Benedict Kingsbury

Kia whakatōmuri te haere whakamua
(Walk backwards into the future with eyes on our past)
Whakataukī (traditional Māori precept)

⁝

Many scholars of political power and public law contributing to this volume, alike with much of the world's population, have been driven in the 2020s epidemics to turn our minds to medicine, government and justice in ways we have not turned them previously. For myself – and I suspect for numerous academics – the starkest questions usually came prefaced in my mind with 'why had I not done enough to have thought more about this before?' Power and law in these kinds of troubled times were infused with, and bound into, the great issues of virus justice and vaccine justice with which the world and every kind of society is required daily to grapple. More abstractly, many of the initial questions for me were located in the large puzzle of how to place life-essential medical-scientific knowledge and associated technologies into these politico-social spaces and their governance. My own work recently has been on physical and digital infrastructures and the workers within and around them, and on the legal and infrastructural governance of data-information-knowledge-wisdom-justice.

In nearly every society, the existential importance of the visible and non-visible work of medical professionals as well as many other workers and caregivers on the front line in infectious disease epidemics was at the forefront in coping with COVID-19. Considerable notice and thought has long been given to this work by the people doing it, of course, and in academic terms it is also prominent in feminist and STS traditions, as well as in rich historico-cultural studies of many kinds, including specific histories of professions. Much of the deep thought about this outside Euro-Atlantic political theory has barely been absorbed inside it. In this little note, though, I write just about asking what is said (and not said) on medics in epidemic disease times within the traditional (male) power-focused Euro-Classical political theory canon – Thucydides, Hobbes, Foucault and the rest.

A place to start is the well-known frontispiece etched for Thomas Hobbes' *Leviathan* of 1651. A nearly-empty walled city is drawn immediately under the imposing (Stuart king-like) Leviathan – the humans of all sorts, the body politic which had hitherto been the multitude, are drawn within the torso and arms of the sovereign. But the city is not quite empty of human beings. A few soldiers move purposefully about in the military quarter of the town. The only other humans in the city, standing watchfully in the lower center, are two plague doctors, readily identifiable by the long-beaked masks (in which were placed anti-miasmic herbs and spices), which had become a prominent symbol of their office in the preceding decades.[1] The doctors (like the soldiers) work under the oversight of the sovereign, but they stand special and apart from the multitude, and their office is highly distinctive.

Why are the plague doctors depicted there? The expert Hobbes scholars have much insight on this which I do not, but the exegetical answer is not going to be easily reached. This is Hobbes' most notable reference to plague doctors. It is pictorial rather than textual; and not directly by his own hand, for Hobbes certainly did not draw the frontispiece although he seems to have had appreciable influence on it. In any case I take this as a stimulus to speculate in my own thoughts, without any exegetical ambition as to Hobbes'.

War and plague, whether arriving from outside or spreading internally, are the two most fundamental threats, and the responsibility of the Leviathan is to ensure security against them. The depiction of those two sets of security personnel might be nothing more than a way to convey this point. Or possibly the singularity arises from some of the professional plague doctors, like some professional soldiers, being itinerant specialists, for hire at high prices when needed, and gone again when not. A third possibility, though, is that the

---

1   The major work on this is Francesca Falk, 'Hobbes' *Leviathan* und die aus dem Blick gefallenen Schnabelmasken', (2011) 39 Leviathan 247, and the corresponding chapter in her doctoral thesis publication. The portion of the printed 1651 frontispiece showing the city, the rural area, and above these the sovereign is very clear in an image, to which colour was added by Elaine Scarry: 'Engraved title page of Hobbes's Leviathan (1651) by Abraham Bosse' (PBase) <https://pbase.com/hobbes/image/151739118> accessed 19 April 2021. An original drawing inspired by the frontispiece and with the two plague doctors strikingly evident, but with the sovereign's torso now comprised of outward- gazing faces instead of inward-turned and upward-gazing human bodies, was presented to Charles II: 'Drawing of frontispiece of Leviathan, 1651' (PBase) <pbase.com/hobbes/image/151739929> accessed 19 April 2021. An overview of Western infectious disease iconography is Christine M. Boeckl, *Images of plague and pestilence: iconography and iconology* (Truman State University Press, 2000).

specialist knowledge and expertise of the plague doctor, believed not to be adequately substitutable by anything else in the sovereign's armory of deployable power, has a status and standing which is not simply subsumed into the Leviathan. In some way, the itinerant plague doctors might be emblematic of transnational knowledge circulation and located in the complex history of science-experts (and medical experts) in relation to formalized ruling power.

Thucydides' report from his personal experience as a sufferer of the Athens epidemic disease of 430 BCE – whether it was typhus, typhoid fever, Ebola, or something else is not presently known – bleakly notes the struggles of the medics on the front line: 'For at first neither were the physicians able to cure it, through ignorance of what it was, but died fastest themselves, as being the men that most approached the sick; nor any other art of man availed whatsoever.'[2] This note leads into Thucydides' extensive detailing of the symptoms and the societal spread and incidence of the disease, expressly provided as a record to help later people recognize the disease if they encounter it. Thucydides says explicitly that he is not qualified to comment in the contemporary contentions about the disease's etiology. He strives to record his observations with care and precision, much as case reports are written in more modern medical science. Yet when he moves on to offer an account of the aggregate social-legal behavior in Athens during the epidemic, he seems more to make a point than to provide a similar level of observational accuracy in his reportage. He emphasizes the prevalence of wanton human behavior and the degradation or even disintegration of law, virtue and honor.[3] In the classic-realist tradition of thought, Thucydides attests that the high risks of imminent death through fatal

---

2　Thucydides, *The History of the Peloponnesian War* (Thomas Hobbes tr, Bohn 1629) para 47. An edition of Hobbes' translation of Thucydides appears in William Molesworth (ed), *The English Works of Thomas Hobbes of Malmesbury; Now First Collected and Edited by Sir William Molesworth, Bart.* (Bohn 1839–45) 11 vols. Vol. 8, <https://oll.libertyfund.org/titles/771> accessed 19 April 2021. Richard Crawley's 19th century translation put it thus: 'Neither were the physicians at first of any service, ignorant as they were of the proper way to treat it, but they died themselves the most thickly, as they visited the sick most often; nor did any human art succeed any better.' Thucydides, *The History of the Peloponnesian War* (Richard Crawley tr, The Internet Classics Archive, 1994–2009) <http://classics.mit.edu/Thucydides/pelopwar.2.second.html> accessed 19 April 2021.

3　Thucydides, *The History of the Peloponnesian War* (Thomas Hobbes tr, Bohn 1629) para 53. In Hobbes' English translation of Thucydides' Greek: 'Neither the fear of the gods, nor laws of men, awed any man: not the former, because they concluded it was alike to worship or not worship, from seeing that alike they all perished: nor the latter, because no man expected that lives would last till he received punishment of his crimes by judgment. But they thought, there was now over their heads some far greater judgment decreed against them; before which fell, they thought to enjoy some little part of their lives.'

infection during virulent plague, like the risks posed by intrigue of opportunists and opponents in the civil anarchy (*stasis*) of Corcyra, spur people to abandon established institutions and social norms in sufficient numbers that anomie appears and even itself becomes normative, begetting antinomianism.[4]

Evidence to confirm or contest Thucydides' report of Athenian anomie on such a scale in 430 BCE does not yet appear to have been found. In practice in other cases, however, it does not seem that well-ordered societies collapse into nomic disintegration in the face of even the more fearsomely virulent and non-discriminating diseases;[5] although fear of contagious risks posed by some group (usually the poor or a minority) is often used to call forth ferocious controls.

To take the example of Northern Italy, from the Black Death onward there was consolidated an organized administrative structure and practice for bubonic plague response in particular, measures that were also tried in England in plague outbreaks of 1631 and 1665.

Larger towns had standing health magistracies with very strong powers to act in plague emergencies (although they had difficulties exercising these against members of religious orders or their abodes). Sealing plague-suspected houses from the outside, closing the city to ingress and egress, shutting down some industries (such as silk production which produced bad aromas and was suspected of contributing to plague miasmas), compulsory 'hospitalization' (in lazarettos or pesthouses), quarantine, and perfuming (much later transformed into disinfecting) were well established responses. Quite substantial public relief was also provided by these magistracies (usually with charitable funds) to the repressed poor, including food, changes of clothing and bedding, and provision for newly-orphaned babies. Large cadres of essential services workers were enlisted, and special quite lucrative contracts were made with plague doctors.[6] The rich were generally treated more favorably than the poor, but overall few were happy about the measures. (There do not seem to have been for the plague epidemics, many equivalents of what British politician Stanley Baldwin reportedly called many of his fellow MPs after 1918: 'hard-faced men

---

4   Clifford Orwin, 'Stasis and Plague: Thucydides on the Dissolution of Society' (1988) 50 Journal of Politics 831.

5   Paul Slack, *The Impact of Plague in Tudor and Stuart England* (OUP 1990) 4 and passim. Foucault also acknowledged this, treating this anomie as literary rather than sociological description.

6   A detailed study of one such contract is in Carlo M Cipolla, 'A Plague Doctor' in Harry Miskimin, David Herlihy, and A.L. Udovitch (eds), *The Medieval City* (Yale University Press 1977) 65.

who looked as if they had done well out of the war.') Distilling his observations from extensive study of archives in Italy, Carlo Cipolla noted that the health ordinances were:

> sources of great annoyance and severe privation and thus met with strong opposition. The segregation of entire families, the separation of kindred in the horror of pesthouses, the closing of markets and trade, the consequent rise of unemployment, the burning of furnishings and goods, the prohibition of religious assemblies, the requisitioning of monasteries for use as hospitals – all these and similar measures provoked reactions which often acquired violent tones. Life was not easy for the health officers of the time. They fought a desperate battle against a formidable and yet invisible enemy. Paradoxically, their action made them highly unpopular among the people whom they were trying to protect.[7]

Thomas Hobbes (who was Thucydides' first English translator) regarded the provision of capacity to deal with plague (here a general term not limited to bubonic plague) and war (civil or external) as important drivers for sovereign power – including lawmaking. The Leviathan combats the disintegration described by Thucydides, or enables an exit path in its aftermath, through consolidation of the multitude into a sovereign body politic and construction of a fearsome authority to secure and maintain order.[8]

The simulacrum of perfected surveillance and control in the design of repressive measures against disease in the 17th century, with everyone locked in houses and intendents moving through the streets insisting on seeing everyone at windows and recording every detail, became one of Michel Foucault's major cases of power through discipline and knowledge: 'the penetration of regulation into even the smallest details of everyday life through the mediation of the complete hierarchy that assured the capillary functioning of power; not masks that were put on and taken off, but the assignment to each individual of his "true" name, his "true" place, his "true" body, his "true" disease. The plague as a form, at once real and imaginary, of disorder had as its medical and political correlative discipline.'[9]

---

7   Carlo M. Cipolla, *Fighting the plague in seventeenth-century Italy* (University of Wisconsin Press 1981) 5–6. (At p 10 is reproduced a printed drawing from 1661 of the waxed black robe and mask then widely known as plague doctors' attire.)

8   Cf Thomas Poole, 'Leviathan in Lockdown' (*London Review of Books*, 1 May 2020) <https://lrb.co.uk/blog/2020/may/leviathan-in-lockdown> accessed 19 April 2021.

9   Michel Foucault, *Discipline & Punish: The Birth of the Prison* (A. Sheridan tr, Vintage Books 1995) 195–228.

In both the Hobbesian and the Foucauldian accounts, fearsome state power is a central focus, and the means of its exercise closely specified. It is not difficult to see Hobbes as a student of biopolitical power *avant la lettre* (as Agamben does), if the foregrounding of relations between the political-state and the medical in the Leviathan frontispiece is taken as the outward symbol of an aspect of Hobbes' thought and its later reception. But can we see something different – inspirational even – in that same image?

The state's police powers predominate in the most usual readings of the literature of *salus populi* and biopolitics. But the 'plague doctors' and their roles nonetheless seem to have – must have – a special character. Perhaps reflection on what this place is, or how it should be deepened and cherished, might add something for long-term planning and structures. Or at least, such reflections might differ from the escapism of the 'emergency imaginary' or of a counterbucolic re-rendering of 'As You Like It' pastoralism, the real origins of which are so readily forgotten again when the sleepwalker awakes, 'normalcy' returns, and the generations change. Science- knowledge and science-roles not worked into institutions and deliberated publicly do not get transmitted between generations and across communities, and hence tend to peter out or be displaced, as the agnatologists remind us.

A feature of medical practice is that even when to some extent co-opted into disciplinary power or made into a tactic of government through laws and bureaucracy, it still retains an aura and power of separate expertise and a degree of institutionalization. There is a capacity in a massive crisis such as a human health epidemic, for medicine and its practitioners to transcend cruder aspects of governmentality and to stand, courageously, against both the disease and misguided or delinquent governmental or transnationalized power. This potential is actualized in critical care, in legions of medical personnel and transporters and mortuary personnel, in whistleblowing, in epidemiologists speaking out fearlessly even if it is risky to do so. Transposing this professional identity into the bureaucratics of a multi-cultural inter-governmental organization such as the WHO, is a hard project and a thankless one, but worth doing and re-doing. Transposing that same professional ethos into written law such as the International Health Regulations seems to have been beyond the possible in the early 2000s and may still be now. At many moments in the near and distant past, in places and cultures and local forms of practice all over the world, one lawyer or many have found ways to stand up and act despite or without fear, as Hobbes' Frontispiece has the plague doctors stand. The more the world seems to be that of Hobbes and Foucault writ even larger, the more the role and inspiration of the plague doctors beckons the rest of us.

CHAPTER 17

The COVID-19 Crisis, Indigenous Peoples, and International Law

A Vulnerability Perspective

Malgosia Fitzmaurice

> Contemplating our shared vulnerability it becomes apparent that human beings need each other, and that we must structure our institutions in response to this fundamental human reality.[1]

∴

Research undertaken globally in the wake of the COVID-19 pandemic indicates that resilience gaps that are already the status quo in respect of indigenous peoples are situating numerous communities at imminent risk of disaster. This short essay presents a brief risk profile analysis carried out by reference to Martha Fineman's theory of vulnerability. Extensive vulnerability manifestations are identified according to different sets of relationships, featuring significant differential barriers for access to goods and services, which place indigenous peoples in a situation of alarming exposure to the impacts of COVID-19. This author argues that awareness of these relationships and obstacles can and should guide State responses, and highlight the role of law as a necessary tool for enabling and maintaining much needed, appropriately targeted resilience work.

One of the principal callings of international law is the establishment of frameworks for State conduct as pathways through which to address shared challenges. Yet, most scholarship involving the transcendent crises of our time, from human rights to the erosion of the Earth's natural resources and environment, illuminates how the solidarity demands placed on States by such crises often expose the limitations of international law. The current COVID-19

---

1 Martha Fineman, 'The Vulnerable Subject: Anchoring Equality in the Human Condition' (2008) 20(1) Yale Journal of Law and Feminism 1, 12.

pandemic evidences these limitations once more, both in respect of the search for effective international responsibility, and in meeting the urgent, broader, more complex protection and support needs of vulnerable populations. Nevertheless, it is difficult to imagine the articulation of successful international responses to stem the crisis without apposite international frameworks. In this paper, appropriate State responses for indigenous peoples are explored , as they face the COVID-19 pandemic in a marked position of comparative disadvantage, with exposure to the disease situating them in danger of increased mortality.[2]

COVID-19 is having a particularly nefarious impact in regions predominantly inhabited by indigenous populations where health systems were already fragile, and may now have collapsed leaving vulnerable groups in an unprecedented state of exposure and risk. Diverse but often compounding factors are relevant in driving this undesirable outcome for many indigenous communities. Biological characteristics can play a part,[3] but they are not always the main factor, with different cultural, political, and socio-economic causes also driving this alarming trend. As this author has previously argued, the personal and socio-economic characteristics of many human communities, including indigenous groups, merit the application of Martha Fineman's theory of vulnerability.[4] In Fineman's own words: 'The theory is based on a descriptive account of the human condition as one of universal and continuous vulnerability'. She adds further that: 'The potential normative implications of the theory are found in the assertion that State policy and law should be responsive to human vulnerability. However, the call for a responsive State does not dictate the form responses should take, only that they reflect the reality of human vulnerability'.[5] The key implication of the theory is that formal equality, whilst at times an appropriate response, as in the case of for example voting rights, is in many other aspects of life not achievable as an aspirational objective, and may even result in manifest unfairness in cases where individuals are differently situated across diverse societal contexts.

---

2 Tamara Power and others, 'COVID-19 and Indigenous Peoples; An imperative for action' (2020) 29 Journal of Clinical Nursing 2737.

3 Tony Kirby, 'Evidence mounts on the disproportionate effect of COVID-19 on ethnic minorities' (2020) 8(6) Lancet Respiratory Medicine 547.

4 See Martha Fineman, 'Vulnerability and Inevitable Inequality' (2017) 4(3) Oslo Law Review 133.

5 ibid 133.

1   Fineman's Vulnerability and Its Implications

From Fineman's perspective, vulnerability is a constant for all peoples, but one that has different manifestations across society resulting in varying degrees of social dependency across the population spectrum. Fineman illustrates the theory in the context of the family, where gender inequality has historically been a feature, relying on the example of reform efforts premised on formal equality in spite of less than equal outcomes. Fineman suggests that institutional responsibility may imply unequal treatment in favour of persons who are either inevitably dependent (such as children, the elderly or those with a severe disability), or those whose vulnerability is not inevitable, but who are less resilient due to their position and role in society (for example, carers or socially excluded or structurally subordinated groups). Hence, vulnerability responsive laws and policies are intended to account and compensate for unequal needs across different social contexts.[6]

Under the vulnerability lens, resilience is thus not innate to the human being, but rather conferred by inclusion in the social and institutional relationships, many of which will be underpinned by public institutions, and defined and maintained by law. This approach has the effect of relieving the onus that the liberal focus places on individuals to transcend the specific vulnerability contexts in which they are situated. Physical, social, cultural, and material wellbeing and development are not innate to the human being, but dependent on inclusion and maintenance within the social, economic, and institutional relationships that promote resilience. Social identities that may or may not reflect the individual characteristics of people may promote inclusion or exclusion from such networks, processes, and relationships. Some of those social identities may change through life (e.g. infant, adult, elderly) but others are stable and can influence an individual's options throughout his or her lifetime. The State, through its public organs and agencies, has the responsibility of modulating and redefining such relationships for the facilitation of resilience, taking care that they do not perpetuate egregious inequality.

This approach has considerable implications for the development and reform of law and policy, including in the international context. As Fineman explains: '[t]he abstract and inevitably contested legal principles often referred to in human rights literature, such as equality, liberty, and dignity, are not the measure for this inquiry, however'. Nevertheless, individuals and

---

6   Fineman (n 4) 138–141.

their characteristics, both in respect of permanent vulnerability features as well as life stages, are as relevant to the analysis as the set of social institutions and relationships to which they pertain. Particularly important is the need to identify the differential relationships that characterize indigenous communities. Sets include institutions and relationships that either favour or impede sanitation, education, employment, health, connectivity – to name a few. The first task of vulnerability informed policy is monitoring these institutions and relationships so that the relevant State organs can perceive situations of vulnerability, and respond to them in order to promote resilience. According to Fineman, such resilience is strengthened *via* access to categories of goods and services, as follows: Human capital goods such as education and training, and social resources such as family, community including ethnicity, and political networks. Fundamental, of course, are physical goods, such as food, sanitation, savings, housing, and transport. Environmental resources refer to the lived environment and its services and threats, whereas existential resources refer to beliefs, including religion but also culture, allowing an understanding of the world and life events. These are the resilience categories through which the State can assess and address the vulnerability of fragile human communities.

2   Facilitating Opportunities for Resilience

, I will commence my analysis with an enquiry on access by indigenous communities to the institutions or processes whereby the allocation of resources by the State takes place in order to outline a broad vulnerability pathway. The analysis intends to assist in the definition of a strategy able to alleviate the vulnerability status of indigenous communities in the specific context of the pandemic. The point of departure is to identify whether the structural features of exclusion and deprivation that affect indigenous communities relate to any of the above categories.

Now the physical goods and services category will be addressed. Abundant evidence indicates that, throughout the world, many indigenous populations have been and continue to be excluded, remaining chronically disengaged from the provision of basic public services, such as access to clean water and other necessary infrastructure. Women, children, and people living with disabilities suffer particularly grievously from the effects of such marginalisation. The impact of the pandemic means that these groups are likely to be facing even more precarity, and be disproportionally affected by severe risks. The consequences of the pandemic are likely to exacerbate already significant levels of insecurity in matters of sustenance and health.[7] Elevated rates of transmission are also due to the conditions of poverty in which many of these communities are forced to live. Poor housing quality and lack of sanitation, crowding, and precarious infrastructures result in a diminished capacity for adaptability when confronted with the social and economic restrictions that are being adopted as mitigating responses to COVID-19.

t I will address now human goods category, which is closely connected to the existential sphere in a significant way, as information and cultural acumen enables individuals to process and understand the significance of events, and their implications for themselves and their families and communities. Communication limitations and ensuing exclusion thus have the potential to unfairly place entire peoples in situations that limit or prevent timely responses against critical events, such as the onset of a pandemic. Cultural difference and marginalisation play a significant part in the vulnerability of indigenous groups, and communication strategies can and often do fail to be incorporated into community systems. This can result in reduced opportunities for understanding and implementing adequate responses, potentially with disastrous consequences. The lack of visibility of some extremely marginalized groups can also be a factor in causing and/or compounding those barriers, resulting in increased exposure and ultimate defenselessness against COVID-19. These issues are not unique to particular geographic areas, and similar trends have been observed across different continents.[8]

Next, I turn to the overview of the category of environmental goods and services. Many indigenous communities live in rural areas, relying on the harvesting of wild species of plants and animals for nutrition as well as medicine. This context is also proving to be a risk factor, particularly at a time when the pandemic is accentuating the impact of climate change on food productivity, compounding pressures on traditional custody chains, and eroding already fragile life and community supporting practices and structures.[9] In this regard,

---

7 'COVID-19 and the world of work: A focus on indigenous and tribal peoples' (International Labour Organisation 2020) <https://www.ilo.org/wcmsp5/groups/public/ – -dgreports/ – -dcomm/documents/publication/wcms_746893.pdf> accessed 25 September 2020.

8 See, for example, Melissa McLeod and others, 'COVID-19: we must not forget about indigenous health and equity' (2020) 44(4) Australian and New Zealand Journal of Public Health 253; Sergio Meneses-Navarro and others, 'The Challenges facing indigenous communities in Latin America as they confront the COVID-19 pandemic' (2020) 19 International Journal for Equity in Health 63; Lucas Ferrante and Philip Fearnside, 'Protect Indigenous peoples from COVID-19' (2020) 368 (6488) Science Magazine 251.

9 Carol Zavaleta-Cortijo and others, 'Climate change and COVID-19: reinforcing Indigenous food systems' (2020) 4(9) The Lancet E381–382.

the particularly acute situation of crisis that is being experienced by indigenous groups can, at least in part, be traceable to the fragility of the natural environments in which they live, the often stressed and unprotected ecosystems that sustain their livelihoods, and their dependency on the essential services emanating from them.

A pertinent example may be seen in the impact of the coronavirus on small-scale fisheries, including capture, processing and support activities along the production and custody chain, all of which supports the food and work security of numerous subsistence communities globally, including indigenous communities. Despite the emergence of limited governmental, grassroots, and other initiatives to counteract the effect of COVID-19 on small-scale fisheries and fishing communities across the world,[10] high dependency on small-scale fisheries for food and work makes this a high-risk area. Beyond subsistence, the concentration of transactions in a relatively small number of key markets means impacts have the potential to be devastating for communities that depend on such trade, highlighting an acute need for adaptation and resilience mechanisms to provide viable alternatives in the event of closures.[11] To put risks in context with some figures, it is estimated that circa 52 million people are employed in small-scale capture fisheries around the world, with the livelihoods of an even higher number being supported by the provision of services provided on land to the custody chain of small-scale fishery products.[12] In addition, the nature of fisheries production means that product survival is dependent on critical services such as the provision of ice and other cold or freezing facilities that may not be available during the pandemic. Further, some aspects of the custody chain present enhanced risk of contagion, due to exposure to crowded working conditions on board and on land,[13] and other possible contributory factors such as the handling of raw produce.

Of course, environmental contexts extend beyond rural and coastal settings. Other production scenarios also present enhanced vulnerabilities to COVID-19, particularly those in which informal and precarious work is significant. These

10   'Information on COVID-19 and small-scale fisheries' (Food and Agriculture Organization of the United Nations 2020) <http://www.fao.org/3/ca8959en/ca8959en.pdf> accessed 25 September 2020.

11   Christopher Knight and others, 'COVID-19 reveals vulnerability of small-scale fisheries to global market systems' (2020) 4(6) Lancet Planet Health E219.

12   Hilary Smith and Xavier Basurto, 'Defining Small-Scale Fisheries and Examining the Role of Science in Shaping Perceptions of Who and What Counts: A Systematic Review' (2019) 6 Frontiers in Marine Science 236.

13   Nathan Bennet and others, 'The COVID-19 Pandemic, Small-Scale Fisheries and Coastal Fishing Communities' (2020) 48(4) Costal Management 336.

contexts include other food production sectors, as well as urban settings in which domestic work, hospitality, transport, manufacturing, and construction services are abundant. According to the International Labour Organization (ILO), indigenous peoples are significantly over-represented in these work contexts. The ILO's work focusing on indigenous and tribal people indicates that long-standing marginalisation factors can explain their particular exposures to COVID-19. These vulnerabilities cannot be accurately described as exceptional, as indigenous and tribal populations constitute circa 6% of the world population.[14]

The social category will be now analysed, noting that it extends into the political sphere. According to the ILO, public institutions dedicated to the situation of indigenous people and their development and integration into public life, whilst present and in development in some countries, are still absent in many others. The ILO has called for the creation and strengthening of such institutions, in order to combat the systematic exclusion of indigenous groups in many countries.[15] In the context of the pandemic, porosity across these categories is likely to compound vulnerability. For example, the absence of dedicated institutions is likely to make access to information regarding health adaptations more difficult, thus also highlighting a human capital need.

3   The Need for Legal Responses

Understandings of vulnerability and its causes in respect of the plight of indigenous peoples have extended beyond material concerns, to include a historical lack of rights to access resources and opportunities in the context of modern societies.[16] The most comprehensive international legal instrument concerning the protection of indigenous communities is the 2007 Declaration on the Rights of Indigenous Peoples, adopted by the United Nations (UN) General Assembly. This document covers extensive collective rights of indigenous people, as are considered indispensable not only for their survival, but also for their well-being, culture, resources, and self-determination. Yet, indigenous communities still face immense obstacles for the recognition and substantiation of their rights and dignity, which in effect places them in a situation of comparative disadvantage vis-à-vis other communities. In 2019, the UN reported that, although indigenous rights are recognised internationally, more

---

14   ILO (n 7) 6.
15   ibid.
16   Amartya Sen, 'Sobre Conceptos y Medidas de Pobreza' (1992) 42(4) Comercio Exterior 1.

work needs to be done to ensure their implementation, and to facilitate their enforcement, so that they are safeguarded and respected by public and private entities alike, and to prevent abuses.[17] In many countries, this lack of rights has led to pervasive and long-standing inequality, preventing access to services that are essential to human health, basic education and development. As a consequence of these and other compounding causes, indigenous communities suffer from a higher rate of morbidity and mortality in comparison to other groups, and are now facing the effects of the pandemic from a starting point of long-standing deprivation and fragility.[18]

There is little dispute that the collective and individual frailty of physical, economic, and communicative resources, and lower health baseline, places indigenous individuals and communities in an alarming position in the face of the COVID-19 pandemic. There is a need to incorporate this urgency into State responses to the pandemic, to substantiate the rights and meet the needs of indigenous communities across the physical, human, socio-political, environmental, and existential spheres. This approach can inform the focus, dissemination, substantive content, and granularity of policies. This approach is consistent with the urgency, coordination and sharing of resources that is required in a global pandemic, and fully in line with the objectives of the UN Declaration on the Rights of Indigenous Peoples. Nevertheless, given that domestic implementation obstacles have been a persistent factor in impermissible and persistent discrimination, resulting in indigenous exclusion and abandonment, the focus from a legal perspective should specifically be placed on the responsibility of the State, as authority with the furthest reaching powers and duties. Even though many countries have taken measures against poverty, it is noteworthy that they have seldom been successful in addressing the causal conditions that keep indigenous populations in a particularly high vulnerability status. Nevertheless, the States that have implemented the 1989 Indigenous and Tribal Peoples Convention are likely to possess a more solid point of departure, as implementation will result in economic assessments likely to cover some of the categories described above.

---

17   United Nations Department of Economic and Social Affairs, 'State of the World's Indigenous Peoples: Implementing the United Nations Declaration on The Rights of Indigenous Peoples' UN Doc ST/ESA/371 (SOWIP vol IV 2019) 69.

18   United Nations Department of Economic and Social Affairs, 'State of the World's Indigenous Peoples: Indigenous Peoples' Access to Health Services' (SOWIP vol II 2016) 7.

4   Concluding Observations

Through the prism of vulnerability, structural safeguarding needs are revealed as foundations for action, highlighting the necessity of embracing resilience as a guiding objective for the development of international law. COVID-19 has increased the need for urgency in protecting and supporting vulnerable individuals and communities. The vulnerability framework can guide law making efforts and the establishment of policies to effectively provide relief where it is most needed. The plight of indigenous communities, where enduring conditions of exclusion and marginalisation have already been documented, should be prioritised in order to eliminate egregious systemic inequality. Implicit in the brief analysis presented in this paper is a call for swift State responsiveness, and for action to support the facilitation of resilience to these communities. In the short term, prioritisation should be given to the protection of the physical systems that support vital needs, especially food security, and adequate sanitation and health preservation measures. Ensuring the human services necessary for the establishment of effective and vital communication strategies will need to be incorporated into health safeguarding strategies. Towards the medium term, these urgent objectives should be reinforced with mechanisms to protect indigenous and traditional knowledge sources with regard to food availability and medicine effectiveness, availability, and accessibility. Understanding the impact, viability, and protection of extraction methods from already fragile natural environments will be key, as is the implementation of work safety and security policies. Much of this work implies looking beyond immediate emergency actions, and reaching further towards increased collective autonomy, and meaningful inclusion of indigenous peoples in sociographic and political processes.[19] This task cannot be accomplished without a commitment to resilience, and without appropriate legal tools capable of ensuring that it is achieved, and maintained. The shock of COVID-19 has been shattering, and there is a clear need to secure as well as redefine the structures that contain, protect, and support people and communities. This time, work should commence with the most vulnerable.

---

19   For further insight, see Per Axelsson, and Peter Sköld, 'Indigenous Populations and Vulnerability: Characterizing Vulnerability in a Sami Context' (2006) 1(III) Annales de Demographie Historique 115.

CHAPTER 18

COVID-19 and Research in International Law

Fuad Zarbiyev

If you can think about something which is attached to something else without thinking about what it is attached to, then you have what is called a legal mind.[1]

∴

Lawyers have a notorious reputation for being boring at parties. The episode of COVID-19 confirmed that they are also bad intellectual company. The former may not be remediable – while boredom may well be a suitable object of investigation for cognitive neuroscientists, it is hard to explain why we find some people or experiences boring. The latter is more easily amenable to rational discussion and it is what this short essay will concern itself solely with.

Because it was experienced as an unprecedented crisis on several grounds and/or because it generated a considerable amount of free time for professionals of intellectual labour at least in the Global North, COVID-19 has triggered reflections about governance and governmentality, the politics of science, modes of crisis management, the place of humans among the living and many other cross-disciplinary themes.[2] Obviously, a global crisis of such magnitude could not leave international law scholars indifferent – after all, theirs is 'a discipline of crisis', as Hilary Charlesworth put it in a celebrated essay. Most of the scholarship produced by international legal scholars on COVID-19 seems easily vulnerable to Charlesworth's devastating critique given its unproblematic assumption of facts, oversimplification of history and the inflated role assigned to international law. But it is possible to approach that scholarship from a different angle. One of the most remarkable things about international legal scholarship on COVID-19 is that it has largely remained limited to more

---

1   Thomas Reed Powell as quoted in Pierre Schlag, The Enchantment of Reason, Durham and London, Duke University Press, 1998, p. 121.
2   For an interesting collection, see Collectifs, *Tracts de crise: Un virus et des hommes* (Gallimard 2020).

or less imaginative descriptions of relevant legal instruments and possible remedies offered by the latter. Some themes such as the International Health Regulations of the WHO or the power of States to derogate from their obligations under human rights treaties have received extensive attention due to their immediate practical relevance under the circumstances. Others such as the question of whether China could be sued before the International Court of Justice might seem more far-fetched but were squarely within what lawyers are expected to discuss. Common to most of these contributions was the depressing lack of anything that could be dignified with the adjective 'intellectual' if one means by 'intellectual' the quality that furthers one's understanding beyond what should be obvious immediately or in a matter of minutes to any decently trained international legal professional capable of competently reading and interpreting legal materials.

It would be impossible to properly discuss within the limits of this short essay what this state of affairs tells us about research in international law in general, or crisis scholarship in particular. What I want to do instead is to reflect on some conditions that make this reality possible or even unavoidable and conclude with a deliberately provocative proposition.

In a famous passage of *Dawn* dedicated to the perspectival nature of all knowledge, Nietzsche writes that 'We hang within our web, we spiders, and no matter what we capture in it, we can capture nothing whatsoever other than what allows itself to be captured precisely in *our* web'.[3] This point can be reformulated as a general law governing research. In Pierre Schlag's words, this law would state something like this: 'One can only find what the search allows in the sense that the search fails to recognize anything else.'[4] What this means among other things is that what we find as a result of our research is a function of the tools that we use. Just as we have to use appropriate telescopes instead of eyeglasses to see far away galaxies, we cannot be expected to find something that our research – because it is designed the way it is – cannot allow us to find.

If this is so, the question that arises immediately is what is lacking in international law scholars' toolbox: what prevents them from saying something intellectually edifying on COVID-19, something beyond the issue of what some rules mean or whether a lawsuit could be brought against a culprit? Part of the response can be found in what sociologists would call international law scholars' attentional socialization. What is relevant and what deserves attention in a profession is not determined by some natural laws, but by disciplinary training

3 Friedrich Nietzsche, *Dawn: Thoughts on the Presumptions of Morality* (Brittain Smith trs, Stanford University Press 2011) 88.

4 Pierre Schlag, *The Enchantment of Reason* (Duke University Press 1998) 4.

and professional socialization. In other words, international law scholars do not even attempt to say anything intellectually edifying on COVID-19, because they have not been trained and socialized in such a way that could make them *see* something beyond rule description and lawsuits as relevant to their profession.

It is sometimes assumed that this is a perfectly normal situation because law is a vocational trade. Another widespread assumption is that narrow-mindedness, resistance to 'the temptation to stray into other fields' is part of the very definition of law.[5] But these assumptions ignore that law can give rise to numerous professional roles, and that if international law is what a group of professionals do in various professional capacities (academic, judge, arbitrator, litigation counsel, activist, legal advisor to a government or an international organization etc.), it would be misleading to assume that all these profession-als pursue the same projects. What is central for the purposes of this essay is to realize that an academic perspective on law cannot legitimately be the same thing as the perspective of a legal professional engaged in legal practice and acting in that capacity.

What do international legal scholars miss when the toolbox they use to study law is 'nothing but the self-replication of legal practice itself'?[6] The most obvi-ous problem with such a toolbox is that it is unlikely to enable international legal scholars to see that at least sometimes law may be part of the problem rather than the proper remedy: the tools of legal practice are hardly suited to diagnose that same legal practice as a problem. Another intellectual limitation of this approach has to do with the fact that mainstream legal scholars enter a scene that is already completely configured by law: if the tools of legal practice are all they have, those scholars will have a hard time re-imagining law because legal discourse is successful in making legally sanctioned social arrangements look natural or unavoidable. It seems as if, for mainstream legal scholars, law only comes into the picture if and when applied by official institutions. That law and its distributional consequences may have something to do with the state of affairs prevailing in the world at any given point in time even outside law's formal application can hardly cross the mind of the legal scholar whose conceptual tools are the ones provided by legal practice.

'[T]he distinction between the subject studying the law and the legal practice that is the object of study'[7] – or, what ethnomethodologists call the

---

5   Gerald Fitzmaurice, 'The United Nations and the Rule of Law' (1953) 38 Transactions of the
    Grotius Society 135, 142.
6   Paul Kahn, *The Cultural Study of Law. Reconstructing Legal Scholarship* (University of Chicago
    Press 1999) 27.
7   ibid 7.

distinction between topic and resource -is not an option that only some highly theoretically minded academics could find attractive; it is the raison d'être of legal academia in the sense that anyone who does not endorse that distinction has nothing legitimate to do in academia. The possible objection that mainstream international legal academics do something different from legal practitioners misses the mark. When a scholar's objective is to clarify the state of the law, clear up any confusion surrounding it and deliver a verdict on what the international law is on a particular issue, that exercise is no different from what practitioners do simply because it is not performed before an official institution like a court. A scholar may come up with a more nuanced account accompanied with more footnotes, but that would be a difference in degree, not in kind.

There is a social cost that a society pays when an academic does not do the job that they are expected to do and does the job that is expected from members of a different professional occupation. To be fair, there may be a social gain when those professionals and academics join forces to do the same job. But it is hard to believe that such a social gain necessarily justifies the social cost of a reduction in serious academic research worthy of the name. Hence an invitation to international law academics: if for any reason, you don't feel that you can conceive of academic work in any terms other than the terms of legal practice, please leave academia and engage in practice as a full-fledged practitioner. You will then have no impostor syndrome, which you must experience from time to time, and who knows, the academic position you will have made available by leaving academia can be occupied by someone actually willing and able to do the job that the society at large considers – and rightly so – as part of a separate professional occupation.

CHAPTER 19

A Narrative of Crises from the Perspective of a Young Scholar

Iga Joanna Józefiak

> The saddest aspect of life right now is that science gathers knowledge faster than society gathers wisdom.[1]

∵

The last several months have been filled more than ever with frustration, emptiness, and a sense of powerlessness. The notion of crisis is deeply embedded in this world. The surrounding reality tends to be perfectly imperfect, in the sense that the human strive for perfection constantly encounters numerous problems. The coronavirus pandemic, however, is a very unique problem. Unlike the notions of financial crisis, increase of the ocean's acidity, or the hurricane that hit a distant place, concepts that are abstract for many people, the COVID-19 pandemic has a truly global dimension, i.e. perceptible and experienced by each and every person. Without belittling other problems or catastrophes, it is difficult to find such a tangible crisis in recent years as the COVID-19 pandemic. The world has been changing beyond recognition in the past few decades. Even a few years make a huge difference when it comes to the development of knowledge, technology, or population size and shrinking space. Certainly, in the past there occurred health problems on a global scale, but the world was a completely different place; less globalized, less connected, less international. Accordingly, the earlier approach to the crisis is no longer correct or effective. The international community must accept the fact that the principles it followed so far are obsolete and require, using youth slang, "a quick update".

The world today has entered an era of disinformation. Despite the so-called fake news being present for at least several centuries, it is the past few decades

---

1 Isaac Asimov, Isaac Asimov's Book of Science and Nature Quotations, Grove Pr, 1990.

that made it so widespread due to the common and facilitated access to the Internet. The possibilities for acquiring knowledge in developed countries seem to be endless but the opposite may be true for its quality. Virtual freedom of speech should not be confused with spreading false or unverified information. There exists very little regulation of what the media can claim, let alone individuals. There is a complete flexibility in this regard. Today, anyone can write that two plus two equals five, that a cold shower in the morning heals cancer, or that the virus causing COVID-19 does not even exist. And while in some cases the general knowledge of the public is at a high enough level that the author will rather be disgraced for his lack of knowledge of basics mathematics, in others (especially those related to something new, unknown, and unexplored), it arouses controversy and spreads disinformation. Such a low level of critical thinking is worrying. Modern schools focus on memorizing information from textbooks and reproducing teachers' expectations, but in times of stress or crisis, students are not able to distinguish between facts and manipulation. This leads to a formation of a generation that cannot even check whether the information on the Internet is from a reliable source, let alone being able to reason independently. Today, more emphasis should be put on educating an aware, responsible, and rational society. Critical thinking skills would be particularly useful when it comes to the coronavirus crisis, especially since the actions of the international community are rarely in line with science. Some people may drown themselves in the sea of illusion of a close cooperation between states and various academic or research institutions, however final decisions tend to be dictated by other reasons, as demonstrated by successive examples.

The Polish Minister of Health at one point, in an interview on public television, suggested protective face masks were completely ineffective and useless. When asked for his opinion on the reason why people wear masks, he expressed his incomprehension and full disapproval of this method. A couple of weeks later, wearing masks became obligatory in Poland and the Minister himself placed an order for hundreds of thousands of protective masks, proclaiming this decision to be lifesaving. Moreover, the ordered masks turned out to have a forged certificate, which provokes a reflection on whether the protection of the life and health of citizens was actually the main motivation for this order.

In Poland the first lockdown happened in the middle of the presidential election campaign. The ruling party did not want to declare a state of emergency that would force the election to be postponed. While the whole of Europe was preoccupied with the alarming information from Italy or Spain, Poles waited in suspense for the announcement of the date of the presidential elections. On television, instead of health experts, one could only see politicians convincing people about the pandemic being under control and persuading society not to be scared of coronavirus. Such political speeches were daily intertwined with increasingly stringent restrictions. How can one expect a society to obey the rules if such contradictory information and lack of consistency are so evident?

Finally, despite earlier assurances of Polish politicians that the country was well prepared for a pandemic, a full lockdown (in the sense of closing shops, bars, even parks and forests, etc.) was introduced very early. Back then, there were only a few cases of COVID-19 a day, but people were determined to obey the restrictions. The deep understanding among the society and the will to unite and subordinate could be really felt. However, over time, as people began to notice some contradictory information and lack of logic and consistency presented earlier, they ceased to care or worry. The government began to unfreeze the economy, because it could not afford the long-lasting downtime. As a result, most of the people have changed their approach. They started to think that the pandemic was over and stopped treating the situation with the same gravity and prudence as before. While playing this political and economic game presented above, has anyone thought about science? What do doctors or statistics say? In some states, like Switzerland or Germany, for sure scientific opinions were taken very seriously into account, but not in many others. Well, it is enough to say that currently there are over twenty-five thousand cases in Poland a day.

This lack of consistency, along with basing regulations on political and economic premises rather than on scientific evidence, is very common all around the world. This pandemic has shown that the international community is not all that united, as one would have thought before, and that the lecture about cooperation should be once again attended by representatives of most of the states. This can be supported by a few examples.

Firstly, it is worth having a look at the coronavirus tests. How is it possible that such a global crisis is tackled with such local means? Why is it allowed to have a variety of tests in different countries? How can states compare the number of COVID-19 cases if it is openly admitted that some tests are more accurate than others? In recent months, one could hear doubts, especially among young people, about the reliability of the information provided by states. Some argued that the numbers regarding cases or tests were underestimated, others, in turn, believed the fear of pandemic was exaggerated. Where do such contradicting opinions come from? The lack of transparency is to blame, together with the poor international cooperation and non-existent unification of rules at the international level. This absence of relevant and competent information makes people doubt, takes away their trust, and at the same time is a propeller for skeptics and conspiracy theories. The more such inaccuracies and contradictions, the weaker the confidence of people at the local level, the worse the further cooperation at the international level. The international community more than ever needs a strong core of trustworthy, fair, and equal states that have honest and supportive relations with their citizens.

Secondly, similar discrepancies apply for precautionary measures. In some countries, such as Switzerland, it was already known in June 2020 that the protective visors are not an effective method of protection against the virus and should not be used interchangeably with masks. In Poland, a few months later, this method of protection is not only still allowed, but also widely used, for example, by the staff of the Warsaw airport. It is worrying to observe how poor the knowledge transfer between the states is. Certainly, the research is made public, but there is no incentive for countries to apply to it. International law by its principles is based on recommendations and voluntary applications, however as soon as there is scientifically confirmed research, it would be much more effective, from the point of view of fighting the pandemic, if certain restrictions were unified in the world and countries were even obliged to comply with them. Some of the readers could now raise concerns about states' independence, equality, or freedom, however, it is not about restricting the freedom or questioning the equality of states, but simply about the necessity to uniformly follow scientific facts and validated research. Under such unusual circumstances as a global fight against an invisible enemy, all the states without exception should be guided primarily by what research and facts say. Of course, there remains a question of what should be considered a valid or sufficiently good quality research that could be acknowledged by the international community. Although there is no standardized and precisely declared rules that would define what credible research means, each field has independent, trust-worthy journals that have existed for many years, which publications are commonly accepted and respected.

Lastly, the manner in which states have closed their borders and implemented travel restrictions reminds one of a game of chess, rather than of the way to protect citizens' health. With one exception – chess tend to be more logical. By this humorous comparison it is worth reflecting on the politics that is being played under the guise of a pandemic. Some countries have introduced quarantines, some in turn have closed their borders completely. Others, such as Greece or Croatia took advantage and opened to attract tourists. At the very beginning of the lockdown, LOT Polish airlines suspended flights from China. Air China, on the other hand, was still allowed to land at the Warsaw Chopin airport a few weeks later. The Polish government introduced the "Flight Home" campaign, which aimed to safely bring Poles from abroad. How much better it would be if countries could count on mutual support and international

cooperation, instead of inventing such expensive and logistically complicated campaigns? If the actions were really guided by safety reasons, and not
by financial motives, the states could conduct a dialogue, negotiate, and help
each other, and Poles could get home safely taking a different carrier. The quarantine implementation rules also aroused controversy and were neither completely transparent, nor unified, which was an incentive for some individuals
to search for loopholes. If the overriding reason behind such travel restrictions
was really to inhibit the spread of the virus, the measures would be introduced
evenly. Unfortunately, the pandemic seems to constantly be a pretext for economic and political motives to be brought to the forefront. The COVID-19 crisis has not only struck global health systems, but above all has demonstrated
existing economic, social, and political weaknesses. It has exaggerated even
the slightest tensions between countries, up to the point that dealing with
the pandemic has actually become a pretext for a political game. The younger
generation usually observes these political skirmishes with a pinch of salt,
sometimes though with a pity, or with an idealized desire and hope for future
changes. However, in the face of a global crisis, such political games should be
set aside, and all restrictions should be coordinated and based solely on scientific recommendations.

Analyzing the above-mentioned local and international examples allows to
perceive that the coronavirus crisis has highlighted the international community's weaknesses particularly in the form of poor cooperation, lack of transparency and consistency, and economic and political plaintiffs preferred over
science, which prevents states from building strong, trusting relations with citizens. After such a pessimistic diagnosis, it would be constructive and valuable
to think about the solutions, which would allow to better deal with the prevailing pandemic and to prevent similar discrepancies and mistakes in the future.

The first and most important weakness that flashes through all the examples analyzed above is the feeble bond between the actions of the international community and science. Over the last couple of months, the world has
been put in a situation of scientific uncertainty with regards to the COVID-19
virus. This is not surprising as reliable research requires financial means and,
most importantly, time. However, actions based independently of scientific
recommendations (e.g. use of protective visors), no regulations regarding the
required quality of tests, lack of specified rules to implement quarantine or
travel restrictions, have led to public distrust, which favors conspiracy theories and internal rebellion, especially among young people. International law
should be effective, coherent, and transparent enough to build trust among
all, taking into account different nations, different religions, different cultures,
and different levels of education. The most effective way to build trust with

individuals is for regulators to meticulously collaborate with science and be very explicit about it. Existing instruments turned out not to be sufficiently effective, as the WHO cannot impose any actions, and its recommendations are often disregarded, or simply fade when juxtaposed with a multitude of other information.

The beginning of this chapter mentioned the era of disinformation and the surplus of low-quality knowledge; problems that seem futile to tackle with. Due to ubiquitous digitization the next generations will be increasingly exposed to fake news and virtual manipulation. The only solution that can balance these disadvantages of modern technology is an adequate education of a society, which is not an action of quick, but certainly permanent, results. Young people must be taught to think independently, to express their own opinion in an argumentative way, as well as to sift online information through a rational sieve. Moreover, international law should regulate the basis on which states act in the event of a global crisis such as a pandemic. The international community has a number of independent, strong scientific institutions which it should trust, and which should constitute the main source of information – both those given to individuals and those on the basis of which restrictions are being introduced. The present responsibilities and challenges of the states are therefore to educate, inform, and act in harmony with science.

Eventually, observing the futile efforts of individual countries provokes a reflection on the effectiveness of international law. The law, which has cooperation between states as one of its fundamental principles, has suddenly been ignored in the face of such crisis. States seem to exchange too little information, as if they were not sufficiently trusting each other. Of course, in a world ruled by money, where the overriding goal is economic growth, it is natural for states to compete in discovering a vaccine or finding effective ways to protect citizens. However, annihilating the virus that has affected every country, regardless of the state of the economy, size, or political system, can only be done by all the states playing together in one team. And what kind of team fouls its own players when no one is watching? This metaphor reflects USA withdrawing from the WHO, or certain states disregarding the results of credible research, or implementing quarantine rules based on political relations. It is clear that politics and economics will always play a central role, however having the health and safety of the human species at stake should require a little more international effort with transparent and undisguised cooperation. The young generation can constitute a source of inspiration and set an example. While seeing climate strikes around the world, one can see this enormous determination, power, and faith among millennials. It is a generation of ideals, transboundary values, and joint efforts. Climate change, terrorism, or a pandemic – all these are global problems against which it is impossible to win alone. Common problems often unite; therefore, the COVID-19 pandemic should be turned into something positive, namely better international cooperation and stronger ties.

The current crisis has a completely different dimension from many other political and economic problems of the past. Until now, it was either a fight between one group and another (e.g. in the event of war) or a destruction of the place of living (e.g. Earth's degradation), however it was hard to imagine that in this modern world based on freedom and democracy, people will be forced to destroy relationships and social ties. This crisis showed more than anything before that man is a social being, who truly needs close bonds with others. However, it has also indicated that in this ever-rushing world ruled by money, existing relationships are often superficial, hence so many divorces during the lockdown when people were forced to really spend time and get to know each other. This pandemic has proven to also be an opportunity to work on oneself, on relationships with loved ones, on reevaluating priorities and slowing down. The law can work both for the benefit and disadvantage of citizens. Currently, while all restrictions are introduced to protect physical health, at the same time they devastate mental health. Consequently, there is a growing number of divorces, suicides, and mental illnesses. It is daunting to imagine that future generations will only know the world of social distancing, surrounded by people wearing masks, that they will be afraid to shake hands or get close with others. Physical intimacy lies in human nature and prolonged attempts to limit it are inhuman and have a negative effect on social ties and mental well-being. Therefore, a critical analysis of the last several months in terms of what international law could do differently is necessary to make sure that a similar problem in the future will not have such severe consequences. Out of respect and concern for future generations, the international community should make every effort and go beyond its comfort zone to fill the gaps and activate mechanisms in international law, that will allow it to operate more ably and successfully in the future.

Despite all the challenges and downsides, one positive aspect of the coronavirus pandemic should be perceived, which is the improvement in the quality of the environment. Smog decreased to the extent that the inhabitants of northern India could see the Himalayas again after many decades, dolphins appeared off the coast of Sardinia, greenhouse gas emissions sharply dropped. "Isn't it ironic, when we can't breathe, the planet breaths?" – what a pertinent question asked by the Black-Eyed Peas in their new album.[2] Very often the

---

2   Black Eyed Peas, "News Today" accessed 1 July 2021.

gument of overpopulation is brought forward as a major problem in the fight against climate change, however the coronavirus crisis refuted this argument, as the global population has not been significantly reduced. Instead, the lockdowns contributed to amelioration of the environment without the need to decrease the population size. Restriction of flights and decreased use of vehicles for commuting contributed the most to the reduction of greenhouse gas emissions and improvement of air quality in cities. This forced new lifestyle, with decreased travel and partially remote jobs, could mark a beginning of a permanent behavioral change. It would make society more aware and sensitive to the surrounding environment, and more grateful for simple things like clean air, meetings in person, or the power of embrace.

This chapter has shown some of the international law constraints with regards to the coronavirus pandemic, mainly the weak relationship between international law and science, as well as a clear primacy of politics and economics over scientific research. It has also pointed out a prevailing manipulation across media and among politicians, up to a point where a confused society is no longer able to distinguish between facts and fiction. For this reason, the most crucial task in the next decades is to educate a new generation of informed, aware, and responsible citizens. Analyzing the efforts of different countries shows how resourcefully some of them have coped with the crisis. Unfortunately, the rest have been struggling, and paraphrasing Thomas Reid,[3] the international system is only as strong as its weakest link, hence the necessity of appropriate cooperation between states, transfer of knowledge, and mutual support. The lack of transparency and consistency showed in numerous examples results in weak relations between states at an international level, as well as between countries and their citizens at a national level, undermines trust, and leads to emergence of a rebellious society full of skeptics and conspiracy theories. What is missing the most to effectively combat the pandemic is an international crisis management body that would serve as an "umbrella" coordinating the actions, that would be recognized and respected by all states and authorized to impose certain standards and reporting methods. Such a mechanism would avoid numerous confusions and discrepancies and would assure that no similar crises will be so impactful in the future. Crises are an inherent part of the world, and it is even expected that in the next decades, due to climate change, the planet will be increasingly affected by extreme weather events or natural disasters. Subsequent struggles are therefore certain and unavoidable, but it is up to current leaders whether they will draw

---

3   Thomas Reid, *Essays on the Intellectual Powers of Man* (John Bell 1785).

conclusions, learn their lessons, and be prepared to effectively cope with similar global misfortunes.

This chapter could not be finished otherwise than with an expression of hope. A crisis like this should be the basis for strengthening the international community. It serves as an opportunity to instill the need to act according to "sustainable development", which can be translated into not behaving self-ishly i.e., identifying the committed mistakes, critically addressing the weak-nesses and reflecting on the possible changes, and finally acting by taking into account a decent future for the succeeding generations.